LIFE BEYOND DEATH

By

Anil Sharma

The radiance of consciousness-bliss, in the form of one awareness shining equally within and without, is the supreme blissful primal reality. Its form is silence and is declared by jnanis *(those who have realized the Self), to be the final and unobstructable state of true knowledge* (jnana*).*

- Sage Sri Ramana Maharshi

Published by

Invincible Publication Pvt. Ltd.

Published by:
Invincible Publication Pvt.Ltd.
201A, SAS Tower, Sector 38, Gurugram, Haryana – 122003
Phone: +91-124-4034247, +91 9599066061
Website : www.invinciblepublishers.com

Sales Office : - 4760-61/23, Basement, Pratap Street, Ansari Road, Daryaganj, New Delhi - 110002
Phone: +91-11-40198405
Email: invinciblepublishers@gmail.com

ISBN : 978-81-94279-91-4

Book Name : Lofe Beyond Death

Anil Sharma

Contents

Preface

Life does not end with sleep, but continues when one is awake.. Life does'nt end with death, it only continues into the regions beyond death. Nothing really dies though everything experiences a change of form and activity. This book gives an overview of superphysical regions that are entered at the time of death. It assists to formulate a kind of mapping of the route, which one follows upon leaving the physical world during death.

As the great Sage Bhagavan Sri Ramana Maharshi stated '...pramada (forgetfulness of Self) ... is the cause of birth and death. The impure mind which functions as thinking and forgetting, alone is samsara (the state of mundane activity or worldly existence), which is the cycle of birth and death The ego is described as having three bodies, the gross, the subtle and the causal, but that is only for the purpose of analytical exposition. The ego's phenomenal existence is transcended when you dive into the source from where the `I'-thought rises.'

Anil Sharma

Sage Sri Ramana Maharshi Centre of Learning,
Sydney,
Australia
25 March 2008

Foreword

Sage Sri Ramana Maharishi taught that an essential aspect for knowing and experiencing our reality of self-awareness is the necessity for the ego to subside. We then become aware of our reality which is always shining forth. An important aspect of subsidence of this personal feeling of 'me' in us is to gain an understanding of why this feeling of 'me' exists in us and its function. Once one knows and fully understands a particular phenomenon, like the individual feeling of 'me' in us, it is an effort in the right direction; it'll no longer continue to trouble us anymore.

Sri Anil Sharma is a devoted follower of Sage Sri Ramana Maharishi, who undertook an in depth study and also personally experienced through meditation the life of the 'ego' at the physical and other planes of phenomenal existence, as mentioned by Sri Ramana Maharishi while answering the many questions about reincarnation and rebirth put to him by his followers in search of reality. He came across the teachings of the Sage Sri Ramana Maharishi in the year 2000, and since has gained knowledge and experience of our reality as Self-awareness.

I am happy to recommend this book for reading and general knowledge in relation to the life of the ego on the physical plane and beyond, written by him just prior to coming across the teachings of Sri Ramana Maharshi and taking him on as his Sat-Guru.

Vasuki Seshadri

Rajajinagar
Bangalore, India
25 March 2008

Acknowledgements

- To Sage Sri Ramana Maharishi for the advice, guidance and encouragement given.

- To Sri V.S.Ramanan President Board of Trustees Sri Ramanasramam for the advice given and permission to reprint extracts of the teachings and sayings of Sage Sri Ramana Maharshi from the books listed in the bibliography which is copyrighted by Sri Ramanasramam.

- To Sri Vasuki Seshadri for his constructive advice during the final editing of the book and for undertaking all necessary activities towards its publication.

- To Sri Thakor Patel, Dr. Srinivasa Murthy, Sri Lajpatrai Sardana and Sri Ulpiano Manlangit for the advice and assistance rendered in the preparation of the book.

- To all the devotees of Sage Sri Ramana Maharshiwho wish to remain unnamed for their assistance in bringing the publication of this book to fruition.

- To Sri John Pater, whose summary of each chapter of the book has been appended at the end of each chapter in this volume in the name In a Nutshell.

Special Note from the Author

John Pater is a rare human being present among us who possesses intricate knowledge of life beyond the physical plane. According to John not only is it important for us to realize out true nature of 'Self' or 'Awareness' as taught by sage Sri. Ramana Maharshi, it is also important to balance out outlook both inwardly and outwardly, so we can help others not only at a spiritual level but also share the shortcomings and grief of others during our sojourn on the Earthly plane. John has gone to great lengths to edit and make recommendations to the current publication of this book. If you have any questions relating to life beyond physical death, particularly with reference to the correlations between the processes of evolution and Self realisation you can contact John by sending an e-mail to him. His e-mail address is -

john_pater@hotmail.com

or write to him at the following address –

Mr. John Pater
10 Edward Bennett Drive,
Cherrybrook
NSW 2126
Sydney, Australia.

SRI RAMANA MAHARSHI

Brief Biographical Sketch And Teachings

Rarely one comes across a sight, where the blending of sparkling tranquil awareness the Self and its manifestation in gross physical form can be seen at its purest best. Such an entity is Sage Sri Ramana Maharishi, an embodiment in human form of the pure subtle invisible awareness – Self, who occupies a unique place both in the history of spiritual sages of both India and humanity as a whole.

He was born on 30th December 1879 in Tiruchuzhi a small village thirty miles southeast of the city of Madurai famous for its temples situated in state of Tamil Nadu, in South India. At the age of 12 he lost his father as a result of which he and his elder brother went to live with their paternal uncle in Madurai.

It sometimes happens that one who is on a spiritual path, or even who has not yet begun consciously seeking, has a glimpse of self realisation during which, for a brief eternity, he experiences absolute certainty of his divine, immutable identity of Awareness Self. Such an experience arising out of fear of death came to the Maharshi on 17th July 1896 when he was a lad of sixteen., while sitting alone in a room on the first floor of his uncle's house, as stated by Sri Ramana in his own words: "The body dies but the Spirit that transcends it cannot be touched by death. That means I am the deathless Spirit.'...... Fear of death had vanished once and for all. Absorption in the Self continued unbroken from that time on" Later when Sri Ramana was relating his experiences in Madurai of the vision of death he said, "In the vision of death, though all the senses were benumbed, the aham sphurana (Self-awareness) was clearly evident, and so I realised that it was that awareness that we call 'I', and not the body. This Self-awareness never decays. It is unrelated to anything. It is Self-luminous. Even if this body is burnt, it will not be affected. Hence, I realised on that very day so clearly that that was 'I'."

Soon after this change occurred after an arduous journey the great sage made his way to Tiruvannamalai, the town at the foot of the holy hill of Arunachala arriving there on 1st September 1896. He spent the remaining 54 years of his life in the shade of Arunachala. The first half of them was spent in its caves, the last half in an Ashram at the foot of it named Sri Ramanasramam after the great sage.

In order to realise while in the physical body our True identity of Awareness which is the changeless witness of the changing world Sri Ramana has described two methods. The spiritual paths the Maharshi taught were simple and direct. He would often say: "Ask yourself 'Who am I?' or submit." These two paths both lead to the same goal. The one that he offered first was always Self-enquiry. It means concentrating on the pure sense of being, the pure I-amness of me. And this, one discovers, is the same as pure consciousness, pure, formless awareness.

Arthur Osborne writes "The power of his presence was overwhelming and his beauty indescribable, and yet, at the same time, he was utterly simple, utterly natural, unassuming, unpretentious, unaffected." He wrote some small treatises, his main work being Ulladu Narpadu, Forty Verses on That which is, Upadesa Saram, Essence of Instruction and Five hymns on Arunachala, and translated some texts which he considered important and useful for those who were following his advice.

On April 14th, 1950, the maharshi left his physical body. The site made holy by his presence is visited as a place of pilgrimage by spiritual seekers all over the world and the presence of the great sage is always felt there. Many spiritual aspirants have felt his presence there and attained enlightenment, to experience the truth behind these words one has to visit Sri Ramanashramam to experience it firsthand.

About The Author

Are we eventually reborn again in a physical body after death? Does the soul pass on into another body after leaving the physical body? Is there any connection between Self realisation and rebirth? There are many questions in relation to reincarnation which need to be understood logically and rationally, before the doctrine of reincarnation can take hold and become part of a person's life.

The ability to commune with the Self is in all humans, but its degree of existence is not the same in everyone. This difference is reasonably understood and explained if one accepts the theory of reincarnation. The peculiar nature and the attributes which characterize rebirth prevent anyone from proving it completely if one uses using normal thinking and sense perception. However, its acceptance helps us to understand our evolution, history, capacity, inequalities of characteristics, our habits and also find a reasonable answer to the question why we are here on Earth. Sri Ramana Maharshi once stated 'This body has birth and death and when this body falls another body arises which is called reincarnation. But are you the body? If you find that you are not this body but the spirit, you will be free from gross or subtle bodies, and then there will be no limitations.'

Dating back to 11 November 1938 Mr. Ranganatha Ayyar, a devotee of fourteen years standing, on a visit to Ramana Ashraman asked the maharshi 'How long is the interval between one's death and reincarnation?' The maharshi replied 'It may be long or short. But a Jnani (one who has realised the Self)does not have any such changes; he merges into the universal Being, so says the Brihadaranyaka Upanishad. Some say that those who after death pass into the path of light are not reborn, whereas those who after death take the path of darkness are reborn after they have enjoyed the fruits of karma in their subtle bodies. If one's merits and demerits are equal, they are directly reborn here. Merits outweighing demerits, the subtle bodies go to heavens and are then reborn here; demerits outweighing merits, they go to hells and are afterwards reborn here. A yogabrashta (one who has slipped from the yoga)is said to fare in the same manner. All these are described in the sastras (scriptures). But in fact, there is neither birth nor death. One remains only as what one really is. This is the only Truth.'

The author of this book Sri Anil Sharma was born in Ambala, a small town in north India in March 1958. He graduated as an electrical engineer in 1980 from Delhi University, after which he travelled for a period of three years throughout the length and breadth of the Indian subcontinent, in search of wisdom, in search of truth, reflections of which can be seen in this book.

In December 1993 he experienced the dramatic rising of cosmic currents (also known as the phenomena of Kundalini in ancient Hindu scriptures) in his body, as a consequence of which his own spiritual search for reality intensified, as a result for the next seven years he experienced the various states of higher consciousness. This book is the outcome of his spiritual experiences, and the guidance received from sages and spiritual masters during altered states of consciousness and deep states of meditation. During these seven years he read more than nine hundred books written and referred to by great spiritual masters, attained various siddhis (supernatural attainments), toured many countries around the world, gave lectures, wrote books and helped many spiritual aspirants both at the material and spiritual level. However, in spite of experiencing the rising of cosmic currents in his body, having attained a heightened awareness of reality, and achieving many tasks in spirituality, like writing books and genuinely helping many aspirants in the path of spirituality, his own quest of knowing and gaining personal experience of self realization remained unfulfilled. In the year 2000 the cosmic currents gradually settled down, also in the same year he came across the teachings of Sri Ramana Maharshi, in whom he found all the answers to his spiritual quest and took him as his Sat guru.

The author currently resides in Australia and works in his profession, but will continue to serve humanity in the form of such books and writings. He runs a small centre in Sydney called Sage Sri Ramana Maharshi Centre of Learning Sydney. If you wish to correspond with the author or know more about the teaching of Sri Ramana Maharshi visit the website -

www.sageramana.org

John Pater

Sydney, Australia

3 March 2008

At the lotus feet of my Sat Guru...

The reincarnating ego belongs to the lower plane, namely, thought. It is transcended by Self-realisation.

- Sage Sri Ramana Maharshi

CHAPTER 1

JOURNEY TO THE REALMS OF DEATH

A man might have performed many karmas in his previous births. A few of these alone will be chosen for this birth and he will have to enjoy their fruits in this birth. It is something like a slide show where the projectionist picks a few slides to be exhibited at a performance, the remaining slides being reserved for another performance. All this karma can be destroyed by acquiring knowledge of the Self. The different karmas are the slides, karmas being the result of past experiences, and the mind is the projector. The projector must be destroyed so that there will be no further reflection and no further births and no deaths.

Sage Sri Ramana Maharshi

DEATH - TRANSITION INTO OTHER WORLDS

Death is an entry into the regions of life beyond the physical plane. The life one leads on earth represents only the tip of the iceberg. The human mind can produce figures and things never known in the waking state in addition to accumulated impressions of the past. It is also capable of creating impressions of a future life that persists beyond death. Death is a change of life from one state to another. In spiritual philosophy the term death is used to denote the passage of life from one phase to another while in everyday language death means the end of the body.

Nothing really dies, it is true the physical body separates and this separation takes place because the life force itself departs and moves on to another state of existence. The question definitely arises in one's mind - Is there really another world, another state of existence after this passage or transition of so called death or are these mere empty words? This is the question which needs to be answered by practical first hand experience, by being able to come in touch with these so called mysterious planes of life after death in an absorbed state of meditation. In a dream one may reconstruct an entire city in one's mind in minutes and shortly later when awake realise that it was not a real city in terms of physical actuality. Similarly in an absorbed state of meditation, it is possible to verify the existence of the regions or planes of life after death before birth.

One may not be aware of the mechanically - produced radio-transmitted waves which may exist in a room wherein one happens to be. When a radio set is switched on it will catch and convert these waves into sounds of melodious music. The waves are there even when the room is silent, but inaudible without a radio. The fact that one's eyes, ears and fingers cannot register them, does not diminish their reality. In the same way, the fact remains unchanged that death is not the end but a change of state into the regions beyond death. It is apparent that one must bifurcate the life of man into the divisions of life after death and life before death. Life before rebirth is no less real or less conscious than the current manifested one. One may begin to formulate a correct opinion about the fact that death is a change of state but one's emotions, feelings and thoughts in connection with it may be so strong that the truth quickly sinks into the background, ignored and forgotten.

Is death not ultimately a process of critical change whereby life passes from one shape into another? Is not everybody somehow and somewhere and in some form reborn anew? If Nature destroys it, it is only that she may create afresh. This is true of every part of her domain, whether in the life and fate of human beings or whether among the lands and waters of the globe. Destruction and death are only part of her game, in the end they are but illusions, although quite often painful illusions to those who suffer them and don't go to the extent of searching for the truth.

If life is sadly stamped with transiency, it holds true for death too. If anything changes and passes away, this is only because it turns into something else. There is no need to fear this passage from one's inferior personality to one's higher individuality. It is not a step towards annihilation, but an advance towards true fulfillment. The individual consciousness is not lost. It is expanded, and enlarged. The very thought of death drives one to look for the deathless i.e., continuation of life beyond death. A person dies to be reborn. One dies from childhood to become a youth, and from youth to become the mature adult, and finally one dies from maturity into old age. Yet throughout all the cyclic changes there is an unbroken continuity of life. Everyone is clear that one is the same person whose life so many years ago was that of the child. Self-identity is preserved despite all modifications that occur. In a similar way self-identity continues through the changes beyond the body's death.

One must always keep in mind that no world becomes real for one until one thinks about it, experiences it and makes it a part of one's consciousness thus absorbing it fully into oneself. Spiritual knowledge tells us that death is a change of dress, that we have gone through many times before in the past and will probably go through many times again in the future.

When someone has passed away, he has only laid himself to sleep for a while, later to wake up into the next world after death. To disturb this rest with noise of lamentation shows that one knows very little of the life that continues beyond death. It appears that death has an effect which one seemingly cannot overcome and one gives every possible outward expression of having forever lost a beloved one. However for those who have acquired the knowledge and understanding of the illusion of death, these frightful emotions have faded away, they naturally feel the sorrow of temporary separation. To them the loved one is seen to have simply passed on to another phase of life, and nothing has been lost - nothing has perished.

Death is a name given to explain a certain phenomenon. Life has many phases and one transitory phase is called death. Nothing really dies - though everything experiences a change of form and activity. There has always existed a definite body of knowledge about the super physical regions that are entered at the time of death. Such information has been accumulating for ages from many sources. Studies of comparative ancient and modern sciences and religions have yielded rich stores of knowledge that have been further confirmed by direct observation through the use of powers that are latent in all humans, and are awakened in some - powers such as extra-sensory perception and even subtle kinds of direct knowing. This accumulated knowledge, together with its philosophical implications, constitutes what is termed as the ancient wisdom of mankind. From this source may be derived a kind of mapping of the route which one follows upon leaving the physical world at death.

Death consists of a repeated process of uncovering, or unsheathing. At death one sheds the physical body and takes on the emotional body, one leaves the physical world and enters the next world known as the astral world. One who has realized by logic and personal experience that death does not lead to annihilation but leads to a vastly extended freedom of life, need not fear the casting away of one's physical body at death.

The truth is that there is no death but there is only everlasting life. Listen to this wisdom in silence, for there alone can its vibrations reach your ears. Affirm- there is no death but only life - Everlasting Life. The statement appears to be true in every respect and every aspect of its meaning.

THE LAW OF CORRESPONDENCES

Prior to embarking on a journey to understand the realms of life and death before birth it is essential to gain a basic understanding of certain cosmic principles on which these regions have been modeled. Two such cosmic principles are the law of correspondences or analogy and the law of cause and effect. The law of correspondences tells us that everything contained in the realms of life after death has a corresponding equivalent in the human body. Hence it is essential for one to observe and study one's physical, emotional, mental and spiritual make up. In addition a study of the nature and environment that surrounds one and the correlation to the regions of life beyond death helps one to gain a good understanding of the mysterious planes of life and existence beyond death.

The human organism is a microcosm, an exact replica of the universe or macrocosm. Hence between man and the universe there are points and zones which correspond. Not only the whole of esoteric science but also the study of the realms of life after death is based on this law of correspondences. Man is infinitely small while the cosmos is infinitely vast, but between them there is a correspondence. Thanks to this law, one can establish contact with forces, centers and worlds in the regions of life after death which correspond to certain elements within a human being. Based on this law, the physical body of man corresponds to the physical plane. The feelings, emotions and desires of man correspond to the plane of desires or astral world, the thoughts and intellect of man correspond to the mental plane and so on.

Based on the law of correspondences the trinity of body, soul and spirit is just another way to explain the phenomenal activity of the creative power of our Creator. This activity is carried out in a veiled, hidden and invisible fashion in this act of creation. Everywhere, on every level of the universe, matter contains energy and man's material physical body possesses its own specific energy. It is this energy which one calls as the soul, the body is the form or container and soul is the energy which animates. Using the law of correspondences one can understand that the whole creation is built according to one identical structure or pattern with only a few minor modifications. Using this key of analogy or correspondences, wherever one looks one can find the same three divisions, form, content and meaning or body, soul and spirit. An egg, for example is an image of the universe. What does one see in an egg? The yolk which contains the living germ, the white that is the albumen, and the shell. The yolk is the spirit, the white is the soul and the shell is the body. The germ, therefore is in the centre, the white is in between and the shell is on the outside. When one breaks the shell of an egg, the white albumen and the yolk run out and the life is lost. So just as an egg shell protects the germ of life in an egg, the human body serves as a protection for the life inside it, i.e. the soul and the spirit. When the body is broken, life departs, the soul and spirit escape. But what is the soul? Just as the white of an egg contains the nutrient necessary to nourish the embryo chic, so does the soul contain all the nutrients necessary to sustain human life. Life itself belongs to the spirit, and it is this life that the soul sustains, nourishes and causes to circulate.

There is one thing which is very important to understand that inspite of the fact that one always speaks of spirit, soul and body as different realities, they are in fact the same essence. The difference between them lies in their consistency, there degree of materialization and manifestation. The body is a condensed form of the spirit, the spirit is a subtle, more rarefied form of the body and the soul lies half-way between the two. Similarly based on the law of correspondences the physical plane is a condensed form of the astral plane or the plane of desires, and the mental plane or the plane of thought is a subtle and rarefied form of the astral plane and so on. When one takes the case of water, it is normally found in the liquid state, but it also exists in the solid state as ice, and in the gaseous state in the form of vapor. It is still water, the same substance, but in varying forms which differ in their degree of subtleness. In its normal state water is a liquid, when it is exposed to low temperatures it hardens into ice, and when it is heated it is converted into vapor, but it is always the same substance. Ice is solid enough but it is only a form, a temporary appearance, since it can become liquid or vapor. In the same way body, soul and spirit and the regions of life after death like the physical, astral, mental planes and so on are of the one and the same substance in more condensed or more subtle states. Thus one can see how much light can be thrown upon the understanding of the life in the regions beyond death if one can attain a clear understanding of this law of correspondences.

According to the law of correspondences every thought one thinks of and every deed one performs has a corresponding effect on the individual. Based on the law of correspondence every human emits a ceaseless flow of waves, beneficial by one's thoughts, feelings and acts, these waves journey through space until they come up against the outer limits and bounce back to strike the sender in the form of rewards and punishments. Those who are conscious of this law take care to send out waves of purity, kindness, tolerance, love and warmth. Similarly based on this law if one were to use one's thoughts, feelings and desires to direct oneself to attain knowledge of the regions of life beyond death then the corresponding effect will be that one will end up reading such metaphysical books that contain knowledge about these regions, or one will come in contact with such people, who will guide and assist the individual in attaining such knowledge. Similarly if in meditation one directs one's attention towards these regions like the astral plane or the mental plane and so on, then the corresponding result will be that one will get suitable responses from these worlds which will assist in confirming one's knowledge of what one has read and discussed with others about these mysterious regions of life after death.

Every place of worship be it a mosque, church, monastery or temple has a striking corresponding resemblance to the physical make up of human beings. The building has a hall called the place of worship and in that hall is placed the statue of a deity representing a being of divine nature. A parallel can be drawn between the physical body and this place of worship. The building and hall represents the physical human body and the deity represents the soul and spirit manifesting and residing in the physical body. What is the corresponding effect of visiting a place of worship like a church, temple or a mosque? These visits to places of worship are a constant reminder to man to continue to make spiritual progress until the ultimate goal of his own evolutionary target is attained. Every ritual has an equivalent corresponding spiritual meaning. The very reason for lighting a candle or burning incense when one prays is that the burning candle or incense is a symbol of sacrifice. The incense sacrifices the very material it's made of so that it may burn and scent may appear, and candle sacrifices its wax so that the flame may appear. Similarly if one wants to grow spiritually one has to learn to sacrifice to transform one's brute instincts which are one's vices, passion, lust and sensuality. In India there is a ritual of taking a holy dip in the river Ganges. The purpose of taking this dip in the river is that one will be cleansed and freed of one's sins, but the truth is that this is only symbolic. According to the law of correspondences, when one takes this holy dip, just as one's exterior physical body is cleansed of any dirt, sweat etc, similarly one has to cleanse and purify oneself internally i.e., get rid of one's bad habits, improve one's character and perform deeds of a noble or divine nature, only then can it be possible to free oneself of one's sins.

According to the law of correspondences, human nature is two-fold in nature. One part consists of the lower earthly self which is a body or vehicle which thinks, feels and acts but is only a corresponding reflection of one's true self (similar to one's image reflected in a mirror). The other part is one's true individuality made up of the trinity of divine will, divine love and divine wisdom. If one tunes oneself to one's divine nature it is possible not only to attain but also verify the wisdom and knowledge of the regions of life beyond death.

The law of correspondences is the most important key that explains everything - the structure of human beings, their intelligence or stupidity, their kindness or cruelty, their fortunes and misfortunes, their wealth and their poverty

- everything. If day represents the region of physical life then corresponding to it night represents the regions of life after death before birth. Having thus gained knowledge of the law of correspondences one should put it to use to understand not only the regions of life after death but also man's individual relationship to the universe and his corresponding purpose for being on earth to gain knowledge and grow in wisdom.

CAUSE AND EFFECT

According to the law of Cause and Effect or the law of karma everything one does has a reaction. The word karma is a Sanskrit (ancient Hindu language) word which means action. For every energy that one puts forth there is a reaction, and these reactions that one goes on evoking constitute karma. Each moment one is building karmas of different types. Now if one betrays someone, one immediately forges a karma, one will be betrayed by someone, at some point in time. It may not happen in this birth; but till then this deposit of a karma opening the possibility of somebody betraying one stays. Similar potentials accumulate. Thus there are two types of karma - accumulated karma and dynamic karma. The karma that one is building up all the time continues to be accumulated in one's consciousness and is termed as accumulated karma. Hence the sum total of one's karma of past lives up to the present is termed as accumulated karma. Each time one takes birth, one decides what part of this previous accumulated karma is to be worked out in that birth, what part is to be postponed to the next, and according to that decision one comes with one's own choice of karma which begins to fructify. The karma that begins to bear fruit in this life is called dynamic karma and this karma which has now begun to work is fate. Every individual is the author of one's fate, because one has done these actions in one's previous births and in this life one has to pay for them. So if one wants to negate that karma one has to build an opposite karma. If one has been nasty, mean, harmed and made people suffer one can negate that karma by being very kind, by being very useful to people in this birth. To a large extent that old karma get cancelled. One can change the level of one's living consciousness, so that the level at which the karma was created is relegated to a lower level, the old karma does not touch one anymore. That level can be changed when one starts living a spiritual life; that is why it is also said that a horoscope does not apply to the true spiritual aspirant. However there is some part of one's karma which one cannot negate and that is a karma which has to be experienced. Murder, suicide etc are heinous crimes which one has to pay for.

The question of destiny has intrigued man for centuries. To what extent is man free or bound to a predetermined fate? It is a grave error to believe that all human beings without exception are necessarily bound by the same laws. Obviously if one behaves like animals do i.e., obey one's sensations and passions and one's purely instinctive impulses, then one is ruled by fate. Whereas those who are much more highly evolved, escape the clutches of fate and enter into the world of Grace. The great masters of humanity belong to this second category, but most humans drift in a middle zone; i.e. between animals and the divine. One must not think that everyone is free, not that everyone is subject to an implacable fate. The truth is that freedom depends on one's level of evolution. Until such time as one attains total freedom, one is still subject to law of Karma in some areas of one's life, whereas in others one is free.

Many types of different philosophies concerning freedom are in circulation and they all set out to convince individuals that one is free. Yes, one may think that one is free just as long as one knows nothing of the pattern on which the universe is built or of the cosmic forces which influence humans. Hence one imagines that when one has to decide on a course of action, one is free to choose and decide what to do. It never occurs to one that most of the time one is a pawn in the hands of forces that one knows nothing about. The ancient astrologers used to say that the stars influence but do not determine or that the wise man is above being influenced by stars. The stars, therefore do influence human beings in one direction or the other. When one is very highly evolved one feels their influence, but they cannot force one into anything against one's will. However, when one is weak it is a different matter, one behaves as though the stars drive one on irresistibly, without one even being aware of it. This can be illustrated with an example - when a pretty girl is attracted to a boy she does not have to say 'come with me'. She simply smiles and behaves in such a way as to egg him on and it is he who starts besieging her with his attentions. She does not say or do anything and yet she manages to attract him and he being weak, lets himself be influenced. The stars are similar to the pretty girls, they arouse something in you - anger or sensuality for instance - and then they leave you alone, because they know very well that you will go all the way. Then they say, 'but we didn't force you, you were free to do as you wanted!' By then one has gone too far and the damage has been done.

Let's say that one is highly evolved and has a debt to pay, instead of being obliged to pay it on the physical level, one can pay it on the astral or the mental level. One way or another, one has to pay but one is free to choose and decide on what level one will do so. But others, who are still on the lowest rungs of the evolutionary ladder, are not free to choose, they have to pay in whatever way they are told to. Be sure to remember that whatever one does one should not imagine that one can ever get out of paying one's debts. One may be allowed to pay this in different ways, but one must pay them. The only freedom involved is in the choice of currency one will use, but no one is free to avoid a karmic debt. On the other hand, if one decides to go back to a life of selfishness everything will change once again. One will again go through suffering and disillusionment, even though one maybe unaware of one's actions.

One's present life will not all change at once because one still has some funds of good karma accumulated in reserve and one does not see the dark future one is preparing for oneself. As soon as these reserves of accumulated good karma run out, that horrible future takes over. It is easy to create the future but it is very difficult to erase the past. In fact one does not create one's future, it is figurative and it would be more precise to say that one chooses the direction one wants to go in. One does not create one's evil fate but one steers oneself towards it. One decides only what direction one will take, that is all.

Why does one have certain talents or one lacks in certain talents? Why is one ill or healthy? Why is one prone to accidents? Why is one liked or disliked? Why is one active or disinterested in the life around oneself? Why is one attached to morality or immorality? Why is one attracted to spirituality or materialism? The questions are answered by examining one's karma or individual karma and its laws. What one sows in this hour is reaped by one's posterity for several generations and one can then call it the karma of the family. What the men of today or community resolve upon and execute, comes back with a blessing or a curse upon the future of their race when they themselves have passed away and are no longer there to rejoice or to suffer, this can be called as karma of the nation. Mankind as a whole has a karma, which can be called as world karma, what is wrought in its past will shape its future destiny though individuals may come and go but the karma of the race which they have helped to form continues through time.

The working of the karmic forces can be better understood by having an understanding of the various levels of consciousness. For the sake of simplicity one may consider that there are three mind levels, the conscious, the subconscious and the super conscious. Each level plays a different role in one's life. Conscious mind consists of will, reason, logic and the five physical senses. Subconscious mind consists of imagination, memory, habits, emotions and past life records. The super conscious mind consists of the creative force, psychic abilities and unlimited unknown powers. The conscious mind, working in conjunction with the brain, is what takes care of one during one's waking hours. The subconscious mind is that part which takes care of the physical body while the conscious mind sleeps. The subconscious mind is that part which is brought forth from one life time to the next according to the theory of rebirth. The super conscious mind is the life giving force or connecting link with God or one's Creator. One is familiar with the general working of the conscious mind, but few people have an understanding of the subconscious. In addition to imagination, memory and emotions it is responsible for one's habit patterns. The subconscious mind is also a complex storehouse of knowledge. From the metaphysical viewpoint of rebirth, the subconscious mind carries the memories and influences of all of one's previous experiences. A person is the sum total of all of one's previous lives. It explains one's natural affinity for some things and aversion to others. As an example - a person who for no apparent reason is fearful of going out on the ocean in a boat may have drowned in the ocean in a past life. This theory offers an explanation for the existence of problems that cannot be traced back to a cause in this life time. Once the soul leaves the physical body after death it is no longer entrapped in matter. It is free. All that it retains from its sojourn in its earth shell is the total recall of its worldly experiences now safely stored in its memory bank, only the conscious mind has been discarded. The subconscious mind has survived because it neither consists of nor depends on matter. It now becomes the conscious mind of the soul and will continue to function as such until the soul returns into the earth's dense matter to begin its next life. Meanwhile the super conscious mind assumes the functions relinquished by the subconscious mind, and the soul is now articulate as it could never be on earth. When the time comes for the soul to return to earth and assume its next body, the process is quite simply reversed. The conscious mind returns to the subconscious level and the subconscious mind returns to the super conscious level where it subsides back into a womb - like a sanctuary in the flesh body. It neither seeks nor desires emotional association with the pursuits of the subconscious mind and the new born conscious mind, as they accustom themselves to their new ego.

One does not have to look very far to understand the Law of Cause and Effect. If one looks at the day-night cycle, one goes to sleep because one remains awake and works throughout the day. Hence if sleep is the cause then remaining awake is the effect. Day and night are also corresponding cause and effect of each other. When one sees an effect in the physical world one can be sure that there has been a cause. If one throws a rock into a lake, it will send out ripples. The rock is the cause, the effect is the ripples, and the person or the individual is another cause when one threw the rock. The river washed the rock down to the place where one found it. Before that a volcano erupted, forming the rock. The chain of cause and effect would trace everything that has ever happened in the universe back to some original cause. When the effect is felt in man the cause was set in motion in the mind. The effect one is feeling now, both positive and negative are the results of causes from this lifetime or from previous lifetimes. The seed (cause) one is sowing now will bring forth the effects yet to come in this lifetime or future lifetimes. One's entire life - one's mental state, health, relationships with others, the money one has or has not made - all are effects, but somewhere in one's background in this life or in previous lives these effects were set in motion by causes

One is one's own judge, and executor - one's own bestowal of rewards. But the Judge who sentences the reward or punishment is not a power outside of itself, but a Power within - in short one's own conscience. A man's own conscience when allowed to speak clearly and forcibly, is the most severe judge that exists. One finds oneself unable to escape from the judgment seat of conscience, and one leads oneself away to one's rewards or punishments. Such is the poetic justice of Nature which far exceeds any concept of man in his religious speculations. There are two great principles at work in the matter of karmic law affecting the conditions of rebirth. The first principle is that whereby the prevailing desires, aspirations, likes and dislikes, love and hatred, attractions and repulsions etc., presses one into conditions in which these characteristics may have a favorable environment for development. The second principle is that which may be spoken of as the urge of the unfolding spirit which is always urging forward towards fuller expression which thus exerts a pressure upon the soul awaiting rebirth. This causes it to seek higher environments and conditions than its desires and aspirations, as well as its general characteristics would demand. These two apparently conflicting (yet actually harmonious) principles acting and reacting upon each other, determine the conditions of rebirth, and have a very material effect upon the karmic Law. One's life is largely a conflict between these two forces, the one tending to hold one to the present conditions resulting from past lives, and the other ever at work seeking to uplift and elevate one to greater heights.

Like a bee, collecting honey from every flower, one collects only the nectar of moral qualities and consciousness, from every terrestrial personality in which one has to clothe oneself, until at last one unites all these qualities in one and becomes a perfect being. Every earth life is an opportunity, carefully calculated, for such development that is most needed by the individual; a failure to use that opportunity means the trouble and delay of another similar incarnation, and suffering probably aggravated by the additional karma incurred. The coils of karma which entwine themselves around the wrong - doer are primarily there as a natural consequence of one's own acts, not as a fate of punishment. Time is educating and developing one to perceive the right. When one has the humility to face the responsibility for one's own past errors, one may see how many of one's troubles were self earned. Where one cannot trace the cause to one's present personality, one must believe it to lie in one's previous ones.

Karma is not merely a law of inheriting previous impressions or of self reproduction or of moral retributive justice but is also something much larger. It is an eternal law which tends to adjust the individual operation to the universal operation. It works for the universe as a whole to keep its innumerable units in harmony with its own integral balance. Retribution merely falls inside this activity as a small concentric circle falls inside a larger one. The results of each individual's existence, his storehouse of thoughts and actions have to be controlled so that they shall in the end be in accordance with the cosmos itself. Every part is bound to the whole. Everything thus tends to ultimate rightness. It is indeed comforting to perceive that the universe has such significant equilibrium at its secret core. A person's freedom from or imprisonment in matter, therefore is dependent on one's motivating ideas. Within the framework of the Law of Cause and Effect one creates one's own destiny, works out in time one's own salvation and wins one's way to the freedom of immortality. The karmic pattern that is inherited by each individual, therefore is the governing factor in the process of rebirth. It determines when one will be born, in what kind of a body, under what circumstances, who the parents will be, with whom there will be close relationships, what teachers, friends there will be a possibility of meeting. Each condition brings further self-knowledge, releasing some fragment of the divine potential. No single life of an individual is isolated from his other lives. Each life is the child of all the preceding lives on earth and the parent of those that follow it.

REALMS OF LIFE AFTER DEATH

If one were to study the human body and desire to understand the working of its various systems, one needs to classify each system into the various organs it is composed of and study in detail the structure and functions of each organ to come to a full understanding of the system. Only by such an analysis can the complicated phenomenon of life activity in the human body be understood. Similarly to gain a comprehensive knowledge of the regions or realms of life after death one needs to study in detail the nature and activity of each of these planes of life after death. There are seven such planes or realms of life – adi, anupadic, atmic, buddhic, mental (consisting of causal and lower mental), astral and the physical plane.

1	ADI – first Cause
2	ANUPADIC – MONAD
3	ATMIC
4	BUDDHIC
5a 5b	CAUSAL OR UPPER MENTAL LOWER MENTAL PLANE
6	ASTRAL
7	PHYSICAL

Fig 1 – Planes of Life after Death.

In the life on the other side, there are no tears, no sighs and one gets the opportunity to realize oneself to one's full perfection. Adi means first; the Adi plane refers to the first cause, the divine light, the Father or the Creator. It is from this plane that the forming of the other realms and further creative activity takes place. Next come the Monads or units of consciousness, for whose evolution in matter the field of a universe is prepared. These units of consciousness are generated within the divine life on the Adi Plane before the field for their evolution is formed. Thus many arise in the one by that act of will of the divine life, the first cause or God on the Adi plane. The Monads are described as sparks of the Supreme Flame. As is written in the Scriptures – 'I sense one Flame, O Gurudeva (or Master/Spiritual Guide); I see countless undetached sparks shining in it. The Flame is the Lord or Ishwara in His manifestation as the first cause on the Adi plane and the undetached sparks are the Monads. A Monad may thus be defined as a fragment of the divine life, separated off as an individual entity by the rarest film of matter. The matter is so rare that, while it gives a separate form to each, it offers no obstacle to the free intercommunication of a life with surrounding similar lives.

Many times in altered and deep states of meditation I have encountered this shining white flame and many individual white lights contained in it signifying the white flame as God or Creator and the small lights as the monads or the individual sparks. A monad is consciousness plus matter. The Monad is the jivatma of Indian philosophy, the Purusha of the Samkya, the particularized self of the Vedanta. While the roots of their life are on the Adi plane, the Monads themselves dwell on the Anupadaka plane. No English equivalent exists for Anupadaka which means without vesture or without clothing or without any additional veil. The Monads are in tune with and respond to the divine vibrations of the Adi plane, but are not in tune with and do not respond to the vibrations of the lower planes,. The divine light or Lord of the Adi plane is in tune with the vibrations of all the lower planes. These Monads have not yet been made perfect through suffering. Hence each of the Monads is to go forth into matter in order to be sown in weakness that he may be raised in power. Whilst omniscient, omnipresent on his own plane – the Anupadaka – he is unconscious on all the others, he is to veil his glory in matter that blinds him, in order that he may become omniscient, omnipresent, on all planes, able to answer all divine vibrations in the universe, instead of only to those of the highest levels. As the Monads derive their being from the Divine Light of the Adi plane, the will of the Divine Light is also the will of the Monads. Hence the whole process of the evolution of the individual 'I' is an activity chosen by the Monads themselves. We are here in the world of matter, because we as Monads, willed to live, we are Self moved, Self determined.

1	ADI PLANE	
2	ANUPADKA PLANE	MONADS
3	ATMIC PLANE	ATMIC BODY
4	BUDDHIC PLANE	BUDDHIC BODY
5A	UPPER MENTAL OR CAUSAL PLANE	CAUSAL BODY
5B	LOWER MENTAL PLANE	MENTAL BODY
6	ASTRAL PLANE	ASTRAL BODY
7	PHYSICAL PLANE	PHYSICAL BODY

Fig 2 – Man's corresponding bodies/vehicles to the Planes of Life.

The next stage is the forming of the 5 lower planes i.e., atmic, buddhic, mental (consisting of causal and lower mental), astral and the physical planes. This stage of development also brings with it evolved beings, at various stages of development, who are the typical inhabitants of these planes. These beings have been brought over by the divine light which manifests on the Adi plane from a preceding evolution. They are now sent to inhabit the plane for which their development fits them, they co-operate with the work of the divine light and later with man in the general scheme of evolution. There are many grades of these beings known by different names in various religions for example the Angels of Christianity or the Dewas or shining ones of the Hindus. The 330 million Gods of the Vedas belong to this category. These beings of various grades inhabit the various planes below the Anupadaka plane.

The next phase of study is the constitution of man as Monad, Ego and Personality. The fragment of Divine life known as the Monad, manifests itself upon the plane of atma as the triple spirit. The spirit itself, remains upon its own plane, that of atma. The second that of intuition, or pure reason, as it is sometimes called puts itself down one level and expresses itself through the matter of the plane of buddhi. The third aspect that of intelligence, puts itself down two planes, and expresses itself through the matter of the higher mental or causal plane. The expression of the Monad, on the planes of atma, buddhi and causal, is the ego or individuality,. Individual means that which is not divisible without loss of identity, subsisting as one and individuality is defined as separate and distinct existence. The ego expresses itself in the lower planes as a personality, which is also triple in its manifestation and is, moreover, an accurate reflection of the arrangement of the ego. But, like other reflections it reverses itself. Intelligence of the causal plane reflects itself as thought in the lower mental plane.

Pure reason, or buddhi, reflects itself in the astral body and in some way much more difficult to comprehend, the spirit or atma reflects itself on the physical plane.

Atmic Body	Higher Action
Buddhic Body	Higher Feelings
Causal Body	Higher thoughts
Mental Body	Thoughts
Astral Body	Feelings
Physical Body	Actions

Fig 3- The Six bodies of Man

(a) The Immortal, Divine Nature or the Individuality of Man –

Atma	-	Will
Buddhi	-	Intuition
Causal	-	Intellect

(b) The mortal/perishable Nature or Personality of Man -

Mental	-	Thought
Astral	-	Feelings
Physical	-	Activity

Fig 4 – The Higher and Lower Nature of Man

The personality consists of the transitory vehicles through which the true man, the Thinker, expresses himself in the physical, astral and lower mental worlds, i.e., the physical, astral and lower mental bodies, and of all the activities connected with these vehicles. The individuality consists of the Thinker himself, the Self in the causal body. As a tree puts out leaves, to last through spring, summer and autumn, so does the individuality puts out personalities to last through the life periods spent on the physical, astral and lower mental planes. Just as the leaves take in, assimilate and pass on nutrient to the sap, which is eventually withdrawn into the parent trunk, and then fall and perish, so does the personality gather experience and pass it on to the parent individuality, eventually when its task is completed, falling and perishing. The ego incarnates in a personality for the sake of acquiring definiteness. The ego on his own plane is magnificent, but vague in his magnificence, except in the case of men far advanced on the road of evolution. The personality with its transient feelings, desires, passions and thoughts thus forms a quasi-independent entity.

In man's cycle of death and rebirth one is concerned principally with the three lower planes, the physical which is fully perceived, the invisible emotional world usually referred to as the astral plane, and the mental plane where thoughts take shape. When the outer body is physical the invisible thoughts and feelings are given expression through physical activities. But if the consciousness is removed from the physical world, and the astral body becomes the outer vehicle, the thoughts and feelings are expressed through that body in the astral world. In a similar manner, when the outer vehicle is mental, the consciousness is experiencing life through that medium. The Monad thus radiates his life outward into the denser planes of matter in order to awaken his latent divine nature. This uncovering requires experience in the physical, astral and mental worlds, enduring their conditions and responding to them. The object of the ego is to unfold its latent powers and this it does by putting itself down into successive personalities. Men who do not understand this and a great majority of humanity – look upon the personality as the real self, and consequently live for it alone, regulating their lives for what appears to be its temporary advantage. Another point to make a note of which will be covered in detail later is the difference between the upper mental or causal level and the lower mental or thought level. In the lower mental plane the vibrations of consciousness give rise to the images or pictures, every thought appearing as a living shape. Whereas the causal levels are concerned with the expression of abstract thoughts, ideas and principles; for these levels pertain to pure reason. The lower mental body deals with particulars, what are known as concrete thoughts e.g., - a particular book, house, triangle etc, whereas the causal body deals with principles, with abstract thoughts e.g., the principal of triangularity common to all triangles. The mental body thus deals with form thoughts, the causal body with formless thoughts.

If one considers the phases of involution and evolution, one may think of them as consisting of seven stages. During the first three stages the spirit descends. As it descends it broods over matter, imparting qualities, powers and attributes. These three stages of materialization which constitute the coming down or descent of spirit into matter or the lower planes is called involution. The fourth stage is the conflict between spirit and matter. The spirit comes into innumerable relations with matter. At first it is overpowered; then comes the point of balance, then slowly the Spirit begins to triumph over matter, so that when the fourth stage is over, the spirit is master of Matter and is ready for its ascent through the next three stages that complete the seven. Thus the fourth stage of conflict results in a point of balance between spirit and matter, this eventually results in the changing from involution to evolution. The next three stages constitute the phase of evolution in which the Spirit ascends gradually attaining mastery over matter. During this phase of evolution or the last three stages the Spirit organizes matter which it has mastered and endowed with a soul, turns it to its own purposes, shapes it for its own expression, so the Matter may become the means whereby all the powers of the Spirit shall be made manifest and active. The last three stages are thus taken up by the spiritual ascent. These three phases may be summarised as below –

Phase 1 – Stages 1,2 & 3 Involution – Spirit Descends into matter

Phase 2 – Stage 4 Conflict – Between Matter and Spirit

Phase 3 – Stages 5, 6 and 7 Evolution – Ascent of Spirit – Spiritualization

To briefly recapitulate and summarize what has been discussed so far referring back to figures 2 and 3 – just like the physical body corresponds to the Physical plane, the emotions, feelings and desires in man correspond to the astral plane, the thoughts in man correspond to the mental plane, the divine nature in man corresponds to the still higher and more subtle planes i.e., the intellect in man corresponds to the higher mental, causal plane, the intuition corresponds to the bauddhic plane, the divine will of man corresponds to the atmic plane and then are still two higher planes namely the Anupadic which corresponds to the Monad or the individual spark of God and the Adi plane where God himself or light resides.

Just like one needs the physical body to live in during the course of one's life on earth, so too one needs to live in one's emotional body during the course of one's life on the astral plane, one needs to live in one's mental body during the course of one's life on the mental plane, one needs to live in one's causal body during the course of one's life on the causal plane, one needs to live on one's bauddhic and atmic bodies respectively during the course of one's life on the bauddhic and atmic planes. The astral body is the seat of one's feelings and emotions, the mental body seat of concrete ideas, that is to say, ideas that relate to matter, the causal or higher mental body allows man access to the comprehension of sublime truths, to the mysteries of the universe, the buddhic body which like the astral body is the seat of emotions and feelings, but of a higher divine order, universal love and sacrifice. Finally, there is the atmic body, seat of that immortal spark which is the omnipotence of God. The first three bodies – physical, astral and mental – are fairly equally developed in all human beings, but the stage of development reached by the three higher bodies varies enormously from one individual to another. Only a certain number of philosophers and spiritualists succeed in rising to the level of the higher mental body and begin to live in the sublime realm of light. The brains of these few achieve such a fine degree of perfection that new centers awake into activity within their being and enable them to grasp the reality at the core of things. This is the world of intuition. Intuition is a vision, an instantaneous apprehension, an immediate and total grasp of the real world which lies beyond the mental plane, for, even on the mental plane, error and illusion are still possible.

An important aspect to understand in these studies is that a plane is a state and not a place. One must learn to eliminate the idea of place from that of plane. It is difficult to conceive of these planes as a state than a place. A plane is a condition or state of activity. It may be objected that these planes of life are but varying forms of vibration of matter? Not at all. Each plane represents a different degree of vibratory energy – but not of matter. Matter is merely a very low form of vibratory energy. The concept of planes has nothing whatsoever in common with that of space. When one speaks of rising from a lower to a higher plane or of descending from a higher to a lower plane it is wrong to picture it as an ascent or descent of steps. Nor is one picturing a rising or descending from one layer or strata to another. Even the familiar symbol of rising from the ocean depths to its surface, is incorrect. The nearest mental picture possible to be made of the transition from plane to plane, is that of increase or decrease of vibrations as evidenced in sound-waves, light waves, or waves of electricity. The transition from higher to lower, or lower to higher may be thought of (if desired) as a change of vibration in the energy of which all things are composed.

The astral plane must not be confused with the idea of being a place. It is always a state or condition and not a place. It is rather a degree of vibration, rather than a portion of space. Its dimensions are those of time – not that of space. When one uses the word 'region', 'realm', 'higher or lower', 'above or below', one uses them merely figuratively, just as one speaks of a 'high rate of vibration', or 'a rate of vibration above that, etc'. It is necessary to repeat this caution, for the reason that one easily erroneously connects the idea of plane with that of place, whereas there should be no mental association between the two. Throughout the book instead of saying that the individual life force or soul passes from one state of vibration to another, it will be spoken of as proceeding from one sub-plane or plane to another.

These planes interpenetrate and those dwelling on one plane are not conscious of those dwelling on another, nor can they pass from one plane to another with this exception – those dwelling on a higher plane are able to see (if they desire) the planes below them in the order of development, and may also visit the lower planes, if they desire to do so. However those on the lower planes are not able to either see or visit the higher planes. There are planes upon planes of disembodied existence. As discussed there are seven great planes but each great plane has seven sub-divisions and each sub-division has seven minor divisions, and so on. When one speaks of a man rising from one sub-plane to another one refers to transferring one's consciousness from one level to another. In the case of a man with an astral body, the focus of his consciousness shifts from the outer shell to the next within it. In course of time the outermost shell or ring disintegrates, the man then becomes able to respond to the vibrations of the next higher level of the astral plane and thus rises to the next sub-plane, and so on from one sub-plane to another. The period of stay on each sub-plane corresponds to the amount and activity of the matter in his astral body belonging to that sub-plane. Thus gradually one becomes unresponsive to the vibrations of one order of matter and answers instead to those of a higher order. Thus one world and its scenery and its inhabitants would seem to fade slowly away from his view while another world would dawn upon him.

One must not form the idea that it is only who functions as intellect in the causal body. As described previously, man is a Spark of the Divine Fire i.e., Monad, and that Monad manifests as its three aspects Spirit in the World of atma, as Intuition in the world of buddhi, and as Intelligence in the higher mental/causal world. It is these three aspects taken together which constitute the ego which inhabits the causal body. Thus man, as one knows, though in reality a Monad residing in the monadic world i.e., the plane of Anupadaka, shows himself as an ego in the higher mental world, manifesting the three aspects of himself which are designated as Spirit, Intuition and Intelligence. The development of the ego is thus the object of the whole process of descent into matter – the ego assumes veils of matter precisely because through them he is able to receive vibrations to which he can respond, so that his latent faculties may thereby be unfolded. All the activities that we call evil, whether selfish thoughts (mental) or selfish emotions (astral), invariably show themselves as vibrations of the coarser matter of those planes, while good and unselfish thought or emotions set in vibration the higher types of matter. As finer matter is more easily moved than course, it follows that a given amount of force spent in good thought or feeling produces perhaps a hundred times as much result as the same amount of force sent out into coarser matter. If this were not so, it is obvious that the ordinary man could never make any progress at all while one is probably entitled to assume that 90% of the thought and feeling of the undeveloped man is self-centered, even if not actually selfish, yet, if 10% of it is spiritual and unselfish, the man must already be rising somewhat above the average. The effect of 10 percent of force directed to good ends enormously outweighs that of 90 percent devoted to selfish purposes so that on the whole such a man makes an appreciable advance from life to life. A man who has even 1 per cent of good makes a slight advance. A man whose account balances exactly, so that he neither advances nor retrogrades must live a distinctly evil life, while in order to go downwards in evil a person must be an unusually consistent villain.

When life terminates, the physical body dies, consciousness recedes in stages towards its source centre. Following one's physical life the period of life in the astral world commences. One has to become dissociated from one's recent involvement in physical matter. This purgation process takes place in the astral world where the nature of desires and feelings that developed during the past earth life undergoes reconditioning and refining that permits at length, the further withdrawal of consciousness into the mental world. For some individuals, the time spent in the astral world is brief, for others it is more extended. This is so because disentanglement from all desires and feelings that were identified with physical matter is undertaken in the astral world. Naturally the person given to coarser sensual cravings and their gratification will require a longer time. Eventually this is accomplished and the astral period terminates. Following it, is passage into the mental or heaven world where the major period of time is spent by all people whose aspirations and pursuits have been less material. The discarnate soul now becomes completely freed of investiture in lower matter. The harvest of one's life experience is translated into spiritual capacity, into added faculties and growth of the individual, as a preparation for return to earth. Hence during this longest after – death period, which is the closing phase of the total cycle of an incarnation, the incarnated ego of man reaps the full benefit of his recent life time on earth, preparing in due season, for the return known as reincarnation. Having glanced in this way at the chart of the after – death course, we are ready now for a more detailed description of the various stages that will be experienced.

AWAKE – DREAM – SLEEP CYCLE AND DEATH

In gaining the experience of and knowledge of life after death there is nothing more important than to have a clear concept of the universe and this is done by making a comparative study of the day-night i.e., awake – dream and sleep cycle and how it relates to the regions of life after death. Each night one dies and each morning one rises from the dead. To go to sleep, is something one practises every night in order to be ready when the time comes for one's true departure to the next world. Someone who is not good at going to sleep will be no better at dying. There is no difference between dying and going to sleep, except that, when one dies one leaves one's present house for good, whereas, when one goes to sleep, one leaves one's present house or environment temporarily i.e., in sleep one is not aware of one's physical surroundings. If one is on earth it is because one has work to do here, one has something to learn here, and one of the things one has to learn and experience is the understanding of the regions of life after death related to the day to day awake-dream and sleep state cycle which every single human undergoes every-day.

The possibility of rebirth is explained by the analogy of sleep. In sleep one disappears into dream or unconsciousness. In death one does exactly the same. Every morning one reappears out of apparent blank nothingness with all of one's character and particular tendencies intact. The marvel of rebirth is thus not different from the marvel of waking up the same person every morning except that in the case of rebirth it is a different body and a different personality. Dream is an entry into the first hinterland of the mind. Sleep in general is something more than a mere physiological and psychological fact, when its profound significance is fully grasped it is a password into a higher comprehension of truth. A condition whose continuous loss would ordinarily cause insanity or death and one in which one spends roughly one third of one's life cannot in any case be deemed an unimportant one. A sixty-year-old person spends nearly twenty years in dream and deep sleep. Those fantasies of the night which one calls dreams and those blank moments of the mind which one calls slumber must surely have an important place in Nature's scheme. Human experience is not limited to the waking state alone but extends itself through these two other states also. Consequently a thorough scientific and philosophical view of human existence must bring all three states into consideration, otherwise it will be incomplete. These three states embrace the many varied aspects of a life beyond death.

A question that arises in one's mind is - what is the necessity to do a comparative study of the awake – dream and sleep cycle and the death-rebirth cycle? A possible answer to this can be given by the following story – There was once a monastery in which one of the monks regularly drank too much. Thanks to his great thirst, the level of wine in the barrels sank very rapidly. Every evening, feeling a little ashamed, he would say his prayers and ask God to forgive him, after which he would lie down with a clear conscience and sleep the sleep of a just man! The next day, the whole thing would repeat again. This went on for years until, one night he forgot to say his prayers before going to sleep. In the middle of the night he was woken up by someone shaking him and saying, 'wake up – you didn't say your prayers tonight. Get up and say them at once!' Rubbing his eyes, he looked to see who had woken him and found that it was the Devil, yes, the Devil had woken him, because it was he who encouraged him to say his prayers at night so that he would not feel the need to reform. With this prayer he put his conscience at rest and felt free to start drinking again next day....to the huge delight of the Devil! History recounts that when the monk realized this he was so terrified that he swore he would never drink another drop. One must always continue to make an effort to free oneself and get rid of one's bad habits if one wants to grow spiritually and gain knowledge of topics like life after death, wake-dream – sleep cycle and so on. If it is not so, one will be surrounded by vices and will make very little spiritual progress.

The process of dreaming fascinates all. It possesses a mystery and magic of its own. How do dreams originate? There is no theory of the origin of dreaming that is universally applicable. Only a broad comprehensive view is possible. Quite clearly there is an occult power at work during the dream which magically turns thoughts into things and ideas into forms for the perceiving mind. If the mind can create its own dream world of cities, forms or people, why should it not be able to create its own wakeful world too? When one remembers all the varied experiences which the mind creates during the dream state, one should ask oneself about a similar possibility in the waking state. Similarly the Cosmic Mind has created the regions of life after death. All dreams are necessarily a product of this image making power of the mind. The revelation of a dream is thus a revelation of this innate power. Nature teaches every individual that through one's dreams one has in miniature the same creative capacities as the Cosmic or World Mind. The wakeful world is a common one, being shared with other individuals, where-as the dream world is an individual one. No one else other than the individual has any part in its making. One may perceive other persons in one's dream but it is certain that ordinarily those persons do not simultaneously see the one dreaming in their own dreams, whereas in the wakeful state each does perceive the other. The still face of a dreamer reveals nothing what one is experiencing in the dream state.

The world into which one enters is the dreamer's own secret, even someone in an adjoining bed, whether awake or asleep, cannot enter it. The scientific explanation of the continuity of the waking world as contrasted with the discontinuity of the dreaming world, is of course, the fact that the former draws its existence primarily from the Cosmic or World Mind's permanent master-image whereas the latter draws it solely from the individual mind's ephemeral visions. It is of profound significance that each dreamer's world belongs to that individual alone whereas the waking world is common to all mankind. Here nature gives every person, in one's own personal experience a key to the mystery of world creation. In fact an individual is able to create one's own image of one's dream environment, one can then comprehend how one can receive and reproduce one's own image of the waking world emanated from the Cosmic Mind. Most people do not know that this larger being exists within them; even those who do know it do not know what an important element it really is in making their world experience; while those who realize its importance know very little about its operations anyway. Here, in the image making power of the finite self, they are provided with a suggestive glimpse of the image making power of the infinite Self.

Imagination is the first characteristic of the Cosmic Mind. Consequently it is also the first characteristic of the conscious beings who are its progeny. This wonderful image-making faculty is a natural possession of the mind. The faculty of forming pictures is as innate in the individual as in the Cosmic Mind. It is perfectly natural for the restraint-free mind to go on evolving pictures. This is the very same faculty with which one unconsciously creates the form of one's world during waking hours, but it works then under the stimulus of the world-image provided by the Cosmic Mind's Karmic potential. The seed-like karmic energies of the world-image are transmitted from the habitat of the Over self (or the habitat of a part of the individuals cosmic spirit) in the heart and received within the head. Here in a sensitive centre within the brain's outer layer it undergoes tremendous magnification and through the other specialized brain centers breaks into the individual consciousness as one's sense – impressions of external world experience.

Why is it that rational order and natural unity seem to disappear so often in these motley dreams? Figures and events appear and disappear haphazardly without logical connections. The disorder and confusion are explicable when one remembers again that the brain-reception has been partially and temporarily set free from the heart-transmission so that the image making faculty works mechanically to a large extent on its own. In the dream state awakened consciousness recedes to the heart centre. The force of suggestions drawn from the memory of waking experiences motivates many of these dreams. The episodes are fed either by previous thoughts, emotions, passions and action, when both scene and circumstances can be easily traced to something said, thought, felt or done during the previous twenty four hours. In addition the creative fancy draws upon forgotten but stored up previous impressions of the past for constructing its dream edifices. They may re-appear wildly and fantastically distorted, however, because the restraining influence of the higher intellectual faculties of reason, critical reflection and judgment are outbalanced by the wild running of the image-making faculty. There is then a partial failure in discriminating and classifying the images. Although the higher intellectual faculties of rational judgment, adequate discrimination and proper classification are retarded or reduced during dream they are not suspended altogether. They exert a certain degree of control, which is not always uniform, being generally feeble. It has already been noted that imagining is the basic activity of the universe and that therefore it is the first characteristic of an individual. From an evolutionary standpoint one has retreated in the dream condition halfway back into one's original self, when one's image-making faculty worked in a freer, fuller and less restrained manner. Hence the profuse outpouring of imagination is natural during dream.

There are large changes of bodily conditions, which separate dreaming and waking life into two different classes. When one lies stretched upon one's bed and enters the sleep state the pulse rate falls, the blood flow is slackened and all the organic functions slow down. The heart beats, the lungs breathe and repair-work starts on the tissues. Ordinarily as the sensations which describe environment fade away, attention begins to wander and one begins to relax the control by will and critical intelligence which operates during fully conscious life. The number of thoughts grow less and less as sleep approaches. Finally the room melts away and vanishes into nothingness as one's consciousness is mysteriously and entirely isolated from the physical world, it sees nothing, hears nothing, smells nothing, feels nothing and tastes nothing and then a dream enters it. Similarly at the instant of death consciousness loses touch with the sense organs i.e., sight, sound, taste, smell and touch and one goes into deep slumber or a state of dream and sleep before one becomes conscious or enters the next world i.e., the world of desire or astral world or Kamaloka. It is easier to explain deep sleep although it is a profounder state when compared to the dream state.

For if some dreams are symbolic and will bear interpretation, many others are not and mean nothing. Who has not awakened after experiencing a nightmare wherein one was being suffocated by some grim monster, only to find that the weight of unduly heavy bed clothes was the cause? Who has not undergone a series of startling fights with a wild animal, only to find that an undigested supper was the reason. The dreamer may turn a knock on the door of a bedroom into a clap of thunder. Most dreams are of no consequence; however it is equally true there is a class of uncommon dreams which possess special significance. Discrimination is therefore required in one's examination. A purely materialist explanation of dreams will not account for all of them. Nor is it right to assert that our dreams draw their material solely from waking experience, past or present, forgotten or remembered.

Where a dream is really significant, is when the consciousness has completely retreated into the heart centre, has dispensed with the contribution of the brain, and is once again working in complete accord with the master world-image which it finds within the heart. Such a dream then has nearly the same status as the waking state but it is a different kind of experience. Its significance will be intuitively felt after awakening. It may happen that one dreams things and thoughts, persons and events, which cannot be ascribed to earlier waking perceptions by any stretch of theory. Such dreams leave extremely vivid after-images and their memory is hard to shake off, even after several years have passed. The sense of familiarity with new places or persons may, on rare occasions, be due to this cause. These dreams arise out of one's karma and are either actual transcripts or vague reminiscences of former happenings. Their roots are deep down in earlier incarnations and they revive events, which happened then. Then there are rare dreams, which are most important because they originate from an altogether different level of mind than the animal part of one's being. One who will not listen to the sublime whisper of one's Divine Self (or a part of one's Cosmic Spirit that resides in the heart) during waking hours will respond more easily during one's dreaming periods, when the veil is thinner, partly because one's egoistic will is more relaxed and partly because one is actually nearer the source of consciousness. It is dreams of this superior character, which bear good fruit after one awakes. Akin to them but also rare are those half-remembered dreams wherein one who has learnt to live in the Divine Self appears to a friend, student or follower to exalt, warn, guide or encourage at a critical time and invariably in a clear connected vision at the moments preceding death.

One must realize that the body has a very important role to play in spiritual life; if it is not well trained it can prevent the spirit from leaving it and doing the work it has to do. There is more than one kind of sleep. Most people would be horrified if they knew where they spent their nights, the psychic regions they went to when they were asleep. They spend their time floundering in the swamps of their own bad habits and coarse appetites. Very few are sufficiently detached to free themselves from their sensations and desires of the physical i.e., earthly plane. When one's soul manages to escape from one's sleeping body, it is never idle; it moves about, contemplating and communicating with Heavenly spirits and gaining greater understanding of love, wisdom and truth. When it re-enters one's body, it brings with it the memory of all the revelations it has received and attempts to pass them on to one's brain. It is these memories that are called dreams. This is why one should try to recall one's dreams as soon as one is awake, for at that moment; the principal images are still floating in one's brain.

Dreams will sometimes come back to one during the course of the day, but it is better to try and recapture them as soon as one wakes up. If one can get into the habit of doing this, it will be easier for one to remember an experience or, perhaps, a warning or some advice received during the night which will help one see what one should do during the day. One may sometimes come across the following experience, while meditating one may suddenly find oneself fact to face with something that terrifies one and one cannot think what had happened. It is simply that one had gone out from one's body and been lured into the shadowy regions of the astral plane, where one sensed that one was being harassed and threatened. For one must not forget, the encounters one may have on the astral plane will not always be very reassuring. If one finds a mole creeping about in one's garden and tries to catch it, it will immediately run into its underground burrow, because that is where it feels safe. How does it know that it can escape by hiding in a hole in the ground? As for human beings, depending on the danger that threatens, one will try to escape into a cave, or up onto the roof, or by climbing a tree or taking to the water. The dangers that threaten human beings are not only physical, they can also be psychic. When one is being pursued on the astral plane, in the regions inhabited by monsters and malicious entities, one must run back, as fast as one can, into one's physical body, in other words, into one's burrow. This is what happens when one is having a nightmare, one escape by waking up, because, by re-entering one's body, one re-enters a different world. Nightmares usually end abruptly, one wakes up with a start and a sensation of immense relief to find oneself in the safety of one's own bed. One says to oneself, 'Thank goodness it was only a dream?' In reality, the safe refuge is neither the bed nor one's room, it is one's physical body. The abrupt awakening was caused by the fact that one knew, subconsciously, that in order to defend oneself against the hostile forces and entities of the astral world, one had to flee to the shelter of one's body which is like a fortress in which one can take refuge. If one had stayed on the astral plane one would have continued to be at the mercy of one's aggressors, by leaving that plane and taking shelter behind the thick, solid walls of one's physical body, one escapes from them. Spirits are not given access to all planes, as they have been created to live and work on one particular plane. The entities of the astral plane, therefore cannot pursue one wherever one goes, if one knows how to move from one plane to another one shall be safe. In fact it is this ability to move from one plane to another that gives human beings their superiority.

It is here in this physical world, which the ascetic despises, which the materialist overvalues and the mystic undervalues that one has to fulfill one's spiritual destiny and realize one's higher individuality, and gain the nature and knowledge of the regions of life after death. For it is only through the maturity of wakefulness and by means of its paramount contribution that can lead to such a realization and gaining of knowledge. Dreams, however, come as tutors to tell wherein one has erred. Nature further breaks up human modes of mental life into the triple degrees of unconsciousness, semi-consciousness and consciousness (corresponding to deep sleep, dream and wakefulness) and thus renders it possible for humans to grasp certain truths. One is so powerfully mesmerized into the belief of world materiality, so strongly chained during one's wakeful condition to self-identification with one's body alone that nature has to enable one to detach oneself periodically from one's bondage by periodically breaking up both the wakeful state and one's earthly life. This she does by interrupting the one with sleep and the other with death. One similarity that can be observed that sleep represents or corresponds to the region of life after death relates to the timing of the two states. One recalls one's dreams in disjointed fragments and sudden revelations. They are rarely remembered as complete parts. The process usually is as swift as it is unexpected. They are quickly lost on awakening, save for blurred broken memories of the last scenes. One often reproaches dreams for this swift transience which makes one remember them only in meager scraps. Similarly often in an occasional flash of one's memory one remembers one's past lives in disjointed fragments. Before one is awake, one cannot understand that what one can see in the dream does not exist externally. Similarly the true reality of the regions of life after death dawn on a human only when one leaves the physical body.

Not only does the mind express itself through the waking and dreaming states, but also in a third state wherein sleep attains its highest intensity and when consciousness completely vanishes. This condition is therefore what must be studied next. It is commonly believed that the profound torpor of mind, the utter inactivity of muscles and the complete stillness of the five senses which characterize sleep have no other meaning other than that of a halt called by nature to the day's activities for the rebuilding of wasted tissues, recuperation of spent energy and the resting of tired mental faculties. That the study of this state, no less than the dream state, could be a gateway to the increase one's knowledge of the regions of life after death is seldom known. Were there not some kind of continuity of selfhood within the mind, one might fall asleep thinking one was one person and wake up thinking one was another person. One cannot therefore rightly set up the waking and dream consciousness as exhausting the continuity of the mind's existence. It is clear that unconsciousness is really an inaccurate description of its most mysterious phase. Both deep sleep and physical death free one from all the fears and pain but they also free one from all the hopes and joy. This is because one then ceases to limit oneself solely to the consciousness of the body.

Problems which agitated many a man prior to falling asleep were solved immediately and spontaneously on waking again the following morning. The same problems seemed impossible to solve prior to sleep. The obvious conclusion is that in some mysterious manner the mind carries on its activity during the night which enables it to present a result hitherto deemed impossible, to consciousness the following day. It is this deeper layer of the mind beneath the threshold of conscious thinking which is the secret source of all those glorious artistic inspirations, all those recaptured missing links of knowledge and all those intuitive decisions which triumph over perplexing problems. These inspirations come from the region of life after death called the mental world or Manas Loka. At some point in one's life, one must have had the experience of waking up in the morning with the feeling that something had become quite clear in one's mind. One has no idea that from where the enlightenment came from, but it is as though one had seen or heard or understood something, one just knows that one has learnt something new and valuable. When one learns things like this, in one's sleep, it is because one has been taught by divine entities. The things one learns in schools and universities are usually no more than a distant reflection of truth; the true reality of things can only be learnt in the world above. Hence, instead of trying to devour all the books that one can find in the libraries, one must remember that one can ask the Entities of Wisdom to enroll one in their school and learn while one is asleep. When one wakes up in the morning, one may not remember all that one has seen and heard but it will all be recorded within one's brain and one day, one will be amazed to see how many things, begin to become clear. It is important to understand to what extent sleep can be something sacred when one goes to sleep with the intention of learning in the world above; this is where one receives true Initiation. Moreover it is at night that a disciple leaves his body and goes to join his master in order to continue learning from him. Here again, when one wakes up in the morning, one will not remember exactly what one saw or understood in one's sleep, but one will have a sensation of something beautiful and luminous that will stay with one all day long.

The day is too short for an Initiate to accomplish all that he wants to; that is why he does much of it at night. Even if he sees each person for only fifteen or twenty minutes, he can fit so few into one day – and they come to him so burdened and tormented by their problems – how can he give them the help they need in such a short time? During the night, an initiate can be in several places at once to help those who need him, his physical body does not move from his bed, but his spirit travels wherever he is needed to help and bring light to others. His Spirit never sleeps, it is always active; this is the difference between an Initiate and an ordinary person. Is there something one really wants to achieve? A weakness one wants to overcome or a quality one wants to acquire? Meditate at length and then go to sleep with this desire in mind and it will continue to work while one is asleep. Suppose for example, that you know that someone dislikes you and is trying to harm you. If you cannot go and talk to him about it, go to sleep with the thought that you will go and see him during the night and tell him, 'Listen, my friend, even if you do manage to harm me, what good will it do to you? You will be happy for a little while and I shall suffer for a little while, but my suffering will make me stronger, and, in the long run, you will be the loser. What's more you will have a karmic debt to pay. You'd be better off to give up the whole thing, because it won't do you any good. In this way you will influence his subconscious and he may decide to change his mind. Even if he doesn't change his mind, at least you will have learnt to do another kind of mental work. One will probably wonder as to what extent one can trust visions and dreams. Both reflect the level of evolution attained by the dreamer or the seer; both always mean something, but the dreams and visions of those who have not yet managed to free themselves from the lower astral plane will stem from that hazy region. Obviously, therefore one cannot rely on them for true answers to one's questions or a clear knowledge of reality. Only one who has reached the causal, buddhic and atmic planes can gain such knowledge.

Every material phenomenon is simply the concrete materialization of a non-material phenomenon. Take the example of a snake, its tail has to always follow its head. The head represents an idea, a plan, and the tail represents the realization of the plan, the materialization of events, which already exist in the subtle world. One must realize the truth about life while yet in the flesh. The more attention is concentrated, the more mental are the images which is a result of the regions of life after death. Such concentration achieves its most intense degree during wakefulness and this is one reason why earthly life seems more real to us than any other. Humanity can attain its fullest spiritual Self-realization only in the wakeful state of the physical world, because the after death regions described as the equivalents to the dreaming and sleeping states only. It becomes necessary for the imperfect spirit to return to earth again, where alone it can find the adequate conditions for its further progress. Whoever has followed carefully the foregoing explanation will understand why it is impossible to give in detail a genuine scientific account of everything that happens to an individual spirit.

Most people usually are misled when reading descriptions which purport to describe post-mortem life, The master key to understanding the psychological experience of it is to keep in view its identity with dream or sleep. The mind is immortal. It remains untouched despite the body's dissolution. One has no more reason to fear its death when the body is destroyed than one has to fear its death when one retires to sleep at night. Sleep affects the body but leaves the mind as active as ever in dream or as potentially active as ever in deep sleep. Death works upon the human being in a somewhat similar manner and the experiences which come to the soul after the body has terminated are nothing else than prolonged vivid dreams or unconscious deep sleep. If one can touch and see things and people without the help of the body during dream, one shall certainly be able to do the same during so-called death. Also if one can take a benign rest from all the problems of personal existence at a later and deeper stage of sleep, one shall certainly be able to enjoy the same rest at a later stage of death. In that stage the one who can survive dream and sleep in the earth-world will likewise survive them in the after world.

THE ETHERIC BODY

Anyone who has seen a corpse, even one prepared for viewing at an open-casket funeral, knows that it looks very different from how the person is remembered. Despite morticians' best efforts, the corpse is unmistakably dead. The very obvious basis of life, what we call the etheric body, is gone. Death can be defined by the etheric body's severance from the dense physical form.

Among the various vehicles utilized by the human Ego for its evolution, the Etheric body, also known as the Vital Body, is an essential component. The Etheric body is not a body in the same sense that the astral or the physical bodies are. It serves two main purposes: a) to act as a link between the physical body and the subtle astral and mental bodies, and b) to provide vitality to the dense physical body. As such, it originates and sustains certain functions in the physical body. Let us first examine the true composition of what is known as the Physical World. Basic chemistry has identified three primordial states: Solids, Liquids and Gases. There are four more, although still physical, they are finer than the gaseous state of physical matter. These finer, more subtle, substances constitute the Etheric Region of the Physical World. The dense physical body - which for convenience will be referred to simply as the 'physical body' - is composed of matter of the three lower sub planes of the physical plane which are solid, liquid and gaseous. The etheric body is composed of matter of the four higher sub planes. Our present focus is on the human etheric body, but animals, plants, and even rocks and minerals all have etheric bodies. However rocks and minerals have their etheric bodies on the next higher plane. We understand that the Earth, the Sun, and all other entities in the universe also have etheric bodies. Despite being considered physical, etheric matter cannot be seen or perceived by the senses nor measured by instruments. The human eye perceptional range nor those of instruments do not reach its vibratory rate hence the existence of this very important part of the Physical World is at present unsuspected by science. But the testimony of trained clairvoyants, plus that of many people who have a natural disposition to perceive beyond the normal range of the eyes, clearly confirm the existence of these ethers. The etheric part of our Physical Body is called the Etheric Sheath.

The Etheric body is also responsible for controlling important functions of the dense physical body. Its etheric matter is divided into four types, each being instrumental to those functions as follows:

1. Reflecting Ether - This Ether owes its name to what has been termed the 'Memory of Nature.' This universal memory is part of the Mental World (Concrete Region) and records all that has taken place during the active life period of the Universe (Manvantar - a period of manifestation, as opposed to dissolution or rest).It is also known as the Akashic Records(also called the Akashic Chronicle it is the enduring record of all that happens, and has ever happened, in space and time).By means of using the reflecting Ether, clairvoyants may have access to this reflected information when required. We are told that all actions and even the thoughts of human beings are indelibly recorded there, making it thus an invaluable source of accurate historical data. However, there could be some difficulties posed for the researcher in that what is being observed is - we must not forget - a reflection and not always a clear one. It is pretty much like trying to see through dirty glasses. Hence, the best method to read the Akashic Records with precision and accuracy is by means of direct contact with the Mental World, where only very high Initiates can have direct access while incarnated. This Ether is also the medium through which thought is transmitted to the human brain by the mind (or Mental Body) because it is closely connected with the fourth or highest sub-level of the Concrete Region of the Mental World, which is considered as the home of the human mind.

2. The Light Ether- Like the other Ethers, this one has negative and positive polarities. The forces acting through its positive pole generate warm blood in man and animals of the higher species. The forces working through its negative pole are concerned with the development and functions of the five senses, especially building and nourishing of the eye. The positive pole of this Ether is also concerned with the circulation of blood in cold-blooded animals. As it has been often observed, when one sense is lost due to illness or accident, this Ether works through its negative pole to strengthen the other senses compensating thus for the handicap. For example, if one becomes blind, then one's sense of hearing will become keener. Nature offers a good example of this in the way it deals with the different animal species. Dogs have poor sight, but their keen sense of smell and hearing, stronger than in man, do compensate for their shorter range in sight.

Forces working through the positive pole of this Ether cause the circulation of juices in plants. When winter arrives, the forces of this pole tend to weaken, this being the reason why plants tend to wither away when there is an absence of sun. The return of spring and summer will energize the force again, and vitality will return to the plant. The color of plants is due to the action of the negative forces of this Ether.

3. Life Ether - This Ether is concerned with the perpetuation of the species through the forces of propagation. Its positive polarity acts upon the gestation process of the female, while the negative enables the production of semen in the male.

4. Chemical Ether - This Ether is concerned with the assimilation of the nutritional elements of the food we eat as well as the excretory functions. Both processes are carried out through forces which do not act mechanically but selectively and whose effects are well known by regular science. The positive pole acts on the assimilation of food, the negative on the excretory functions. Thus the role of this Ether is centered on the growth and sustenance of the physical body. When proper control is not exercised, our astral body may sometimes have a detrimental effect over our physical body in its relentless pursuit of the fulfillment of its desires. Our Etheric Body, on the other hand, works constantly to restore the energy on the flesh vehicle. Also this Ether is responsible for the chemical combination of the elements in fixed ratios to form the compounds.

The etheric body is composed of interlocking and circulating lines of force or pathways, called nadis (complex network of pathways or channels through which prana - life energy passes through the physical body). These nadis, are the carriers of energy. They are in fact the energy itself and carry the quality of energy from some area of consciousness in which the dweller in the body may happen to be focused. The largest nadis, or bundles of nadis, are the sushumna(central main energy channel which extends from the base of the spine to the head),ida(one of the main energy channels running on the left side of the central channel -sushumna, stimulating the right side of the brain) and pingala (one of the main energy channels running on the right side of the central channel -sushumna, stimulating the left side of the brain), which run up the spine, and which are the externalization of the antahkarana (Antahkarana is a way, a conduit, a connection between our intelligent mind and the higher levels of perception and consciousness, it consists of manas - sensory processing mind, chitta - storage of impressions the memory, buddhi - that knows, decides, judges, and discriminates and ahankara – The 'I'- maker,egoitythe ego) composed of the antahkarana proper, the sutratma(the thread soul or that which binds all things together, the chord which conveys the vital force or prana into a body, the consciousness thread passing from the soul to the physical body that connects the physical body to the etheric body onwards to the astral body and finally to the mental body)or life thread, and the creative thread. Of those three, sutratmais the most important to the present discussion. The sutratma, popularly known as the silver cord, is spun by the Ego from within the causal body much as a spider spins a thread. It can be shortened or extended at will. It enters the physical body through the top of the head, and is anchored in the heart to sustain the life of the physical body during the incarnation. The whole etheric body is but an extension of one aspect of the sutratma. The sutratma is lengthened when the astral body and higher vehicles separate from the physical form during sleep or in an out-of-body experience and contracts when the individual returns to waking consciousness.

Smaller nadis correspond to the meridians of Chinese medicine, while the smallest ones permeate the entire etheric body, including the part that extends beyond the physical form. The nadis, we understand, underlie every nerve in the human body, and the centers which they form at certain points of intersection or juncture are the background or motivating agency of every ganglion or plexus found in the human body. Nodes, or points of intersection, in the network of nadis constitute the minor and major chakras, or centers. They are foci for the exchange of energy between the etheric and higher planes, and are entry points for the receipt of prana. The chakras are found in close proximity to, or in relation to major glands or organs. Indeed, the various glands are in reality the externalization or materialization of the centers, major and minor.

At death, the etheric body is withdrawn from the dense physical form. When the lifetime comes to an end the etheric body withdraws from the dense physical form. In due course, after three days, it too is abandoned, as the lessons learned at the physical, astral, and lower mental levels are absorbed into their respective permanent atoms.

Following an understanding of the etheric body as described in the previous pages, we now need to understand and get an overview of our Aura.

Everything that exists, be it human beings, animals, plants or even the stones in the ground, is surrounded by its own subtle, fluidic atmosphere made up of the particles and emanations it is constantly giving off. It is this atmosphere that constitutes the aura. Of course, it is not visible, except to clairvoyants and, in fact, a great many people don't even know that it exists. The aura is kind of halo which surrounds every human being, the only difference being that some people's aura is immense and very brilliant, extending its gloriously varied colors and intense vibrations to great distance, whereas others are meager and lusterless, with dirty, blurred colors.

The aura has exactly the same functions as the skin. You could say that it is the skin of the soul which it surrounds and protects. It is also its sense organ and, finally, it is the means of communication which enables the soul to receive the Cosmic currents flowing through space and to communicate and exchange with others, with other human souls, other creatures of the universe, even with the stars in the heavens, and with the Supreme Universal Soul. The cosmic, planetary and zodiacal influences ceaselessly flowing through space reach out to touch us and, depending on the purity and sensitivity of our aura and the colors it contains, we may capture or fail to capture certain specific forces. Our aura, therefore, is like an antenna, it is an instrument which detects and receives messages, waves and forces coming to us from the length and breadth of the universe. Now, suppose there are certain negative, harmful influences at large in the universe: if your aura is very powerful and very luminous, those negative influences will be unable to reach your consciousness or to upset or harm you. Why? Because before they can get to you they come up against your aura, and your aura is an impenetrable barrier. It is like a wall.

The aura is a combination of all the emanations of all our subtle bodies, each of which, by adding its own unique emanations adds its own shades and tints to the whole. One's etheric body forms an aura which penetrates and interweaves with the aura of the physical body and the combined aura of one's physical and etheric bodies reveals the state of one's health and vigor. The astral and mental bodies, according to their activity or inertia, their qualities or their weaknesses, add their own special emanations, their own coloring, to the initial aura, thus revealing the nature of one's thoughts and feelings. And if the casual, buddhic and atmic bodies have been awakened, they add yet other, brighter, more luminous colors and other, more powerful vibrations.

Following is a brief overview of the various vehicles or bodies which constitute the aura.

1. Physical Body (AnnamayaKosha) - The first body is called Annamaya Kosha. Anna means 'food,' maya means 'form' better known as 'illusion', a different word. So Annamaya Kosha is the food-formed sheath. We may simply call it the physical body because the physical body is indeed built on sustenance – the nourishment we take in, be it water, food, or air. The Annamaya Kosha is the physical body.

2. Etheric Body (PranamayaKosha) - Behind the physical body is the PranamayaKosha or the etheric body. This etheric body is a corpus that has subtle layers of energy, much as a room is permeated with wiring that allows the central lights to go on. If there is any interference with that wiring, the lights go out.

The relationship between the etheric body and the physical body is rather like the relationship between the nervous system and the physical body. The etheric body is a matrix of pure energy, supporting and feeding the physical with life forces.

The etheric body provides a kind of power, a kind of spiritual energy or prana, to move the physical body, including allowing the electrical-chemical operations of the nervous system. It provides the pranic irrigation channels (nadis) or acupuncture meridians that nourish the physical body. It is both the substrata and the matrix supporting the physical body.

Indeed the etheric body is the subtle energy body and it controls many of the body's physical functions

3. Astral or Emotional body(Manamaya Kosha) - Beyond that etheric body is another body. This body is known as Manamaya Kosha, also known as the astral or emotional body. This astral-emotional body is like that part of our nervous system (the limbic system and the thalamus in the brain) that is responsible for emotional reaction. It is body that is glued together or held by emotion or feeling, both positive and negative. It has to do also with the dream world.

4. Mental Body(VijnamayaKosha) - After the astral body is the VijnamayaKosha, or the body of discrimination. We will call it the mental body. This mental body is capable of logic - it holds the buddhi(the higher mind, which is the seat of wisdom, the discerning, discriminating aspect of mind, the ability to make decisions and draw conclusions) or the reasoning faculty, and is capable of pure mental computation and coming to decisions.

5. Spiritual Body (Anandamaya Kosha) - Finally there is the Anandamaya Kosha, the spiritual body. It is also known as the Causal body or Karan Sharira. This is the deepest core of being - our essence. In deep sleep, when the mind and senses cease functioning, it stands between the finite world and the Self. The AnandamayaKosha is a reflection of the Atman (Soul) which exists in a state of absolute bliss. Through it one enjoys the bliss of God.

The Causal body is named 'Causal' because it is the originating source of each personality that incarnates in each lifetime. When the personality ends, one's essence is absorbed back into the Causal Body. The Causal Body is the highest level of one's individual self.

The Causal Body exists for many millions of years, during one's journey as a human being through many lifetimes. When liberated from the cycle of rebirth the human being moves onto higher planes beyond the causal body. The Causal Body is the final sheath around the Soul. Once the individual has worked out one's causal karma the soul is free to return to God and to Oneness.

The Causal Body is the depository for all consciousness and virtues cultivated in each lifetime. The Causal Body stores the will-power, love-wisdom and creative intelligence that one has developed in one's many lives. It is built out of all the experiences of one's past lives. It is the treasure chest that keeps safe the fruits of all past experiences. It is the body of the abstract ideas, high ideals and holds the record of the actions carried out in past lives. It is indestructible, and it lasts as long as the evolution of the individual soul lasts. The Casual Body functions as our karmic bank. It is the vehicle that facilitates the unfolding of one's consciousness.

As the physical body needs air to sustain life, so does the etheric body need life force energy, most of which is extracted from the air we breathe. This vital force is known as 'Prana' in India. This vital energy can be received, stored, and changed naturally in the force centers of the etheric body, as electricity is stored in batteries.

The human etheric body permeates and extends a short distance beyond the physical body and resembles its physical counterpart in shape. It extends about one-half of an inch (a little over a centimeter) beyond the physical body. The astral, mental, spiritual bodies extend much further from the physical body beyond the etheric body and occupy a space up to two to three feet beyond the physical body.

Like the five digits of the hand, we have not one but five bodies and these five bodies integrate. If one looks at this aspect and agrees with it one can then understand a lot of things in one's life. Let us understand this with a physical analogy. The physical body is a conglomeration of actual tissues composed of some sixty trillion cells, stratified into organs and systems. If you walk over to me and kick me in the shins, some nerve endings in the shinbone will fire, this is like the etheric body being brought into action. As the pain impulses register in the limbic system of my brain (deep inside the cerebrum), I get emotional, I get shocked, I get dazed, I get confused and this activation is the astral or emotional body. Then the impulses go up to my cerebral cortex and the frontal lobes take over. "That's got to be an accident because I haven't annoyed you", is the conclusionreached, and this is a function typical of the mental body. The spiritual body, throughout this experience, remains totally uninvolved, functioning as merely the silent witness of my life and events.

The aura as one can infer is a blend of all the different emanations of every aspects of a human being. Compared to the aura of a human being as mentioned previously minerals, plants and animals also have an aura, but theirs is a purely physical aura. Minerals, metals and crystals give off certain forces which form a sort of miniature magnetic field of colours around them. The aura of plants is more intense and has more vitality than that of minerals because their etheric body adds its own vigor, its own compiling urge for growth. The aura of animals is richer again, because animals have an astral body, the body of desire. In general, animals have not yet begun to develop their mental body, although it does seem that there are a few exceptions such as dogs, horses, elephants and monkeys, in which biologists detect a certain capacity for thought.

True, the aura is constant in that it always manifests the fundamental nature of its owner, but subtle variations flit through it continually. It is like a person's face, in the course of the day it registers every possible expression, but that doesn't mean that the shape of one's nose, forehead or mouth have actually changed. Similarly with the aura, it is made up of certain radiations and colors which reveal a person's true nature, and this does not change substantially during one's lifetime, but other, secondary vibrations come and go, reflecting transitory changes and states. Those who give way to certain emotions or weaknesses, therefore, are constantly clouding the atmosphere of their aura, so that when beneficial currents and forces seek an entry, looking for a welcome and a place to rest, they come up against a barricade of muddy, opaque colors. If your life is meaningless and chaotic your aura will be crisscrossed by so many untidy eddies and currents that it will no longer be an effective shield against the hostility of invisible enemies. In these conditions you will be unable to establish a harmonious relationship of mutual exchange with the universe and other living creatures. In keeping with the Law of Affinity you will be receptive only to all that is somber, chaotic and discordant in the universe; all that is luminous will automatically be rejected. Light attracts light; purity attracts purity. So if your aura is impure, muddy and chaotic all the pure, harmonious, luminous forces will keep away. Only those which are muddy and ugly will be able to get in because your aura only opens its doors to forces of the same breed as itself. Like to like.

If your aura is not luminous, therefore, it is not an effective protection, nor is it a good instrument with which to receive signals from the Invisible World and perceive the hidden aspect of reality. This means that you will possess neither intuition nor foresight, nor be able to exchange messages with Heaven; entities dwelling in the far-away regions of space will not notice that you exist. Those who dwell in the sublime heights of the Invisible World will not even see you. Whereas if your aura is luminous they will see you perfectly. How well, suppose you are on a ship in the middle of the ocean at night; if your ship is not carrying any lights no one will be able to see it, but if you send up a flare or switch on a search-light, someone will see you. This is only an example, of course, being communicated here.

So it is not surprising that nobody notices when human beings cry out in pain, and groan and curse their fate? Is it any wonder that no one comes to their rescue? They don't produce any light! They have to send out signals of light, and the aura is the instrument that they should use for this purpose. So one's aura can serve not only to attract the attention of heavenly entities, but it can also give one access to the regions in which these entities dwell.

EXPERIENCING DEATH

To get a clearer prospective on what happens at the time of death, one has to first consider the experience the individual life force undergoes just before, and immediately after, its passage from the physical body. As one approaches the stage generally called death, one experiences a gradual dulling of the physical senses. Seeing, hearing, and feeling grow dimmer and dimmer, and the life of the individual appears to be like a flickering candle flame gradually approaching extinction. In many cases this is the only phenomenon experienced at the approach of death.

The experiencing of death itself is not as painful or fearful as often pictured. It is true its approach is often painful, but with its arrival pain ceases and unless there is some unusual reason, fear is not present. Frequently one is subject to the idea of death as being a final agonizing and desperate struggle. Many such fear producing versions have been created about the subject by uneasy minds. This is definitely not the case. Reviewing further what usually occurs at the time of death, the individual who is conscious during the dying hours will become aware of a growing coldness and inertness in ones extremities, as the vital forces withdraw towards the heart centre and the region of the brain. There is nothing to fear about departure from the physical body. Pain has been reduced to a minimum by science and the average experience of transition, more often than not, is a happy one. It should be revealing that usually the dying person's face relaxes and frequently lights up with a smile, often becoming radiant as with some inner glow of vision. In almost every case the actual passing away appears to be perfectly painless, even after a long illness involving terrible suffering. The peaceful look on the face of the dead is strong evidence in favor of this statement.

Another matter which should be mentioned here is the wonderful phenomenon of the review of the past life of the individual life force, that great panorama which passes before its mental vision. This really occupies but an infinitesimal moment of time – a moment so brief that it can scarcely be spoken of as a point in time, yet in this brief moment, the individual life force witnesses the panorama of the life it has passed on earth. At the actual moment of death, even when death is sudden, one sees the whole of one's past life in its minutest detail. In a moment one sees the whole chain of causes which had been at work during one's life; one sees and now understands oneself as one really is, without flattery or self-deception, one reads one's life, remaining as a spectator. Scene after scene, from infancy to old age, life passes by so it can be reviewed by the one. The most insignificant incident is reproduced in detail as is the greatest event. The sub-conscious planes of memory unfold their secrets to the last – nothing is reserved or withheld. Moreover, the individual life force, by its awakened spiritual discernment, is able to know the meaning, cause, and consequence of every event in its life. It is able to analyze and to pass judgment upon itself and its acts. Like an omniscient and impartial judge it judges itself.

Normally, during this period there takes place a flash review of all that has been experienced in the life now ended. This swift playback of one's life track, the microfilmed history, as it were, of one's entire life, all of its contacts and events, the capacities developed, the powers unfolded and limitations incurred, is the final act of a process that had been operating throughout life. One may object that it is impossible for the mind to grasp the events of a lifetime in the space of a moment of time. However psychology tells us that even in ordinary earth life this is possible. There are many cases in which a person nodding into slumber has dreamed of events which have occupied an apparent period of many years. In ordinary dreams time is practically reduced to a small unit, and in the state just mentioned the process of concentration is intensified and the single point of time covers the entire period of one's life. The result of this process is that the acts of one's past life are concentrated and impressed upon the records of the individual life force, thereby becoming seeds which will produce better fruit in the future. These seeds serve to bear the fruits of future character, in future lives, atleast, so far as the acquired characteristics and desires will admit of. Just like banks of data are stored in a magnetic disc or a tape, just like one carries the history of one's past activities within one's memory, similar to that is the recording of every experience of the individual which is retained by the individual life force or soul, by means of which the individual life force returns to the physical plane life after life, each time in a mortal body that is precisely adapted to one's requirements. This aspect of the subject embraces one of the great ideas that together assembled; render the concept of reincarnation soundly reasonable and logical.

It is a common occurrence for dying persons to manifest a consciousness of what is occurring in a room at another place. Clairvoyance frequently accompanies the approach of death, in some cases being attended by clairvoyance, the dying person being conscious of sights and sounds in distant places. There are also many instances recorded in which the dying person has been able to so strongly project his personality that friends and relatives at a distance have actually seen his form, and in some very rare cases have been able to converse with him. A careful comparison of time shows that these apparitions, in nearly every case, have appeared before the actual death of the person, rather than after it. There are of course cases in which a strong desire of the dying person has caused him to project his astral body in the presence of someone near to him, immediately after death, but these cases are far rarer than the ones just mentioned. In the majority of these cases the phenomenon is caused by a process of thought – transference of such a high power and degree that the visited person became impressed with the consciousness of the presence of the dying friend or relative even while the individual life force of the latter remained in the body.

In many cases, the dying person became psychically conscious of a nearness to loved ones who had passed on before. This however does not necessarily mean that these persons are actually present on the scene. One must remember that the limitations of space are largely wiped out on the astral plane and that one may come into close rapport with the individual life force of another without their existing of any space relationship. In other words, while the two individual life forces may not be in what may be called a nearness in space, they may nevertheless, enjoy the closest relationship in mind and spirit. It is very difficult for one still in the flesh to realize this. On the physical plane, we are governed the laws of space. Telepathy gives the key to the phenomena of the other side. Two persons in the flesh may experience the closest relationship by means of the communion of their mental principles and yet may be on opposite sides of the world. In the same way two individual life forces may enjoy the closest communion and communication without the question of space nearness coming into question. The dying person frequently enters into soul communion and communication with those already on the other side, and is greatly cheered thereby. This is a beautiful fact attending that what we call death. It is also possible that one had been a person of deep faith and devotion and the great master towards whom one was devoted is present in some glorified form to help him upwards.

When the individual life force completely withdraws, the living link with the physical body is severed and the physical body falls apart. One may also see that the individual, who is now in a subtler body, is the consciousness that had united the physical form with its vital forces; the individual is the Immortal, who is now departing. The corpse that remains is but a mere collection of independent cells. As the dying person proceeds through the withdrawal stage, one is suddenly aware of standing aside from the dense physical body, fully conscious in one's vehicle of subtler etheric and atomic matter. It is really a form of material substances, of a degree, so fine, that it escapes the tests, which reveal ordinary matter. However, one has not yet departed from the physical world. One's familiar surroundings are visible, the pictures on the walls, the furniture in the room, one's body lying on the bed. One can see those who may be present at one's demise. One's first realization is most likely to be that, certainly one is not dead. When one steps out of the physical body at death, the immediate awareness is that of freedom, lightness and buoyancy.

Those who die by accident or who are killed, i.e. those who pass out of the body suddenly, find themselves wide awake and in full possession of the mental faculties for some time. They often are not aware that they have died and cannot comprehend the new situation. They are often fully conscious (for a short time) of life on earth, and can see and hear all that is going on around them by means of their astral faculties. They cannot imagine that they have passed out of the body and are perplexed. Their lot would be most unhappy for a few days, until sleep dawns on them. Astral helpers, who are souls or individual life forces from a higher state of existence, who gather around them and gently break the news to them of their real condition and take care of them until they sink into deep slumber, just as a tired child sinks to sleep at night. These helpers never fail in their duty and no one who passes out suddenly is neglected.

Dying is very much the same experience as going to sleep, which everyone does during some portion of the twenty-four hour daily cycle. No healthy person is rendered uneasy or fearful by this routine demand. If one's attitude towards going to sleep were analogous to the common superstitions about dying, there would be endless added fears and occasions for grief. Happily everyone is quite certain that one will wake up the next morning. Is it not significant that one of the joys of life is that of becoming physically unconscious at regular intervals? One looks forward to sleep because of the anticipated renewal of strength and vitality. Sleep refreshes one, returning one to a state of well-being, to continue with one's day-to-day physical activities with renewed interest and vigor. It would be only reasonable to view death and rebirth as a larger cycle of refreshment and renewal. Going to sleep and dying can be equated in many ways, the real difference being that with final departure, the so called dead cannot return to the physical vehicle.The living individual during sleep, goes into the astral world every night, having experiences there which if remembered are fragmentary in nature when one wakes up in the physical body every morning.Therefore one does not go into an unknown realm when one leaves the physical body at death. If this fact is comprehended properly, many anxieties related to death would disappear. If one is aware of this direct firsthand knowledge, death at its proper time could be greeted as though it were a blessing and an event to celebrate!

Death is a departure into conditions of reality that are experienced through means other than the sensate. That such conditions actually exist is evidenced in numerous testaments found everywhere throughout the cultural history of man. The experiencing of life's reality in subtler realms far exceeds the limited aspect of it experienced on earth. It is this happy discovery that crowns the great adventure of discarnation, the first steps of which transport one through the etheric veils of matter. At death one does not simply cease to exist as the individual one has known oneself to be; one does not enter into completely strange and unfamiliar conditions. Rather, the situation is a continuation of one's present life in extended phases. No sudden changes take place at death, on the contrary, one remains after death exactly what one was before, except that one no longer has a physical body. One has the same intellect, the same disposition, the same virtues and vices; the loss of the physical body no more makes one a different individual. Moreover, the conditions in which one finds oneself are those which one's own thoughts and desires have already created for oneself. There is no reward or punishment from outside, but only the actual result of what one has done, said, and thought, while living in the physical body. This is the first and most prominent fact to appreciate, that after death there is no strange new life, but a continuation under changed conditions, of the present physical-plane life.

If knowledge were more widespread about the mechanism of death and the general course of events, people's anxieties would be greatly relieved; and those who have passed on would understand their situation when they try futilely to communicate with friends on the physical plane only to find that they cannot be heard or seen. With knowledge, the departed would realize that they are now embodied in subtler, etheric matter and cannot expect to continue in the same ways as on the physical plane. This experience which might ordinarily be disconcerting is not so because one's attention in that solemn hour is deeply attracted elsewhere. The informed person knows, as does the simple man of faith and devotion, that the way to die is confidently to let go of this world and just as confidently to relinquish the etheric shell that links one with it. This is accomplished simply by not clinging to the world being left behind. A person, who does not let go easily, has his total consciousness focused in the etheric sheath that links the physical and astral regions but is not fully in either one of them. Thus one is temporarily earthbound. Ordinarily there is no awareness at the entire etheric vehicle, because within a few moments or hours after death, deep and peaceful sleep intervenes before entrance into the astral world. Normally after death the individual stands aside from his body,experiencing a brief lucid period of full awareness and general relief about the event, before one falls into the peaceful sleep that intervenes between this stage and one's awakening in the astral world.

THE MOMENTS AFTER DEATH

The individual life force having left the physical body is then plunged into deep sleep resembling the condition of an unborn child for several months prior to birth. The individual life force is being prepared for rebirth on the astral plane, and requires time in order to adjust itself to the new conditions and to gain strength and vigor required for its new phase of existence. Nature is full of these analogies that are birth on the physical plane and on the astral plane have many points in common; both are preceded by this period of rest or deep sleep. During this sleep – like stage, the individual life force dwells in the etheric shell which serves as its covering and protection, just as the womb serves as the protection for the child approaching physical birth.

Normally the individual life force sleeps in peace, undisturbed and protected from outward influences. However, there is an exception to this rule and the peaceful sleep may be disturbed by the so called dreams of the sleeping individual life force. These dreams may arise as a result of intense desire filling the mind of the dying person, such as love, hatred or unfulfilled tasks or duties, or due to the strong desires and thoughts of those left behind. This tends to produce a restlessness in the sleeping individual life force and has a tendency to attract the individual life force back to the scenes of earth, either in a dreamy kind of telepathic communication, or else, in a few rare cases, by something approaching the state of somnambulism or sleep-walking of the physical life. These conditions are regrettable, for they disturb the individual life force and defer its evolution and development in its new phase of existence. The individual whose mind is filled with strong desires concerning earth-life or with strong remorse, hate or great love and anxiety for those left behind is often tormented by these earthly ties and its sleep is rendered feverish and fretful. In such cases there is often also an involuntary attempt made to communicate with, or to appear to persons still on the physical plane. In some extreme cases, there may even ensue the state resembling earthly somnambulism or sleep-walking and the poor sleeping individual life force may even visit its former scenes and what one thinks as ghosts are actually sleeping individual life forces in their etheric vehicle appearing in visual form in the minds of humans already present on earth. In some cases these visualizations can be of a very ghastly nature and may result in such individuals seeking psychiatric treatment. In time, however, these poor earth-bound individual life forces become tired and finally sink into the blessed sleep. In the same way, the strong desires of those left behind often serve to establish a rapport between such persons and the departed individual life force causing it to become restless and uneasy. Many a well meaning person has acted so as to retard the natural processes of the astral plane in relation to some loved one who has passed away and has denied the individual life force that rest which it has merited. Here one may understand why weeping, crying and showing remorse is not really helping the one who has passed on to the other side i.e., the region beyond the physical plane.

The process of sinking into the restful state and its peaceful continuance as mentioned may be interfered with by those left behind. An individual life force that has something on its mind to communicate, or which is grieved by the pain of those left behind, when it hears the lamentations and constant calls for its return, will fight off the dreamy state creeping over it and will make desperate efforts to return. This is similar to a situation where there is something on one's mind really troubling one and one cannot go to sleep. Likewise, the mental calls of those who have been left behind will disturb the slumber once it has been entered into and will cause the sleeping individual life force to rouse itself to answer the calls or at least will partially awaken it and retard it's uncovering. The selfish grief and demands of those left behind often cause much pain and sorrow to their loved ones who have passed over to the other side.

Sometimes the individual life force will fight off the slumber for years in order to be around their loved ones on earth, but this course is unwise as it causes unnecessary sorrow and pain both to the ones who have passed on and to the ones who have remained on earth. Such an awakening is often accompanied by acute suffering and it delays the natural process of the individual life force's withdrawal.Spiritual teaching does not for a moment advocate forgetfulness of the dead, but it does suggest that affectionate remembrance of the dead is a force which if properly directed towards helps their progress towards the higher worlds. Their passage through the intermediate state of slumber might be of real value to them, whereas mourning is not only useless but harmful. It is with a true instinct that the Hindu religion prescribes its sharaddha ceremonies and the Catholic Church its prayers for the dead. Prayers with their accompanying ceremonies, create elementals which strike against the negative forces creating disturbances in the slumber state, thus speeding the progress of the individual life force in the slumber state towards the astral world. One must avoid delaying, as a result of one's selfish demands, the progress of those who have passed on. Those who have passed away should be left alone to sleep on and rest, waiting for the hour of their transition. To do otherwise, is to make them die their death several times in succession. Those who truly love and understand always avoid this, for the individual life force of a near and dear one should be allowed to depart in peace and take its well-earned rest and gain its full development. This period of the individual life force's slumber or soul slumber is like the existence of the baby in the mother's womb, it sleeps so that it may awaken into life and strength. Nowhere in Nature is an entity so carefully and fully guarded as the sleeping individual life forces. So absolutely secure from intrusion are these sleeping individual life forces that nothing short of a complete revolution of Nature's most sacred laws could affect them. No harmful influence can in anyway reach or even draw near them. So secure are these sleeping individual life forces that it would seem as if all of Nature's forces had conspired to guard and protect them. There is a Hindu maxim that says – 'Not even the gods on their high thrones have any power or dominion over the sleeping individual life forces.'

The individual life force carries with it into its slumber state a concentrated record of its entire life, including the seeds of its desires, ambitions, likes and dislikes, attractions and repulsions. These seed-ideas soon begin to sprout and blossom and bear fruit during the life of the individual life force on the astral plane. Some of these seed ideas will bear results in future incarnations of the individual life force but Nature does not impose on the individual life force the task of living and outliving all of its tendencies in future incarnations. It so arranges that many of these strong impulses will be manifested and worn out on the astral plane, so that the individual life force may leave them behind when it is reborn into a new earth life. It is towards this fruition that this soul or individual life force's slumber serves. During the period of slumber the individual life force is prepared for its entry into the astral world and its life therein, a detailed description of which will follow in the next chapter. This state of slumber is as necessary for the individual life force at this stage of its progress, as is the slumber of the unborn baby in the womb of its mother. The idea of rest after the stress and storms of life is so natural and instinctive that it may be said to represent the strongest inclination and conviction of the individual life force or the human soul in connection with the idea of death. It is as fixed as is the conviction of future life beyond the grave. Sleep and rest immediately after death is analogous to the sleep and rest which everyone eagerly awaits and welcomes every night after a day of hectic activity. It is only by means of this sleep every night that one recoups one's lost physical, emotional and mental energies to carry on with one's activity for another day, so too is the soul slumber after death. This enables the individual life force to carry on with its activities on the next plane of existence i.e., the astral plane. It is only in advanced spiritual teachings alone that one may find these striking correspondences between life on the physical plane i.e., earth and the life after physical death.

The period of sleep may extend but a few moments or it may be days or years, and sometimes longer as the case may be, before the etheric matter is disentangled from both dense physical and astral worlds. Here too one finds a remarkable correspondence with the phenomenon of gestation and birth on the physical plane. In the case of those animals whose natural life period is short, one finds as a rule, that their period of gestation in the womb is correspondingly short; on the other hand, animals of a natural long life spend a much longer period in the womb before birth. Thus the baby elephant spends twenty or twenty-one months in the womb; man, nine months; guinea-pigs, three weeks; the natural life of each bearing a relation to the period of gestation. Similarly the gestation period of the individual life force's slumber is found to vary in proportion to the time the awakened individual life force is to pass on the astral plane. An apparent exception to this rule is found in the case of persons of highly advanced spiritual power and knowledge, in which the individual life force is able, by its knowledge and power, to largely control the natural processes instead of being under their general control.

The variations in the time period of individual life force's slumber are due to the fact that during the slumber period the individual life force is being prepared to shed its lower animal nature upon awakening. The individual life force awakens only when it has reached the highest state of development possible for it, when it is able to pass on to the particular plane or sub-plane for which its degree of development calls. An individual life force of low development has very little to shed in this way and soon awakens on a low plane. An individual life force of higher development, on the contrary, must shed and discard sheath after sheath of the lower animal nature, before it can awaken on the plane of its highest attainment. The process of discarding or shedding these lower fragments of personality occurs immediately after the first stage of the awakening. The individual life force feeling the impulses of re-awakened life, stirs itself languidly, as one does in awakening from a sound slumber in earth-life. Then, like the butterfly throwing aside the chrysalis shell, it slips away from the etheric vehicle and in rapid succession unconsciously discards the lower principles of its nature. This takes a short time and occurs while the individual life force is slowly gaining consciousness. At the moment of the actual awakening, the individual life force is free from all these worn out shells and encumbrances and opens its eyes upon the scenes of its new activities and existence in the astral world. Each individual life force is destined to dwell on the plane of the highest and best in it-self, after the dross of the lower elements have been discarded. It awakens on the plane in which the highest and the best in itself is given a chance to develop and expand. The individual life force makes great progress on the astral plane and during its stay there, discards more of its lower nature as it passes on to still higher sub planes of the astral plane. The life of the individual life force in the astral plane will be discussed in detail in the following chapter.

There is often something within one which is much higher and better than one's everyday life and actions would seem to indicate. Material environment and circumstances tend to retard and prevent the expression of the best in one. Hence it is pleasant to know that in the region of life after death the individual life force is relieved of all that tends to hold it back and drag it down, and is rendered free to express and develop those qualities and characteristics which represent the best and truest that is in it. This fact accords not only with the sense of justice and equity; not only with the longings and cravings of the individual life force imprisoned in the physical body but also with the fact and principles of evolution, which tend to move towards a far off goal of attainment and perfection. The awakening of the individual life force is akin to a new birth, an entrance into a new world of experience.

The individual life force manifests no fear of its new surroundings, but is full of activity in the direction of expression and manifestation of its new powers. After the state of slumber, the individual life force awakens into a region of life, and not into a region of death. Like the butterfly, it spreads its wings and enjoys its new state of existence, and does not mourn the loss of the chrysalis form and life i.e., the physical body, the life on the physical plane and the etheric vehicle and shells which transported the individual life force to this new plane of existence. In the following chapters the type of life the individual life force will lead and undergo; the nature, activities and incidents of such a life in these new higher planes of existence after death will be described.

IN A NUTSHELL

The etheric body is the second member of the human being and is the body which provides life and organizes the physical body. It is sometimes called the life or vital body. The etheric body is invisible to the senses and is not directly detectable by instruments but we can see and experience the effects of the etheric body on our physical-mineral bodily nature. The purest visible expression of the etheric body's effects are in a sleeping new born child as its higher members are partially detached in the sleeping state. Also we can clearly see the effect of the etheric body in plants which consist of only of a physical and etheric body and here, if we place before us a plant alongside Apure crystal or mineral, we can see and experience the differences and see the effects of the etheric body on physical substance. However, the human being consists of further, higher, invisible members who provide consciousness, thoughts, feelings, self-awareness and individuality, all these invisible members have outwardly combined integrated visible effect on the physical body which we see before us which makes us different to the plants, animals and minerals. As etheric body was the second separate member of the human being to be formed, in the distant past, it is less perfect than the physical body, which was the first member of the human being to come into existence, but it will become more perfect in the future.

CHAPTER 2

THE ASTRAL WORLD

After the death of the physical body, the mind remains inactive for some time, as in dreamless sleep when it remains world less and therefore bodiless. But soon it becomes active again in a new world and a new body - the astral - till it assumes another body in what is called a rebirth.

Sage Sri Ramana Maharshi

ASTRAL PLANE PRINCIPLES

The term astral is derived from the Latin word astrum that means 'pertaining to the stars'. It originally came into use by reason of the common idea, that the other side is up in the skies or in the regions of the stars. Even at present, when we think of heaven, it is quite natural to raise one's eyes. It is difficult to shake off this habitual concept even though one knows better than to suppose that there is any special 'up or down' in the Cosmos. Prior to proceeding to the experiences of the newly awakened disembodied individual life force, it is important to attain a brief glimpse of the astral plane.

The astral plane is not a place at all - in the usual sense. Its dimensions are those of vibration and not space. The dimensions of the astral plane are the dimensions of time, for vibration can be measured only by rate of motion, and that rate is determined only in terms of time. The same is true of all vibrations whether of astral energy or the lower forms of energy. The higher the rate of vibration, the greater the rate of speed manifested in the vibration. Spiritual masters of the past were fond of stating that there is a rate of vibration so infinitely rapid that it seems to be absolutely still and motionless. From this extreme, one descends until the very grossest forms of matter are reached and there one finds a rate of vibration so slow that it seems motionless. The substance of the astral plane is very much finer than that of the material plane and its vibrations very much higher than the finest form of material substance.

There is a wide range between the vibrations of the lowest planes and those of the highest ones. In fact, the difference between the lowest plane of the astral and the highest of the material plane is far less than the difference between the lowest and highest of the astral itself. So that between these two extremes of astral vibrations, one has the same territory that one would have on the material plane. The fundamental difference however is that the material domain is measured by space dimensions, while that of the astral is to be measured only in terms of time of vibration. For instance, when one travels on the material plane, one must traverse space - meters, feet, kilometers or miles. However, on the astral plane when one travels, one traverses rates of vibration - that is to say, one passes from a higher rate of vibration to a lower, or vice versa. These various planes or sub-planes of vibratory energy constitute the astral plane. There are countless planes and sub-planes which may be travelled, but all astral travel is performed simply by passing from one degree of vibration to another. For the sake of simplicity, we shall speak of travel on the astral plane as the travel between the different planes and sub-planes of the astral - as if it were on the material plane. That is to say, instead of saying that the soul or individual life force passes from one state of vibration to another, we shall speak of it as proceeding from one sub-plane or plane to another. With this understanding, we shall proceed further on our journey of the astral plane.

The planes and sub-planes in the astral plane are inhabited by individual life forces fit to dwell on the particular series of planes or sub-planes upon which they awaken from the soul-slumber. Subtle principles of individual life force attraction draw each soul to the particular place for which it is fitted. The great law of attraction operates unerringly here. The law operates with absolute precision and uniformity; it makes no mistakes. Each soul is restricted in its range by its own inherent limitations and degree of development. There is no need of astral policemen to keep the disembodied individual life forces in their rightful places. It is impossible for the disembodied individual life force to travel into planes above its own immediate series. The law of vibration prevents this. However each and every individual life force may, if it so chooses freely visit the planes and sub-planes beneath its own series and freely witness the phenomena of those lower planes and mingle with the inhabitants. This is a very wise provision of the law, otherwise the higher planes would be open to the influence of those dwelling on the lower and the soul-life and development would be interrupted.

All creeds and religious dogmas are man-made. Underlying these man-made creeds and dogmas eternally exist the intuitive perception of the race regarding the existence of truth. The mind may not be able to correctly interpret the intuitive perception, but it finds itself positively impressed by the fact that the truth does exist. Man has made a God of nearly everything in the material world, and has fallen down and worshipped his own creation; this is so because of his limited power of interpretation. However in worshipping the stick or stone or an image, he was actually worshipping something which was the cause of the religions intuition within his soul. When one studies the various scriptures of mankind, scattered descriptions about the truths of regions of life after death as described in this book will be found. Each individual life force creates for itself and holds to the particular form of religious faith. This happens to be best suited for its requirements at that particular period of its evolution. When one is ready for a higher conception, one discards the old belief and eagerly embraces the new one. The world has witnessed many instances of this evolutionary religious thought. The path of the race is strewn with broken and discarded idols, material and mental, which were once precious to millions of worshippers. As the race advances, many more idols will be overthrown and left crumbling on the paths of time. Each idol had its own appropriate place in the general history of the evolution of the religious thought of the race. Each served its purpose, and its ideals served to aid man in his perpetual and eternal journey towards the absolute truth.

There is a naive belief among many persons which would imply that the disembodied individual life-force is magically and instantaneously transformed from ignorance into absolute knowledge upon passing over to the other side. This is a naive belief and has no true basis. There is very little difference in the general intelligence or spiritual attainment of the individual life force, before or after death. Soul progress is gradual whether in or out of the body. In and out of the body are but successive phases of its continuous life, succeeding each other like day and night. Therefore what is true of a particular soul's feelings and emotions during earth-life will hold well in its life on the astral plane. It will not only find the particular heavens or hells which it expected to find, but it will also find itself in contact with other souls of a similar belief.

Each individual life force is its own absolute law giver; deciding its reward and its punishment. The judge who sentences the individual life force to reward or punishment is not a power outside of itself, but its own conscience. On the astral plane the conscience of the soul asserts itself very forcibly, and the quiet voice that was perhaps smothered during earth-life, now speaks with authority and the soul hears and obeys. A man's own conscience when allowed to speak clearly and forcibly, is the most severe judge that exists. Stripping aside all self-deception, it causes the soul to stand forth naked and bare at its own spiritual gaze. Thus the soul, listening to its own conscience, sentences itself in accordance with its own conceptions of right and wrong, and accepts its fate. One can escape from the judgment of others, but one can never escape from one's own conscience on the astral plane. Such is the poetic justice of Nature, which far exceeds any conception of mortal man.

Man is judged according to the highest standards of his own soul. However it must be remembered that absolute justice has no place for punishment as such. This being true of finite human law, what should one expect from the infinite cosmic law? Surely, nothing more or less than discipline should encourage the uncovering of the good qualities of the soul and the destruction of the evil ones. This is exactly what one finds on the astral plane. Belief or disbelief in a future state does not alter the cosmic law of compensation and astral 'purgation'. The law of karma cannot be defeated by a refusal to believe in an after-life or a refusal to admit the distinction between right and wrong. Every human being has a deep-seated consciousness of some sort of a moral code. These sub-conscious beliefs and opinions come to the surface on the astral plane.

The astral body, as we have seen, is the field of manifestation of desire. It is the mirror in which every feeling is instant. From the material of the astral body, bodily form is given to the dark 'elementals', which men create and set in motion by evil wishes and malicious feelings; from it also emerge beneficial elementals called into life by good wishes, gratitude and love. Man's astral body consists not only of ordinary astral matter, but also of a quantity of elemental essence. During the man's life in the physical plane this elemental essence is segregated from similar matter around and practically becomes for that time what may be described as a kind of artificial elemental, i.e., a kind of semi-intelligent separate entity known as the Desire-Elemental. The Desire-Elemental follows the course of its own evolution downwards into matter without any reference to (or, indeed, any knowledge of) the intention of the Ego to whom it happens to be attached. Its interests are thus diametrically opposite to those of the man, as it is seeking ever stronger and coarser vibrations. Furthermore, finding that association with the mental matter of the man's mind-body brings to it more vivid vibrations, it induces the man to believe that he desires the sensations which it desires. It is a mistake to imagine that by refusing to gratify the desire-elemental with coarse vibrations, a man is thereby checking his evolution, for that is not the case. By controlling the passions and developing the higher qualities, a man drops the lower and helps to evolve the higher type of essence. The lower kind of vibrations can be supplied by an animal in which it is even stronger that those of man. The point is that it is only man who can evolve to the higher type of essence. All through his life, a man should fight against the desire-elemental. He has himself created it and should not become a slave to it, but realize him as apart from it. Sorrow and pain flow through this realm like the wind and the astral-world being the very home of passion and emotion helps those who yield themselves to an emotion experience it with vigor and strength mercifully unknown on earth. While in the physical body most of the efficiency of an emotion is exhausted in transmission to the physical plane, but in the astral world the whole of the force is available in its own world. Hence it is possible in the astral world to feel far more intense affection or devotion than is possible in the physical world, similarly an intensity of suffering is possible in the astral world which is unimaginable in ordinary physical life.

Much of the matter of the astral body is composed of elemental essence which lives blindly, instinctively, and without reason seeks its own ends and shows great ingenuity in fulfilling its desires and furthering its evolution. Evolution for it is a descent into matter, its aim being to become a general monad. Its objective in life is to get as near to the physical plane as it can, and to experience as many of the coarser vibrations as possible. It neither does nor can know anything of the man in whose astral body it is for the time living. It desires to preserve its separate life, and feels that it can do so only by means of its connection with the man. It is conscious of the man's lower mind and realizes that the more mental matter it can entangle with itself, the longer will be its astral life. On the death of the physical body, knowing that the term of its separate life is limited in order to make the man's astral body last as long as possible, it rearranges its matter in concentric rings or shells, the coarsest outside. From the point of view of the desire elemental this is a good policy, because the coarsest matter can hold together longest and best stand friction. The re-arranged astral body in Sanskrit is called the yatand, or suffering body. In the case of a very evil man in whose astral body there is a predominantly the coarsest matter, it is called the Dhruvam or strong body. The effect is to prevent the free and full circulation of astral matter which usually takes place in the astral body. In addition, the man is able to respond only to those vibrations which are received by the outermost layer of his astral body. The man is thus shut in a box of astral matter, being able to see and hear things of the lowest and coarsest plane only. Although living in the midst of high influences and beautiful thought-forms, he would be almost entirely unconscious of their existence. Consequently since being able to sense only the coarsest matter in the astral bodies of other people, he would assume that the person he was looking at possessed only unsatisfactory characteristics. Since he can see and feel only what is lowest and coarsest, the men around him appear to be monsters of vice. Under these circumstances it is little wonder that he considers the astral world a hell. In the course of time, the outermost shell or ring disintegrates; the man then becomes able to respond to the vibrations of the next higher level of the astral plane, and thus rises to the next sub-plane, and so on from one sub-plane to another. His stay on each sub-plane corresponds to the amount and activity of the matter in his astral body belonging to that sub-plane.

When one speaks of a man rising from one sub-plane to another, one transfers one's consciousness from one level to another. In the case of a rearranged astral body, the focus of one's consciousness shifts from the outer shell to the one next within it. One thus gradually becomes unresponsive to the vibrations of the lower order of matter and answers instead to those of a higher order. As the shell usually disintegrates gradually, one finds the counterparts of physical objects growing dimmer, while thought forms become more vivid. If during the process one meets another human at intervals, one will imagine that one's character is steadily improving, merely because one is able to appreciate the vibrations of that character. In fact the rearrangement of the astral body constantly interferes with one's true vision of one's friends at all stages of their astral life. This process of re-arrangement of the astral body, which takes place with most people, can be prevented by setting one's will to oppose it. In fact anyone who understands the conditions of the astral plane, should totally decline permission to rearrange the astral body by the desire-elemental. The particles of the astral body will then be kept intermingled as in life, and consequently one will be free of all the sub-planes, according to the constitution of one's astral body. The elemental, being afraid in its curious semi-conscious way, will endeavor to transfer its fear to the one who is preventing rearrangement in order to deter the individual from doing so. Hence this is one reason why it is so useful to have knowledge of these matters before death.

The individual life force begins to realize the differences between its present life and that which it had lived in the physical world. For example the individual life force soon finds that all pain and fatigue have passed away. It also finds that in the astral world desires and thoughts express themselves in visible forms, though these are composed mostly of the finer matter of the plane. Though an individual life force on the astral plane cannot usually see the physical bodies of its friends, yet it does see their astral bodies and consequently knows their feelings and emotions. The individual life force will not necessarily be able to follow in detail the events of its loved ones on the physical plane, but it would at once be aware of feelings such as love, hatred, jealousy etc, as these would be expressed through the astral bodies. Thus, those living on the physical plane often think that they have lost the dead but the truth is that the dead are never for a moment under the impression that they have lost those living on the physical plane. In fact an individual life force living in its astral body after death is more readily and deeply influenced by the feelings of its friends in the physical world, than when it was on earth. This is primarily because now the individual life force no longer has a physical body to dampen its perceptions. Friends who have become closely united in life, belong together also in the land of spirits. In fact after casting away their bodies, they are in much more intimate communion than in physical life. An individual life force on the astral plane does not usually see the whole astral counterpart of an object, but only that portion of it which belongs to that particular sub-plane upon which the individual life force is present at that time.

The conditions of life referred to above constitute kamaloka, literally the world of kama or desire. Loka is a Sanskrit word that may be translated as place, or world, so kamaloka is literally the place or the world of Desire. Kama is the name of that part of the human organism that includes all the passions, desires and emotions which man has in common with the lower animals. In the Kamaloka dwell all the human entities that have shaken off the dense body and its etheric double, but have not yet disentangled themselves from their passionate and emotional nature. The point to be understood is the existence of Kamaloka as a definite region, inhabited by a large diversity of entities, among whom are disembodied human beings. The individual life force is clothed with the Kama Rupa, or body of Kama, the desire body; a body of astral matter. This state is also called Pretaloka, a preta being a human being who has lost his physical body, but is still retains his animal nature. The Kamalokic condition is found in each sub-division of the astral plane. When an average man or woman reaches Kamaloka, the spiritual intelligence is clothed with a desire body, which possesses considerable vigor and vitality. The lower Manas i.e., thoughts related to the sensual perception/ objects of the physical plane, closely interwoven with Kama (feelings and desires) during the earth life just ended cannot quickly disentangle itself and return to its Parent Mind, the source of its own being. Hence in Kamaloka, there is a considerable delay in the world of transition because the desires need to wear out and fade away to a point at which they can no longer detain the soul.

Many who die are at first in a condition of considerable uneasiness, and others of positive terror, when they encounter the thought-forms which they have been used to. These thoughts are for e.g. thoughts of a personal devil, an angry and cruel deity, and eternal punishment. They are often reduced to a pitiable state of fear, and may spend long periods of acute mental suffering before they can free themselves from the fatal influence of such false conceptions. Very soon they realize that the state in which they find themselves shortly after death is merely a temporary one, and that to transcend them soon is possible by intense spiritual aspiration while they accept any suffering which is necessary to wear away the imperfections in their character, so that they can pass to higher levels. On the astral plane the individual life force is really free; free to do whatever it likes and to spend its time as it chooses. Thus each physical incarnation may be regarded as the ego experiencing the lower planes whose actual home is the higher part of the mental plane. The ego puts the soul out, as though it were an investment, and expects his investment to draw back added experience, which will have developed new qualities within it. The portion of the life after death spent on the astral plane is therefore definitely the period of withdrawal back towards the ego. During the latter part of the physical life, one's thoughts and interests should be less directed towards mundane physical matters. Similarly during the astral life, one should pay less and less attention to the lower astral matter, instead one should occupy oneself with the higher matter, The lower matter is related to physical

It is not so much that one has changed one's location in space, as that one has moved the centre of one's interest. Hence the counterpart of the physical world which one has left gradually fades from one's view, and one's life becomes more a life in the world of thought. One's desires and emotions still persist, and owing to the readiness with which astral matter obeys one's desires and thoughts, the forms surrounding an individual in the astral plane will be very largely the expression of one's own feelings. This in turn results in a period of happiness or of discomfort. To get a complete understanding of the events of the astral body in the astral plane, it is desirable to bear in mind that the astral life is primarily an intermediate stage in the whole cycle of life and death; a preparation for life in the mental plane. As we have seen, soon after the physical death the astral body is set free, expressed from the point of view of consciousness, the desire and thought is set free. From this, that portion of the lower mental body or the thought forms belonging to the mental body of the lower mental plane which is not inextricably entangled with desire, gradually frees itself taking with it such of its experiences as are fit for assimilation by the higher mental body. Meanwhile, that portion of the lower mental body which still remains entangled with desire, gives to the astral body a somewhat confused consciousness, a broken memory of the events of the life just closed. If the emotions and passions were strong and the mental element weak, then the astral body will be strongly energized, and will persist for a considerable time on the astral plane. It will also show a considerable amount of consciousness, due to the matter entangled with it. If on the other hand, the earth life just completed was characterized by mentality and purity rather than by passion, the astral body will be poorly energized and will disintegrate and perish rapidly.

In considering the conditions of one's astral life, there are two prominent factors to be taken into account - (1) The length of time which one spends on any particular sub-plane, (2) The amount of one's consciousness upon that particular sub-plane. The length of time depends upon the amount of matter belonging to that sub-plane which one has built into one's astral body during physical life. One will necessarily remain upon that sub-plane until the matter corresponding to it has dropped out of one's astral body. During physical life, as we have already seen, the quality of the astral body which one builds for oneself is directly determined by one's passions, desires and emotions and indirectly by one's thoughts, as well as by one's physical habits, food, drink, cleanliness, continence etc. A coarse and gross astral body, resulting from a coarse and gross physical life, will cause the individual to be responsive only to the lower astral vibrations. After death one will find oneself bound to the astral plane during the long and slow process of the disintegration of the astral body. On the other hand, a refined astral body, created by a pure and a refined life, will make the individual responsive only to its higher influences. Consequently, one will experience much less trouble in one's post-mortem life, and the individual's evolution will proceed rapidly and easily.

The amount of consciousness depends upon the degree to which one has vivified and used the matter of the particular sub-plane in one's physical life. During the life on earth if the animal nature had been indulged in and if the intellectual and spiritual side had been neglected and stifled, then the astral or desire body will persist for a long time after physical death. On the other hand, if desire had been conquered and bridled during earth life, if it had been purified and trained into subservience to the higher nature, then there will be little to energize the astral body, and it will quickly disintegrate and dissolve away. The average person has by no means freed oneself from all lower desires before death, and consequently it takes a long period of more or less fully conscious life on the various sub-planes of the astral plane to allow the forces which one has generated to work themselves out and thus release the higher ego. The general principle is that when the astral body has exhausted its attractions to one level, the greater part of its grosser particles fall away, and it finds itself in affinity with a somewhat higher state of existence.

To be upon any given sub-plane in the astral world is to have developed sensitiveness of those particles in the astral body which belong to that sub-plane. To have perfect vision on the astral plane means to have developed sensitiveness in all particles of the astral body, so that all the sub-planes are simultaneously visible. One who has lead a good and a pure life, whose strongest feelings and aspirations have been unselfish and spiritual, will have no attraction to the astral plane, and will if entirely left alone, find little to keep one upon it even during the comparatively short period of one's stay. One whose earthly passions having been subdued during physical life will have but little energy of lower desire to be worked out on the astral plane. Consequently one's stay there will be very short, and most probably one will have little more than a dreamy half-consciousness, until one sinks into the sleep during which one's higher principles finally free themselves from the astral body and enter upon the blissful life of the heaven or mental world. Expressed more technically, during physical life the higher mental principles had purified desire with which they were interwoven, so that after death all that is left of the desire element is a mere residue, easily shaken off by the withdrawing ego. Such an individual, therefore, would have little consciousness on the astral plane. There is a point known as the critical point between every pair of sub-states of matter, ice may be raised to a point at which the least increment in temperature will change it into liquid. Similarly, each sub-state of astral matter may be carried to a point of fineness at which any additional refinement would transform it into the next higher sub-state. If a person has done this for every sub-state of matter in one's astral body, so that it is purified to the highest possible degree, then the first touch of disintegrating force shatters its cohesion and resolves it into its original condition leaving the individual free at once to pass on to the next sub-plane. One's passage through the astral plane will thus be of inconceivable rapidity, and one will flash through the plane practically instantaneously to the higher state of the heaven or mental world. Every individual after death has to pass through all the sub-planes of the astral plane, on one's way to the mental plane, but whether or not one is conscious on any or all of them depends upon the factors enumerated. For these reasons, it is clear that the amount of time one may spend on the astral plane before one passes to the mental plane may vary within very wide limits. There are some who pass only a few hours or days on the astral plane, others remain there for many years, or even centuries.

Thus so far it has been observed that (1) the time spent, and (2) the amount of consciousness experienced, on each level of the astral plane depend very largely upon the kind of life the individual has lead in the physical world. Another factor of great importance is one's attitude of mind after physical death. The astral life may be directed by the will, just as the physical life may be. An individual with little will power or initiative is, in the astral as in the physical world, very much dependent on the surroundings which one has made for oneself. On the other hand a determined individual, can always make the best of the conditions, and live his own life. One, therefore, does not rid oneself of evil tendencies in the astral world, unless one definitely works towards that end. Unless one makes definite efforts, one will necessarily suffer from one's inability to satisfy such cravings that can be gratified only by means of a physical body. With the passage of time the desires wear themselves out simply because of the impossibility of their fulfillment. The process may however be greatly expedited as soon as one realises the necessity of getting rid of them and makes the requisite effort. One who is ignorant of the true state of affairs usually broods over one's desires, thus energizing them and clings desperately to the gross particles of astral matter for as long as one can. This is because the sensations connected with them seem nearest to the physical life for which one still craves. The proper procedure for an individual is to kill earthly desires and withdraw into oneself as quickly as possible. Even a mere intellectual knowledge of the conditions of astral life, is of great value to one in the after-death life. It is of the utmost importance that after physical death one should disengage one's thoughts from physical things and fix one's attention upon spiritual matters. By adopting this attitude one will greatly facilitate the natural disintegration of the astral body instead of unnecessarily and uselessly delaying oneself upon the lower levels of the astral plane. Many people unfortunately, refuse to turn their thoughts upwards, but cling to earthly matters with desperate tenacity. As time passes on, they gradually lose touch with the lower worlds, but by fighting every step of the way they cause themselves much unwanted suffering and seriously delay their progress.

Another aspect to be noted here is that these lower plane souls spend but little time in the disembodied state, and are strongly attracted by the material life, the consequence being that they are filled with a great desire to reincarnate, and generally spend but little time between two incarnations. Off course, when they are reborn they are attracted to parents of the same tendencies, so that the surroundings in their new earth - life will correspond very closely to those of their old one. These crude and undeveloped souls progress but slowly, making very little advance in each life, and having to undergo repeated and frequent incarnations in order to make even a little progress.

Smoking and consuming alcohol also poisons the astral body and delays one's progress in the astral world. The effect of excessive tobacco smoking on the astral body after death is remarkable. The poison so fills the astral body that it stiffens under its influence and is unable to work properly or to move freely. One is as though paralyzed but able to speak, yet debarred from movement, and almost entirely cut off from higher influences. When the poisoned part of the astral body wears away, one emerges from the unpleasant predicament. This is similar to when one is drunk and one loses one's presence of mind, but after sound sleep one again emerges into a state of clear consciousness. Coarse food and drink tend to produce a coarse mental body. Flesh foods, alcohol, and tobacco are harmful to physical, astral and mental bodies. The same applies to nearly all drugs. When a drug such as opium is taken in order to relieve great pain, it should be taken as sparingly as possible. One who knows how to do it can remove the evil effect of opium from the mental and astral bodies after it has done its work upon the physical. Furthermore, a body fed on flesh and alcohol is especially liable to be thrown out of health by the opening up of the higher consciousness; nervous diseases, in fact, are partly due to the fact that the higher consciousness is trying to express itself through bodies clogged with flesh products and poisoned by alcohol. The astral body changes its particles, just as does the physical body, but there is nothing to correspond to eating and digesting food. The astral particles which fall away are replaced by others from the surrounding atmosphere. The purely physical cravings of hunger and thirst no longer exist there. The desire of the glutton to gratify the sensation of taste and that of the alcoholic to experience the feelings which result from consumption of alcohol, being both astral, still persist and may cause great suffering owing to the absence of the physical body through which alone they can be satisfied.

The worst that an ordinary individual usually provides for oneself after death is a useless existence, devoid of all rational interests. This is but a result of a life wasted in self-indulgence, triviality and gossip here on earth. One thus makes for oneself both one's purgatory and one's own heaven, and these are not places but states of consciousness. Hell does not exist, it is only a figment of the theological imagination. Neither purgatory nor heaven can ever be eternal, for a finite cause cannot produce an infinite result. Nevertheless, the conditions of the worst type after death are perhaps best described by the word 'hell', though they are not everlasting. Thus, for example, it sometimes happens that a murderer is followed about by his victim, never being able to escape from his haunting presence. The victim (unless himself of a very base type) is wrapped in unconsciousness, and this very unconsciousness seems to add a new horror to the mechanical pursuit. Such conditions are not produced arbitrarily, but are the inevitable result of causes set in operation by each individual. Nature's lessons are sharp, but in the long run they are merciful, for they lead to the evolution of the soul, being strictly corrective.

For most people the state after death is much happier than life upon earth. The first feeling of which the dead person is usually conscious is one of the most wonderful and delightful freedom. One has nothing to worry about; no duties rest upon one, except those which one chooses to impose on oneself. Regarded from this point of view, it is clear that there is ample justification for the assertion that people physically alive, buried and cramped as they are in physical bodies, are in the true sense far less alive than those usually termed dead. The so-called dead are much more free and, being less hampered by material conditions, are able to work far more effectively and to cover a wider field of activity. Astral pleasures being so much greater than those of the physical world, there is danger of people being lured towards them thus hampering their progress? However, even the delights of the astral life do not present a serious danger to those who have realized a little of something higher while on the physical plane. After death one should try to pass through the astral levels as speedily as possible and not yield to their refined pleasures. Any developed individual is in every way quite as active during astral life after death, as during one's physical life. One can therefore help or hinder one's own progress and that of others quite as much after death as before, and consequently one is all the time generating karma of the greatest importance.

An important feature of the astral plane consists of what are often, though mistakenly called the Records of Astral Light. These records (which are in truth a sort of materialization of the Divine memory, a living photographic representation of all that has happened) are really and permanently impressed upon a very much higher level and are only reflected in a more or less spasmodic manner on the astral plane. One, whose power of vision does not rise above this, will be likely to obtain only disconnected pictures of the past instead of a coherent narrative. Nevertheless, these reflected pictures of all kinds of past events are constantly being reproduced in the astral world and form an important part of the surroundings of the investigator.

During the time of purification on the astral plane one lives one's life in the reverse order. One passes again through all that one has experienced in life since birth. One begins with the events that immediately preceded death and experiences everything in reverse order back to childhood. During this process everything that has not arisen out of the spiritual nature of the ego during life passes spiritually before one's eyes. For example, a person who died in his sixtieth year and who in his fortieth year had done someone a bodily or soul injury will experience this event again when passing through his life's journey in reverse order after death, when he reaches the point of his fortieth year. He now experiences not the satisfaction he had in life from his attack upon the other person, but the pain he gave him. From what has been said above, it is at the same time also possible to see that only that part of such an event can be experienced painfully after death that has arisen from passions of the ego having their source only in the outer physical world. In reality, the ego not only damages the other person through the gratification of such a passion, but itself as well; only the damage to itself is not apparent to it during life. After death this whole damaging world of passion becomes perceptible to the ego, and the ego then feels itself drawn to every being and everything that has enkindled such a passion, in order that this passion may again be destroyed in the same way it was created. Only when man in his backward journey has reached the point of his birth have all the passions of this kind passed through the fire of purification that nothing hinders him from complete surrender to the spiritual world. Thus one enters upon a new stage of existence. Just as at death, one threw off the physical body, then soon after, the ether body, so now that part of the astral body falls away that can live only in the consciousness of the outer physical world.

The phase in the astral plane is primarily needed to enable disentanglement of the desire nature which was the main feature during the phase on the physical plane. Also it must be remembered that in each case the individual soul is immortal; and even though one's recent efforts one's life has been a dismal failure, one is not thereby doomed. More accurately understood, the individual is cleaning away the debris during his sojourn on the astral plane. This is a preparation for fresh opportunities and renewed effort when one returns to the physical plane at a later time. Suppose a person while on earth wanted to paint or to express joyously and creatively in some way but could not do so, nothing now will prevent one from turning one's full attention in such a direction. Compared to the physical, the astral world is a place of exhilarated consciousness. One is engaged in a metamorphosis of one's nature from the relatively mediocre condition of the life on earth, into a closer resemblance to the god-like nature of the Inner Self. The process to etherealize induces every, possible intensification of the refining impulses and freedom generating characteristics that have been awakened in the astral nature. There is a stepping up of the emotional life to highest levels. It may be recalled that every facility of the astral world invites creativity. One creates naturally and readily in astral matter, for it is mobile and plastic and responds instantly to feeling, thought and will. Creative people, artists particularly, can anticipate the delights of unhampered inventiveness and expression of beauty through original impulses. From the limitations that we experience in the physical form, there has now come release to relatively limitless, free expression of feeling in astral matter. There is still limitation in the sense that everyone is limited by the desire-habits and emotional patterns that have been one's customarily during one's lifetime on earth. With these boundaries being non-existent, the liberations that follow seem miraculous. An example would be that of a cripple who hobbled about on crutches for many years prior to his death and who continued the same for a time in his astral body. Once he was told that there was no need to walk but that all he had to do was to visualize clearly where he wanted to go and that was all that was needed to get there. On the astral plane there is no longer self-aggrandizement for 'getting somewhere in the world.' Anxiety and fear regarding the necessities for survival are foreign to this place. With the death of the physical body, food and shelter, fine clothes and a new automobile, cease to be of any concern. Education of the finer aspects of one's emotional capabilities has the continuous attention of the dweller in astral regions.

The astral plane is composed of numerous planes and sub-planes, and divisions of sub-planes. At the lowest level they touch the higher material planes and at the highest they blend into the lower strata of the great spiritual planes. Between these two extremes is to be found the greatest possible variety of phenomena and phases of existence. The astral plane may be divided into seven great sub-divisions or sub-planes which will be discussed in some detail in the next section. On the lower planes of the astral are to be found certain forms of the ghosts, spooks, and other apparitions of disembodied souls which occasionally are perceived and sensed by humans and some of the lower animals. On some of these planes also, the astral bodies of humans still in the flesh travel and manifest activity, either during the sleep of the owner of the body, or in certain trance conditions. This also is possible when the owner deliberately leaves the physical body for the time being and projects his astral body on the astral plane. Some of the lower sub-planes of the astral are not nice places to visit, or upon which to function for the untrained person. In fact experienced spiritualists have as little to do with them as possible and advise all novices to stay away from them. Many persons have harmed themselves by attempting to penetrate these lower planes without adequate knowledge; many having wrecked their bodies and minds by foolishly producing or inducing psychic conditions which cause them to function on these lower psychic planes. Some of these lower astral sub-planes are filled with astral forms of disembodied human-beings, the higher principles of whom are still attached to the astral body, and which are held earth-bound by reason of the attraction of the material world. In this region also dwell for a time the very scum of disembodied human life, having every attraction to hold them down to the things of the material world. In the astral world, as might be expected, are to be found certain lower planes in which, dwell the disembodied souls of persons of brutal natures and tendencies, in which the inevitable result of their earth life is worked out. These hells of the astral plane are not eternal, the disembodied soul in turn may work out into a better environment, may be given another chance. The Catholic conception of purgatory, also has its astral existence, in the form of these sub-planes in which the foul crimes done during one's life on the physical plane are burned and purged away, not in the fires of materiality, but the fires of memory and imagination sufficing in these sub-planes of the astral plane.

There are many different kinds of regions on the astral plane as there are on the physical plane and each plane is inhabited by exactly the class of souls which it might be expected to attract. There are to be found the abodes of degraded souls, so steeped in materiality and animality, that they would be veritable hell to a soul of higher attainment. It may well be imagined that a soul of higher impulses has no desire to travel into these depths of the astral, unless, indeed it is some very highly developed soul which is willing to descend into hell in order to help them. On the astral plane, the sinner who believes in a hell of flames, which await him due to his deeds on the physical plane, is not disappointed. His beliefs supply the necessary environment and his conscience condemns him to the punishment he believes in. Even if he has sought to disbelieve these things by use of his reason, and still retains the subconscious memories of the traditions of his race, he will find himself in the same condition. He will undergo thc traditional tortures and sufferings (all in his imagination of-course) until he receives a valuable disciplinary lesson, the dim memories of which will haunt him in his next incarnation. This off-course is an extreme case. There are many other degrees and grades of 'hells' carried over to the astral plane by souls of various shades of religious belief. Each has the punishment which is best adapted to exert a deterring influence and effect over its next life.

Those who in earth-life have deliberately brought themselves to the conviction that there is no life after physical death have a peculiar experience. They meet with their kind on a plane in which they imagine that they have been transplanted to another planet and are still in the flesh. There they are made participants in a great drama of karma, being made to suffer for the miseries which they have wrought upon others, and to enjoy the blessings which they have bestowed upon others. They are not punished for their incorrect belief but they learn the lesson of right and wrong in their own way. This experience likewise, is purely mental, and arises merely from the expression in astral manifestation of the memories of their earth-life. It must be noted that both the heaven and the hell of each and every soul, abides in the soul itself. Each soul creates its own heaven and hell, for neither has any objective existence. The heaven and hell of each soul is the result of its karma, and is purely a mental creation of its own being. However, the phenomena seem real to the soul. There is nothing in its earth-life which ever seemed more real to it. Also it must be remembered, that heaven and hell, on the astral plane, are not given as reward or punishment respectively, but merely as a natural means of developing and unfolding the higher qualities and restraining the lower, to the end that the soul may advance on the path. Hence once again we see that each individual life force is its own absolute law-giver; the one who gives its own reward and its punishment on the astral plane.

The lower class of earth-bound souls are composed of souls of a very low degree of spiritual development and are predominantly driven by their animal nature. These souls are considered as earth-bound by reason of the fact that the attraction to the physical plane far outweighs the urge to reach higher planes. Thus the soul lives on a plane as near the physical plane as possible. In fact, the lower planes of the astral inhabited by this class of souls are so little removed from the material plane that it may be spoken of as almost a transitional stage between the material and the astral plane. These are sub-planes of the astral plane so low and degraded that one hesitates to describe them. They are inhabited by the most degraded and degenerate souls, which are on the sure descent to annihilation, being unfit to serve as carriers of the sacred plan. There is no need to go into the details of these sub-planes. The latter-day investigator says - 'Most students find the investigation of this section an extremely unpleasant task for there appears to be a sense of density and gross materiality about it which is indescribably loathsome to the liberated astral body, causing the sense of pushing its way through some black viscous fluid, while the inhabitants and influences there are unusually undesirable.' It should scarcely be necessary to warn persons not to dabble in psychic phenomena of a material character, which brings them more or less into contact with these lower planes of the astral. There is always the temptation and fascination of the unknown for many persons, especially for those who are not familiar with the phenomena of the lower astral sub-planes. Such persons like fools rush in where angels fear to tread, and attract upon themselves all sorts of undesirable astral entities and conditions. This class of investigators, in opening the doors of the minds and souls to lower astral influences run great risks. Therefore it has been very wisely said that 'beware of the lower astral vibrations,' keep the mind and soul centered on the higher truths and resist the temptation to dabble in the phenomena of the lower states. Live on the spiritual heights, always seek the truth, which, when known makes all other things clear.

Pure and spiritually minded individuals who are the victims of accidents etc., sleep out happily the term of their natural life. In other cases they remain conscious, often entangled in the final scene of earth-life for a time, held in whatever region they are related to by the outermost layer of their astral body. Their normal kamalokic or astral life does not begin- until the natural web of earth-life is lived out and they are vividly conscious of both their astral and physical surroundings.

The karmic consequences of suicide are usually affect the next life and probably more lives than one. It is a crime against nature to interfere with the prescribed period appointed for living out the physical life. For every human has an appointed life-term, determined by an intricate web of prior causes - i.e., by karma, and that term must run out its appointed time before the dissolution of the personality. Deprived of the assistance rendered by the physical body in resolving a situation of stress, the individual who commits suicide simply hurls himself into an astral vortex which is an enormous intensification of every psychic torment and fury that drove him to self-destruction. It is so much possible for an individual to live such a degraded, selfish and brutal life that the whole of the lower mind becomes immersed in desires that it finally separates from the higher ego. This is possible only when every thread of unselfishness or spirituality has been stifled and where there is no redeeming feature whatsoever. Such a lost entity very soon after death finds that it is unable to stay in the astral world and is irresistibly drawn in full consciousness into ' its own place', the mysterious eighth sphere, there slowly to disintegrate after experiences best left untold.

Humans incarnate in physical bodies for a purpose which can be attained only in the physical world. There are lessons to be learnt in the physical world which cannot be learnt anywhere else and the sooner one learns them, the sooner one will be free from the need to return to the lower and more limited life. As wonderful as the astral life turns out to be for the majority of people, the prospect that lies beyond them is still more splendid. Progress continues into higher astral plane regions until the last earthly ties are dissolved and all links with its pain and sorrow are ended.

ASTRAL SUB-PLANES

The difficulty of describing the astral world is a complicated issue as it is not easy to correctly translate from the astral to the physical plane, the recollections of what has been seen by the seers during their sojourns into the astral plane in a state of transcendence or meditation. One of the most prominent characteristics of the astral plane is that it is full of continually changing shapes. One finds there not only thought-forms, composed of elemental essence and animated by a thought, but also vast masses of elemental essence from which continually shapes emerge and into which they again disappear. The elemental essence exists in hundreds of varieties on every sub-plane. Currents of thought are continually pounding through this astral matter, strong thoughts persisting as entities for a long time, weak ones clothing themselves in elemental essence and wavering out again.

Astral matter exists in seven orders of fineness, corresponding to the seven physical grades of solid, liquid, gaseous, etheric, super-etheric, atomic and sub-atomic. Each of these seven orders of matter is the basis of one of the seven levels, sub-divisions, or sub-planes of the astral plane. It has become customary to speak of these seven levels as being ranged one above the other, the densest at the bottom and the finest at the top. The matter of each sub-plane interpenetrates that of the sub-plane below it. The higher astral sub-planes extend further away from the physical earth than the lower sub-planes. A very fair analogy of the relation between the astral sub-planes exists in the physical world. To a considerable extent liquids interpenetrate solids, e.g., water is found in soil, gases interpenetrate liquids (water usually contains considerable volume of air), and so on. Nevertheless it is true that the bulk of the liquid matter of the earth lies in seas, rivers etc., above the solid earth. Similarly the bulk of gaseous matter rests above the surface of water, and reaches much further out into space than either solid or liquid. Similarly with astral matter, the densest aggregation of astral matter forms the lowest sub-plane followed by the next sub-plane of much finer matter and so on.

The seven sub-divisions fall naturally into three groups - (a) the seventh or the lowest, (b) the sixth, fifth and fourth and (c) the third, second and first. The distance between members of one group may be compared to that between two solids, e.g. steel and sand, the difference between the groups may be compared to that between a solid and a liquid. Sub-plane seven has the physical world as its background, though only a distorted and partial view of it is visible, since all that is light, good and beautiful seems invisible. Four thousand years ago the scribe Ani described it in an Egyptian papyrus thus - 'what manner of a place is this unto which I have come? It hath no water, it hath no air; it is deep, unfathomable, it is black as the blackest night, and men wander helplessly about therein; in it a man may not live in quietness of the heart.' For the unfortunate human being on that level it is indeed true that all the earth is full of darkness and cruel habitation, but it is darkness which radiates from within himself and causes his existence to be passed in a perpetual night of evil and horror, a very real hell, though, like all other hells, entirely of one's own creation. Many find the investigation of this section an extremely unpleasant task, for there appears to be a sense of density and gross materiality about it which is indescribably loathsome to the liberated astral body, causing it the sense of pushing its way through some black, viscous fluid, while the inhabitants and the influences encountered there are also usually exceedingly undesirable. The ordinary decent man would probably have little to detain him on the seventh sub-plane, the only persons who would normally awake to consciousness on that sub-plane being those whose desires are gross and brutal - drunkards, sensualists, violent criminals and the like.

Sub-planes six, five and four have for their background the physical world with which we are familiar. Life on number six sub-plane is like ordinary physical life, minus the physical body and its necessities. Sub-planes five and four are less material and more withdrawn from the lower world and its interests. On the fifth and fourth sub-planes, merely earthly associations appear to become of less and less importance, and the individual life forces there tend more and more to mould their surroundings in accordance and agreement with their thoughts.

Sub-planes three, two and one, though occupying the same space, give the impression of being further removed from the physical world and correspondingly less material. At these levels entities lose sight of the earth and its affairs, they are usually deeply self-absorbed, and to a large extent create their own surroundings, though these are sufficiently objective to be perceptible to other entities. They are thus little awake to the realities of the plane, but live instead in imaginary cities of their own, partly creating them entirely by their own thoughts, and partly inheriting and adding to the structures created by their predecessors. Here are found the happy hunting - grounds of the Red Indian, the Valhalla of the Norseman, the houri filled paradise of the Muslim, the golden and jeweled - gated New Jerusalem of the Christian, the lyceum - filled heaven of the materialistic reformer. Nevertheless, many of the creations are of a real though temporary beauty, and a visitor who knew of nothing higher might wander contentedly among the natural scenery provided, which at any rate is much superior to anything in the physical world. The second sub-plane is especially the habitat of the selfish or unspiritual religionist. Here he wears his golden crown and worships his own grossly material representation of the particular deity of his country and time. The first sub-plane is specially appropriated to those who during earth-life have devoted themselves to the materialistic but intellectual pursuits, following them due to selfish ambition or simply for the sake of intellectual exercise. Such persons may remain on this sub-plane for many years, happy in working out their intellectual problems, but doing no good to any one, and making but little progress on their way towards the heaven-world.

GROUP SOULS

When one examines the processes of evolution, one is fascinated by the slow but steady change and improvement in the various forms of life related to the various kingdoms of Nature. Consider a body of water which is to be resolved into millions of tiny dew-drops for a time, and each dew-drop was then to acquire certain outside material in solution. In that case, each dew drop when it again returned to the body of water, would carry with it its foreign material, which would become the property of the whole. Any subsequently formed dew-drops would carry in their substance a particle of the foreign matter brought back home by the previous generation of dew drops, and would thus be a little different from their predecessors. This process continuing for many generations of dewdrops, would ultimately, cause greatest changes in the composition of the successive generations. This, in short, is the story of the change and improving forms of life. From the atoms into the elements; from the lower elements into those forming protoplasm; from the protoplasm to the lower forms of animal life; from these lower forms onto higher forms. This is the story, but it is all counterparts of the dewdrop and the body of water, until the human soul is evolved. The plants and the lower forms of animal life are not permanent individual souls, but each family is a Group Soul corresponding to the body of water from which the dewdrops arose. From these family Group Souls gradually break off into minor groups, representing species, and so on into sub-species. At last when the forms reach the plane of man, the Group Soul breaks itself up into permanent individual souls and true Metempsychosis begins. That is, each individual human soul becomes a permanent individual entity, destined to evolve and perfect itself along the lines of spiritual evolution.

Thus in order that one may comprehend the formation of the causal body as a result of which individualization takes place one must have some understanding of the formation of the field of evolution, the flow into that field of the great streams of life, the coming forth of the Monads, the building of the many kingdoms of life, and the plunging of the Monads into the material universe, and the gradual development of life in the Group Souls, after aeons of existence the point of individualization is reached, when the causal body for the first time appears. The general plan of the evolutionary process, more strictly speaking the evolutionary process, is a gradual differentiation of the great stream of divine life, until, after repeated division and sub-division, definite individualization as a human being is attained, after which no further sub-division is possible, a human entity being an indivisible unit or soul. Group souls, which exist in mineral, vegetable and animal kingdoms, thus represent intermediate stages leading up to complete differentiation into separate human entities or units. Hence in the three kingdoms mentioned, one does not find one soul in a block of mineral, or a plant, or an animal. Instead of this one finds one block of life, ensouling a vast quantity of mineral substances, a large number of plants or trees, or a number of animals. This will be discussed briefly later but currently we are confining ourselves to the general function and purpose of the Group Souls.

The best physical analogy of a Group Soul is perhaps the oriental one of water in a bucket. If a glassful of water be taken from the bucket, it represents the soul or portion of soul of, say, a single plant or animal. For the time being, the water in the glass is quite separate from that in the bucket, and, moreover it takes the shape of the glass which contains it. So may a portion of a Group Soul occupy and vivify a vegetable or animal form. An animal during its life on the physical plane, and for some time after that in the astral world, has a soul just as separate as a man's; but, when the animal comes to the end of its astral life, that soul does not reincarnate in a single body, but returns to the Group Soul, which is a kind of reservoir of soul matter. The death of the animal would thus, in our analogy be represented by pouring the water from the glass back into the bucket. Just as the water from the glass becomes thoroughly mixed and united with the water in the bucket, so does the portion of the soul from the particular animal become mixed and incorporated with the total soul in the Group-Soul. And just as it would not be possible to take again from the bucket another glassful consisting of the same molecules of water, so it is not possible for the same portion of the total soul in the Group-Soul to inhabit another particular animal form. Continuing the analogy further, it is clear that one could fill many glasses with water from the bucket at the same time; equally it is possible for many animal forms to be ensouled and vivified by the same Group Soul. Further, if one supposes that any given glassful of water becomes colored with a distinctive hue of its own, then, when the water is poured back into the bucket, that coloring matter back into the bucket, that coloring matter will be distributed throughout the whole of the water in the bucket, the color of all the water in the bucket being thereby to some extent modified. If one considers the coloring matter to represent experiences or qualities acquired by a particular animal, then, when the portion of the soul vivifying that animal returns to its parent Group Soul, those experiences or qualities will become part of the general stock of the Group Soul and be shared by every other part of it equally, though in a lesser degree than that in which the experience existed in the particular animal to whom it occurred; i.e., one can say that the experiences concentrated in a particular animal are spread, in a diluted form, over the whole of the Group Soul to which the animal is attached.

There is an exact resemblance between the Group Soul in the mineral, vegetable and animal kingdoms, and a human child in its prenatal life. Just as the human child is nourished by the life-stream of the mother, so does the protective envelope of the Group Soul nourish the lives within it, receiving and distributing the experiences gathered in. The circulating life is that of the Group Soul, the young plants or animals are not yet ready for individual life, but must depend on the parent i.e., the Group Soul for nourishment. Thus the germinating lives of mineral, vegetable, and animal are initially nourished by the elemental and monadic essence of the parent Group-Soul.

The process of division and sub-division of a single human cell into a complete human body is an excellent example of how Group-Souls have been formed. Just like the single cell continues to multiply in the initial stages of birth, and eventually from that single cell result the formation of the various similar group cells within the human body like the brain cells, blood cells etc. These in turn form the different families or groups of similar cells, for example red blood cells are one such group, brain cells or neurons is another such group, so too during the process of involution and evolution in a similar fashion cosmic intelligence has molded and formed these so called Group-Souls. The main category of Group-Souls being minerals, plants and animals, which then sub-divide and are classified into various Sub-Group-Souls like various minerals, plants and animals, say for example all the cats or dogs or lions or Palm trees etc each belong to their own individual Sub-Group-Soul. What may be stated as the place of abode or residence of the Group-Souls is the astral world for the mineral and plant Group-Souls, the astral/mental plane for the animal Group-Souls.

Reverting to the simile of the water in the bucket one may conceive of a scarcely perceptible film forming itself across the bucket. At first the water filters through the barrier to some extent; but nevertheless the glasses of water taken out from one side of that barrier are always returned to the same side, so that by degrees the water on one side becomes differentiated from the water on the other side. Then the barrier gradually densifies, and becomes impenetrable, so that eventually there are two distinct portions of water instead of one. In similar fashion, the Group-Soul after a time divides itself by fission, and forms two Group-Souls. The process is repeated over and over again, producing an ever-increasing number of Group-Souls, and contents showing a correspondingly ever-increasing distinction of consciousness, while, off-course, still sharing certain fundamental characteristics. The involution processes according to which the parts of the Group-Soul have plunged and involved themselves into the kingdoms of nature are as yet by no means still clear. There are indications that the evolution of mineral, vegetable and the lowest part of the animal kingdom belongs rather to the evolution of the earth itself than to their corresponding higher counter-parts the Monads, who come, in due course, to the earth to pursue their evolution by utilising the conditions it affords.

At present the knowledge of general configuration and mode of working of Group-Souls is highly fragmented. However to get a general overview of the mechanism and process of evolution of Group-Souls a very generalised picture can still be drawn up. The wall or envelope of a Mineral Group-Soul can be pictured as being circular in shape made up of three layers, the outermost is composed of physical atomic matter; the central one of astral essence; the innermost one of mental elemental essence, i.e., matter of the fourth mental sub-plane. Within the Group-Souls are enclosed Lower Triads, consisting of a physical unit, an astral unit and a mental unit. These Triads as per their evolutionary processes are in due course plunged into the mineral, vegetable or animal kingdoms respectively. These lower Triads are linked to their higher Triads consisting of Causal, Bauddhic and an Atmic Unit which in turn are linked to their respective overshadowing Monads, which oversee the individual development and evolution of the Triads. The habitat of the Mineral Group-Soul may be said to be that of its densest envelope, i.e., the physical, in other words, the most active working of the Mineral Group-Soul is on the physical plane. Every Lower Triad has to pass through the mineral kingdom, this being the place where matter reaches its grossest form, and where the great life-wave reaches the limit of its descent, and turns to begin its upward climbing. Furthermore, it is physical consciousness that is the first to be awakened, it is on the physical plane that life must turn definitely outwards and recognize contacts with the external world. Consciousness thus awakens on the physical plane, and its expression is through the permanent physical unit of the lower Triad. In this unit the consciousness sleeps, i.e., it sleeps in the mineral, according to the well known aphorism; and therein some degree of awakening must take place, so that it may be roused out of this dreamless sleep, and become sufficiently active to pass on into the next stage, that of the vegetable kingdom, where it is destined to dream. The responses of consciousness to external stimuli in the mineral kingdom are far greater than one may realize, some of these responses indicating that there is even a dawning of consciousness in the astral permanent unit. Thus chemical elements exhibit distinct mutual attractions, and chemical compounds are continually being broken up, when another element interludes. For example two elements silver and oxygen forming Silver Oxide, will suddenly separate from one another, in the presence of hydrochloric acid which is made up of the elements of hydrogen and chlorine, the silver from silver oxide uniting with the chlorine from the acid to form silver-chloride, leaving the hydrogen from the acid to form a new partnership or compound with the discarded element oxygen to form a molecule of water. When such active interchanges take place, as a result of the violent physical vibrations set up by the formation of and wrenching apart of, intimate ties, there is a slight stir in the astral permanent unit of the lower Triads. Thus astral consciousness is slowly aroused from the physical, a little cloud of astral matter being drawn round the astral permanent unit by these slight thrilling. This astral matter is, however, very loosely held, and seems to be quite unorganized. This marks the first initiation of the transition from the mineral kingdom to the plant kingdom.

A vegetable Group-Soul can be pictured as being circular in shape made up of two layers, the outer one is composed of astral monadic essence, the inner one of mental elemental essence, of matter of the fourth mental sub-plane. The physical layer, which the envelope of the Mineral Group-Soul possessed, has thus disappeared, as though absorbed, by the contents of the Group-Soul, for the strengthening of their own etheric bodies. Within the Group-Soul are some lower Triads, attached to their respective Higher Triads, these being again linked with their respective over-shadowing Monads. It is not to be supposed that every blade of gross, every plant, every tree, has a permanent astral unit within it which is evolving towards humanity. It is rather that the vegetable kingdom which exists on its own account, and for other purposes also affords the field of evolution for these permanent astral units, the Devas (spiritual beings as per the Hindu Scriptural knowledge) guide these permanent units, from one plant form to another, so that they may experience the vibrations that affect the vegetable world, and again store up these as vibratory powers in themselves as was done by the physical permanent units while they were in the mineral kingdom. The method of interchange of vibrations, and consequently of segregation continues as before. The Group-Souls therefore constantly divide and sub-divide, becoming thus not only more numerous, but also more different from one another in their leading characteristics. During the time that is spent in the vegetable kingdom, there is more activity perceptible in the astral permanent unit, than was the case during the period spent in the mineral kingdom. In consequence, the astral permanent unit attracts round itself astral matter, which is arranged by the Devas in a rather more definite way. In the long life of a forest tree, the growing of aggregation of astral matter develops itself in all directions as the astral form of the tree. That astral from experiences vibrations which cause massive pleasure or discomfort, set up in the physical tree by sunshine and storm, wind and rain, heat and cold etc., these experiences being passed on to some extent, to the astral permanent unit of that particular tree. When the tree-form perishes as a tree, The astral permanent unit retreats within the Group-Soul, taking with its rich store of experiences. Which it shares, in the manner as previously described, with the other Triads in the Group-Soul. When there has been a long separate life, as, for example, in a tree, there will be a slight arousing of the mental unit, which will gather round it a little cloud of mental matter. This marks the first initiation of entry into the animal kingdom from the plant kingdom. As a general rule, in fact, it appears that each lower Triad, during the later stages of its evolution in the vegetable world, will have a prolonged experience in a single form, in order that some thrills of mental life may be experienced, and the Lower Triad thus be prepared to profit, in due time. The rule, however, is not universal, for it also appears that, in some cases, the passage into the animal kingdom is made at an earlier stage, so that the first thrill in the mental unit occurs in some of the stationary forms of animal life, and in very lowly organisms. For conditions, similar to those as existing in the mineral and vegetable kingdom, appear also to prevail in the lowest types of animals.

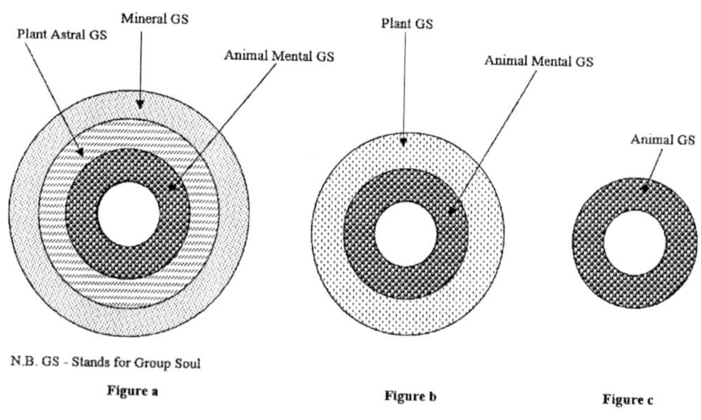

Figure 1 Transition from Mineral to Animal Group Soul

The envelope of an animal Group-Soul has a single layer, consisting of elemental essence of the fourth mental sub-plane. The astral layer, which the vegetable Group-Soul possessed, has been absorbed, for the strengthening of the vague astral bodies of the Triads within the Group-Soul. The activity of the Group-Soul is now transferred a plane higher, to the lower mental plane, and it nourishes the inchoate mental bodies of the contained Triads, thus gradually strengthening them. Just as in the earlier kingdoms, the Devas or Spiritual beings guide the Triads into animal forms. Just as feelings and thoughts of our present life experiences are stored in our brain cells, and can be recalled at a later stage, so too the vibrations of individual minerals, plants or animals experience are stored up and recalled when they return back to the Group-Soul. In the animal kingdom, the mental permanent units receive far more varied vibrations than in the lower kingdoms; as a result they differentiate more quickly. As this differentiation proceeds, the multiplication of Group-Souls goes on with increasing rapidity, the number of Lower Triads in any one Group-Soul, of-course, steadily diminishing. Again and again the Group Soul divides, until eventually each Lower Triad possesses its own separate envelope. The Triad is still within the enveloping case of elemental essence, which protects and nourishes it. It is drawing near to individualization, and the term Group-Soul is no longer strictly applicable to it, because one Lower Triad clearly is not a 'group'. It is a single Lower Triad which has separated off from the group to which it previously belonged.

The next stage is reached when there is only one animal form attached to the Group-Soul. Large numbers of the higher domestic animals has reached this stage, and have really become separate entities; although they have not yet reached the stage of possessing a causal body which is the true mark of individualization. The envelope derived from the Group-Soul serves the purpose of the causal body. One may note here an analogy between the animal, when it is approaching individualization, and the human antenatal life. The animal at this stage corresponds to the last two months of the human fetus. Now it is known that a seven month child will be born, but it will be stronger, healthier, more vigorous, if it profits yet another two months by its mother's shielding and nourishing life. So it is also better, for the normal development of the ego, that it should not burst too soon the envelope of the Group-Soul, but should remain within it, still absorbing life through it, and strengthening from its constituents the finest parts of its own mental body. When the mental body has reached the limit of growth possible, under these shielded conditions, then the time is ripe for individualization to take place.

It has been found that individualization, which lifts an entity definitely from the animal kingdom into the human, can take place only for certain kinds of animals, in fact for each of the seven great types or rays. Also it is only among domesticated creatures, and by no means among all classes even of these, that individualization occurs, we already know certainly the elephant, the monkey, the dog and the cat. The horse is possibly a fifth. Upto each of these heads of types leads a long line of wild animals which has not yet been fully investigated. However, it is known that wolves, foxes, jackals and all such creatures culminate in the dog; and lions, tigers, leopards, jaguars and ocelots culminate in the domestic cat. With regard to the number of separate creatures attached to a Group-Soul, there may be quadrillions of flies or mosquitoes; hundreds of thousands of rabbits or sparrows; a few thousands of such animals as the lion, tiger, leopard, deer, wolf or wild boar. Among domesticated animals such as sheep and oxen the number is still smaller. In the case of the seven animals from whom individualization is possible, there are only a few hundred attached to the Group-Soul, and, as their development continues, they break up rapidly. Whilst there may be a thousand pariah dogs attached to one Group-Soul, in the case of the really intelligent pet dog or cat, there may be not more than ten or twelve bodies to the Group-Soul. This brings to an end the journey undertaken to gain a basic understanding of Group-Souls and the role they play in the evolutionary processes.

ENTITIES OF THE ASTRAL PLANE

To describe every kind of entity belonging to the physical plane would not only be a formidable task but would also take up many volumes of work to cover the entire range of physical species living on earth. So too describing every kind of astral entity would be an equally formidable and difficult task. However in this section a brief description of some of the common entities belonging to the astral plane has been undertaken.

1. The Ordinary humans after Death -

This is a large class and consists of all grades of persons, in varying degrees and conditions of consciousness found in the various sub-planes of the astral plane, as described in some detail in the previous sections of this chapter.

2. The Shade–

When the astral life of a person is over, one dies on the astral plane and leaves behind the disintegrating astral body, precisely as when one dies physically one leaves behind the decaying physical corpse. In most cases the higher ego is unable to withdraw from its lower principles the whole of its mental principles, consequently, a portion of its lower mental matter remains entangled with the astral corpse. The portion of mental matter thus remaining behind consists of grosser kinds of each sub-plane. The astral corpse, which is a mere shadow of the original astral body is known as the shade. It is an entity which is not in any sense the real individual at all but it does bear an exact personal appearance, possesses a part of the memory, and all the little idiosyncrasies of the original astral body. It is in reality merely a soul-less bundle of all its lowest qualities. The length of life of a shade varies according to the amount of the lower mental matter which animates it.Though it may possess a great deal of a certain sort of animal cunningness, it is still able to communicate by borrowing temporary intelligence from a neighboring astral medium. By its very nature it is exceedingly liable to be swayed by all kinds of evil influences since it has nothing in its constitution capable of responding to good ones. The mental matter it possesses gradually disintegrates and returns to the general matter of its own plane.

3. Astral Shells–

Astral shells are the worn out astral bodies of the souls who have awakened from the soul-slumber of the astral plane. A shell is the astral corpse in the later stages of its disintegration, every particle of mind having left it. These astral shells may be galvanized into a semblance of life by coming in contact with the vitality of some astral medium and the subconscious mentality of the medium causing it to manifest signs of life and partial intelligence. They are astral corpses, just like the discarded physical body. Just as the physical corpse may be aroused into apparent life activity by a strong galvanic current so may these astral corpses be galvanized by the vitality of a medium (unconsciously by the latter), if the conditions be favorable. They may be materialized so as to appear as a shadowy form; acting, moving, and even speaking, the only mind in it, however, being supplied by that of the medium. A vitalized shell is always a true demon, whose evil influence is limited only by the extent of its power. The astral shell is nothing dissolved into its original elements.

4. Elemental Essence –

The word elemental has been used by various writers on this subject, to mean various different kinds of entities. This word has been employed here to express during certain stages of its existence, monadic essence which in turn may be defined as the outpouring of divine force into matter. It is important to understand that the evolution of this elemental essence is taking place on the downward curve of the arc, as it is often called, i.e., it is progressing towards the complete entanglement in matter which one observes in the mineral kingdom, instead of away from it. Consequently for it to progress means descent into matter instead of ascent towards higher planes.

In the astral plane one finds a vast store of elemental essence, wonderfully sensitive to the most fleeting human thought. It is incredibly sensitive to a vibration set up in it by an entirely unconscious exercise of human will or desire. The moment by the influence of such thought or will it is molded into a living force, it becomes an elemental, or an entity belonging to the so-called artificial class. When one visits the astral plane either in a dream state or in an altered state of meditation or after physical death, one is inevitably impressed by the various forms of the elemental essence. One marvels at the enormous army of entities temporarily called out of this ocean into existence by the thoughts and feelings of man whether good or evil.

5. The Astral Bodies of Animals –

This is another extremely large class. It does not occupy a particularly important position on the astral plane, since its members usually stay there for a very short time. The astral body of the animal rearranges itself just as in the case of humans and the animal has a real existence on the astral plane. In most cases its existence is no more than dreamy consciousness but generally the animals in their astral bodies appear to be in a happy state. Another interesting point to note here is that in those countries where organized and systematic butchery of animals takes place in slaughter -house and for sport, it sends millions of these into the astral world, full of horror, terror and shrinking from man. The astral bodies of such animals add much to the general feeling of hostility on the astral plane. Humans have yet to learn to live in peace and harmony with the animal kingdom.

6. Nature Spirits –

Nature Spirits are entities of the astral plane which assist in the running of the various phenomena of nature. The nature-spirits belong to an evolution quite distinct from our own, and are divided into seven great classes, thus there are nature - spirits of the earth, water, air, fire (or ether) etc., which are definite intelligent astral entities. At the head of each of these classes is a great Being, the directing and guiding intelligence of the whole department of nature which is administered and energised by the class of entities under his control. These are known by the Hindus as (1) Indra, lord of the Akasha, or ether; (2) Agni, lord of fire; (3) Pavana, lord of air; (4) Varuna, lord of water and (5) Kshiti, lord of earth. The vast kingdom of nature spirits, is in the main astral kingdom, though a large section of it appertains to the etheric levels or regions between the physical plane and the astral plane.

Based on my personal experience, for every feeling and emotion arising in man there exists an equivalent so-called nature spirit in the astral world. As the individual human mind is interconnected to the whole universe, these spirits do influence the well being of humans operating through the sub-conscious, particularly say in a dream or deep states of emotion. A typical example of this is the appearance of a mirage in the mind of a weary and tired traveler in a dry and sandy desert. Another example of this is that these nature-spirits are also responsible, in certain mountainous regions for enabling a traveler, to see for example, houses and people where he knows none really exist. These delusions are frequently not merely momentary but may be maintained for quite a considerable time, the man going through quite a long series of imaginary but striking adventures and then suddenly finding that all his amazing surroundings have vanished, and that he is left alone in a valley.

The life periods of the various classes vary greatly. There is no sex among nature-spirits, there is no disease and there is no struggle for existence. Jealousy and anger are possible but seem quickly to fade away before the overwhelming delight in all the operations of nature which is their most prominent characteristic. Their bodies have no internal structure, so that they cannot be injured, neither has heat or cold any effect upon them. They appear to be entirely free from fear. An adept visiting the astral plane from another higher plane and who may be involved in the process of evolution may use the services of the nature-spirits, and may entrust them with pieces of work.

7. The Devas –

The beings called by the Hindus devas are elsewhere spoken of as angels, sons of God etc. They belong to an evolution distinct from that of humanity, an evolution in which they may be regarded as a kingdom above humanity. The bodies of devas are more fluidic than those of men, they are capable of far greater expansion and contraction, and have a certain fiery quality which is clearly distinguishable from that of an ordinary human being. The three lower great divisions of the devas are - (1) Kamadevas, whose lowest body is the astral (Kama is a Sanskrit word meaning desire), (2) Rupadevas, whose lowest body is the lower mental (Rupa is a Sanskrit word meaning form) and, (3)

Arupdevas, whose lowest body is the higher mental or causal (Arupa is a Sanskrit word meaning formless). For Rupadevas and Arupadevas to manifest on the astral plane is as rare as for an astral entity to materialize on the physical plane. Above these classes are four other great divisions, and above and beyond the deva kingdom are the great hosts of Planetary Spirits. We are concerned here principally with the kamadevas. The general average goodness among them is much higher than among us, for all that is evil has long ago been eliminated from them. It is desirable to mention here the four Devarajas. These four have passed through an evolution which is certainly not anything corresponding to our humanity. They are spoken of as the Regents of the Earth, the Angles of the four Cardinal Points, or the Chatur Maharajas. They rule not over the devas but over the four elements of earth, water, air and fire, with their indwelling nature spirits and essences. References to them are made in the symbology of many religions, and they are always held in high reverence as the protectors of mankind. They are the agents of man's karma during his earth life, and they thus play an extremely important part in human destiny. The great karmic deities of the Cosmos, named Lipika, weigh the deeds of each personality when the final separation of the principles takes place at the end of its astral life, and give, as it were, the mould of an etheric double or blue print, exactly suitable to its karma for the individual's next birth. However, it is the Devarajas, who, having command of the elements proportion so as to fulfill accurately the intention of the Lipika. Also all through life they constantly counterbalance the changes introduced into man's condition by his own free will and that of those around him, so that Karma may be accurately and justly worked out. All the higher nature-spirits and hosts of artificial elementals act as their agents in their stupendous work, but all the threads are in their own hands and they assume the whole responsibility. They seldom manifest on the astral plane, but when they do they are certainly the most remarkable of its non-human inhabitants.

ASTRAL DEATH AND REBIRTH ON THE MENTAL PLANE

During one's investigations into the regions of life after death one comes across many examples which illustrate the principle that Nature is consistent and uniform in her methods, and that Nature has a few fundamental methods of manifestation on the various planes of being. One of these methods of Nature is that by which she always interposes a period of rest or recuperation between the end of one period of activity and the beginning of another. On the physical plane one can see many instances of this, from the momentary pause of the pendulum between its forward and backward swing; the period of sleep between the close of one day and the beginning of another; the period of rest of the unborn child between its formative period and its birth into the world and so on. In the astral world one finds the same phenomenon in the Soul-Slumber which occurs between that which one calls death and the beginning of the new existence on the astral plane. Now, reasoning from analogy, one would naturally expect that a similar phase or period exists between the close of activities of the soul on the astral plane and its passing on to higher spheres of spiritual life. Indeed such a phase does exist and it forms a very distinct feature of the soul's existence on the other side. Such a phase or period is known to the spiritualists as the 'second soul sleep', or slumber. The second soul sleep is preceded by a transition stage of gradually declining activity and consciousness, and a corresponding desire for rest on the part of the soul. The natural processes on the astral plane nearing their close, the soul begins to experience a feeling of weariness, and instinctively longs for rest. It finds that it has lived out the greater part of its desires, ambitions, and ideals, and in many cases has also outlived them. There comes to it that feeling of having fulfilled the purpose of its destiny and a premonition of the coming of some newer phase of existence. The soul does not feel pain at the approach of the second soul-sleep, but, on the contrary, experiences satisfaction and happiness as the coming of something which promises rest and recuperation

The steady withdrawal of the ego causes the particles of the astral body gradually to cease to function. The time taken for this process varies within very wide limits and it entails arrangement of layers by degree of density with the densest being outside. The astral body thus disintegrates as the consciousness is gradually withdrawn from it. During the interval of falling asleep at the close of the astral period and prior to the awakening on the lower mental plane, the last of the separation of matter of the two planes takes place. An imprint of the experiences on the astral plane is retained by the now abandoned astral corpse, which is in a state of disintegration. As at the time of death on the physical plane an imprint of all the experiences undergone during one's life on earth was gathered and stored by the individual life force, similarly an imprint of the experiences on the astral plane will remain stored within the individual life force to be used in the future when the new astral body will be constructed having exactly similar potentialities and capacities that the last one had. In each of the three worlds, physical, astral and mental, these imprints store the total vibratory capacity that has been developed by the soul or individual life force throughout the ages of its evolution in those levels of matter.

This is another fine example of the provision of the necessary tools by nature for the evolution of man towards perfection. Slowly the ego draws into itself the memories of the earth and astral life just ended and it prepares to pass out of Kamaloka into the blissful state of devachan or the lower mental plane/heaven world.

It may be said briefly that the period spent in devachan, is the time for the assimilation of life experiences, the regaining of equilibrium, where a new descent into another incarnation is undertaken. When one passes out of the astral plane into devachan, any thought-forms of an evil nature cannot be carried there as astral matter cannot exist on the devachanic level. Devachanic matter cannot answer to the coarse vibrations of evil passions and desires. Consequently all that one may carry, when one finally shakes off the last remaining remnants of one's astral body, will be the latent tendencies which when they can find an outlet in another incarnation, will manifest as evil desires and passions once again in the astral world. These lie dormant throughout one's life on the lower mental or devachanic plane.

The final struggle with the desire-elemental takes place at the conclusion of the astral life, for the individual life force is then endeavoring to draw back into itself all that it put down into incarnation at the beginning of the life which has just ended. When the individual life force attempts to do this it is met with determined opposition from the desire-elemental, which the individual life force has created and fed. In the case of ordinary people, some of their mental matter has become so entangled with their astral matter that it is impossible for it to be entirely freed. The result of the struggle is that some portion of the mental matter, and even of causal (higher mental) matter is retained in the astral body after the ego has completely broken away from it. On the other-hand, if during the life just completed one had conquered one's lower desires and succeeded in absolutely freeing the lower mind from desire, there is practically no struggle and the ego or individual life force is able to withdraw not only all that it had invested in that particular incarnation, but all the interest, i.e., the experiences, faculties etc., that had been acquired. There are also extreme cases where the ego or individual life force loses both the capital invested and the interest, these are known as lost souls or elementaries.

The exit from the astral body and the astral plane is thus a second death, the individual life force leaving behind an astral corpse which in turn disintegrates. Thus after the second soul slumber the ego or the individual life force wakes up on the lower mental plane and starts its life in its mental body on the mental plane.

JOURNEYING TO PLANES BELOW THE SOUL'S PLANE

The subject of communication between persons in the flesh and souls out of the flesh may be divided into two general classes, i.e., the lower and the higher respectively. The lower is composed of cases in which disembodied souls, of a lower order, the so-called earth bound souls manifest their presence to persons still in the flesh. The higher class consists of cases in which the souls on the higher planes of the astral manifest their presence to persons in the flesh. It is absolutely impossible for a soul to go beyond the plane to which it belongs, although those on the upper planes may freely revisit the lower planes, this being the rule of the astral plane. On the astral plane, the soul with the greatest amount of materiality, and coarsest nature, is stopped by the screen of a certain grade or plane, and cannot pass on to the higher ones; while one which has passed on to the higher planes, having cast off more confining sheaths, can easily pass backward and forward among the lower planes, if it so desires.

As a matter of fact, souls often do so, for the purpose of visiting friends on the lower planes and giving them comfort, and in the case of a highly developed soul, spiritual help may be given in this way. The one exception to the rule of free passage to the planes below that of the particular soul, is the one which prevents the lower-plane souls from entering the plane of the sleepers, i.e., the plane where the individual life forces or souls rest prior to entry into the astral plane. This plane cannot be entered by souls which have awakened on a low plane, but may be freely entered by those pure and exalted souls who have attained a high degree of spiritual evolution. The plane of soul slumber is sacred to the souls occupying it, and it is of a nature which is a distinct and separate state than the great series of astral plane, and sub-planes.

The soul residing on a higher astral plane dwells in an idealistic condition and has very little to do and does not concern itself at all with the affairs of the world it has just left behind it. It however maintains a sympathetic connection with its close ones who have been left behind on the physical plane. However, it must be kept in mind that such a sympathetic connection is entirely of a spiritual nature and has no connections with nearness in space, or physical proximity. The ties and bonds between the disembodied soul and the soul still in the flesh in earth-life may be thought of as a spiritual filament, something like a transcendent form of telepathic rapport. When the disembodied soul is thinking of the loved one on earth, the latter frequently experiences a feeling akin to the physical nearness of the disembodied soul, but this merely arises from the sensing of the mental and spiritual rapport as already discussed. In the same way, the disembodied soul experiences a sense of 'call' or message from the person in the flesh, when the latter is thinking intently of the former. Every one experiences at one time or another in life, a feeling of kinship or closeness to a near or dear one who has passed away and exists in another state of existence.

So far as the continuance of the feelings of love and affection between the separated souls is concerned, nothing but good can be said about the relationship. The soul in the flesh is comforted and strengthened by the feeling of rapport and nearness of the disembodied soul on the astral plane; and the disembodied soul experiences pleasure and joy just it would on earth-life by the physical nearness of the loved one. This relationship is a peculiarly sacred one and is enjoyed by many persons in the flesh, although they may have but little to say regarding it to others who would not understand. Those who have had this experience will fully recognise and appreciate just what is meant by these lines, others, who have not had these experiences, can understand them only by reference to the greatest feeling of soul nearness that they have ever experienced in earth-life. It is indeed a communion of soul with soul, almost approaching the perfection of soul-communion on the astral plane in many of its aspects.

Advanced spiritualist unanimously agree, that the practice of recalling the attention of disembodied spirits for mere entertainment and curiosity purposes is highly deplorable. The best of spiritual authorities condemn this practice. Firstly, the result is always unsatisfactory from a spiritual point of view and secondly, the effect of such recalling is apt to be detrimental to the disembodied soul. This is because it has to withdraw its spiritual attention from the things of the higher plane and turn them back to the things of the material plane, thus retarding its development and also confusing its mind. It is akin to directing the mind of the growing child back to the things of its prenatal condition, if such a thing were possible. Also, to the soul, which does not understand the nature and character of its astral life (and none but only the most advanced souls do understand), the mixing of the things and phenomena of the material and astral planes is most confusing and distracting. The soul should be left to unfold naturally on its new plane and not be called back to earth to satisfy curiosity. This brings to an end the brief overview undertaken in this chapter of the astral plane. Details of the life of the ego on the mental plane will be covered in the next chapter.

In a Nutshell

Astral plane and its principles

There are many sub planes which make up the astral world. Religious faiths are different as they support particular peoples at their level of development. Departed souls are in contact with other souls who held the same religious beliefs. The soul is its own judge after death and leads itself to its own reward and punishment. An individual's astral body is the field of manifestation of desire and thought.

Man's astral body consists not only of astral substance but also of a separate entity known as the desire elemental which is opposed to man's interests. An unimaginable intensity of suffering is possible in the astral realm that is not possible on the physical plane. The desire elemental arranges one's astral body in accordance with one's physical life.

An individual on the astral plane can see their astral bodies with their associated feelings and emotions – love, hate etc. The sojourn in the astral world is known as karmaloka – the place of burning desire. Many individuals, after they die, find themselves in a state of uneasiness. The astral life is an intermediary stage for the mental plane. A life of purity on earth allows one's astral body to quickly dissolve.

The length of time and to the degree of consciousness spent on each sub plane of the astral world depends on one's life on Earth. Unless one has made efforts on earth to purify one's cravings then one will suffer in the astral planes until one has weaned oneself off these cravings and passions to pass into the next plane. Even an intellectual knowledge of life after death is helpful. Those individuals with coarser instincts spend only a short time between incarnations. There can be great suffering on the astral plane if one had physical addictions and cravings. One creates one's own heaven or hell but these are temporary states. One elaborates karma after death. The astral body of animals – After death the animal astral body quickly dissolves but stays longer the more domesticated the animal was.

Nature spirits – Elementals of life, air, water and earth are the forces behind the world of nature. The Devas also known as angels are above humanity. Kamadevas, rupadevas, Arupadevas, Devarajas, lipika provide the fabric of the earth and karma.

Astral death and rebirth on the mental plane

The astral body gradually fully withdraws from the ego as the individual enters the mental plane. An essence of the astral body is retained. Devachan is another term for the lower mental planes or heaven. No evil can enter here.

Journeying to Planes below the Soul's Plane

Two types of communication are possible with the departed. A departed soul has a sympathetic connection to those to whom it had ties with on earth and this connection is entirely of a psychic or spiritual nature. The disembodied soul can experience those who have been left behind if the latter is intensely aware of the former.

Earth life is experienced on the astral plane in reverse order as one had lived on earth and from the perspective of the effect of one's deeds on the other person.

When one's earthly passions and attachments have been purified then one passes into the next plane. Injury may occur if one dabbles with the lower astral plane by the use of psychic phenomena.

The hells of the astral plane are not eternal. Each soul creates its own heaven and hell. The karmic consequences of suicide are monumental. There are lessons to be learnt in the physical world which cannot be learned elsewhere.

Astral Sub Planes

One resides on a higher or lower astral sub plane depending on how one lived here on earth.

Group souls – each species of plants or animal has a group soul and get its experiences from each individual animal or plant. Each human soul is an individuality in its own right. The group soul can, after a long time, divide and become two group souls i.e. two new species.

Devas assist the group souls of plants in their evolution. The group souls, over very long periods of time, evolve from minerals, to plant, to animal. Eventually particular animals of a group soul individualize.

Entities of the Astral Plane

The ordinary humans after death. The shade and astral shell – This is the disintegrating astral body with all its lowest qualities which is left behind by an individual. This can be animated by a medium and can appear as the departed individual.

Elemental essence – Is defined as the outpouring of divine force into the matter. Entities are called into existence by thoughts and feelings.

CHAPTER 3

THE MENTAL WORLD

The quest for and the realization of the source of the ego in the form of aham-vritti (the 'I'- thought) necessarily implies the tuuuranscendence of the ego in every one of its possible forms.

Sage Sri Ramana Maharshi

MENTAL PLANE PRINCIPLES

The closing and longest chapter of the cycle of incarnation is the soul's return home to heaven. This is the most beautiful and inspiring part of the soul's heroic pilgrimage through birth and death. Just prior to leaving the astral plane, the individual soul drops into a serene sleep while final disengagement from astral matter takes place. The astral body is left behind on its own plane and the soul withdraws its consciousness into the mental body, i.e., rises to the mental plane and in so doing enters what is known as the heaven world. This is also called Devachan, which means literally the Shining Land; it is also termed in Sanskrit Devasthan-the land of the Gods; it is the Svarga of the Hindus, the Sukhavati of the Buddhists, the Heaven of the Zoroastrians, Christians and Mohammedans; and the 'Nirvana of the common people.'

The basic principle of devachan is that it is a world of thought. The mental plane is that part or aspect of nature which belongs to consciousness working as thought.

This is not the mind working through the physical brain, but the mind working in its own world, unencumbered with physical matter. Everyone goes to heaven, but not all portions of one's nature can reach there. Astral desires that were identified completely with satisfaction in the physical matter have been left behind. They are dead and do not enter heaven. A person's astral desires that expressed unselfish love and other elements of one's higher nature, are very much a part of the heaven life. Each individual takes into heaven that which is native there; these are the thoughts and deeds that are to be explored and processed into mental character which happens during the profound contemplation in the mental plane. The soul's longer repose in heaven is necessary for mental disengagement from the past incarnation. The length of time one spends there, and the quality of one's experience, depends on one's mental and emotional life on earth. The heaven life seems to be mainly a condition of effects, the causes of which were set in motion in physical incarnation. The content of the experience is unique to each individual but in every case it is a blissful period. While one is in heaven, there remains no link with the physical plane across which pain, sorrow or evil of any kind can reach one. Yet friends and those whom one loved, as well as all of the beauty and glory of nature are resplendent in this place. No want of any kind exists.

In esoteric literature, mental plane or devachan has been described as a plane where all sorrow and evil are excluded by the action of the great spiritual intelligences who supervise human evolution. It is the blissful resting-place of the individual soul where one peacefully assimilates the fruits of one's physical life. Just as one's future condition is determined largely by the nature of one's desires, so is one's life on the mental plane largely determined by one's desires and ideals? In spite of the idea entertained by many people that it is easier to deal with things on the physical plane than those on the astral and mental planes, the truth is quite the opposite. For the very fineness of mental matter, and its ready response to mental impulses, makes it far easier to move and direct by action of the will, than either astral or physical matter. The mental plane gives free expression to the ideals entertained by the individual during earth-life, and in fact, may be spoken as largely a reflection of those ideals. On the mental plane these ideals tend towards a real manifestation. This is true not only of high ideals, but of the lowest as well. If one were to consider the emotional and intellectual nature of the soul of a primitive person, one will see that to put such a soul in the environment of cultured civilized people would make such a soul miserable. In fact, such a heaven would seem like hell.

There are many reports of clairvoyants, seers, and communicators with departed souls, who assert positively the existence of heaven in exact accordance with the religious teachings of their tribe or race. It is very easy to dismiss these reports either as pure fantasy or dreams of the priests. But a closer examination will reveal the fact that there is a striking similarity in the fundamentals although they differ in details. The spiritualist knows that these reports are all truthful and is based on actual psychic experiences of certain members of a particular tribe, class or group of people. Even a little understanding of the nature of the mental plane will explain this matter. The clairvoyants, among the old American Indians, who were able to penetrate the lower planes of the mental plane, were thoughtful when they reported of the existence of the happy hunting grounds of their departed brothers on the other side. The heaven world of the Red Indians was precisely as their medicine men had taught them it would be. When such a soul awakened from the soul slumber, it would find itself perfectly at home, surrounded by all that made life pleasant to it, including great forests, streams, plenty of buffalo and deer to be shot etc though these things exist but they exist only mentally. Like a very intense dream these things appear to such a soul, but it does not realize that it is merely a dream. Even in earth-life, we sometimes experience dreams which seem so real that partake in them as if they were the only substantial reality.

These primitive or savage souls spend only a brief period of existence on the mental plane during which they develop newer desires which blossom and bear fruit in their next incarnation on earth. They also wear out some of their lower desires and in this way, make way for the spiritual evolution which is always seeking to unfold on the mental plane. Their life on the mental plane is very brief compared to their life on earth but these souls really make considerable progress during their short stay on the mental plane. For such souls a hundred earth lives may be equal to one life on the mental plane. Compensation and equity are found on the mental plane as elsewhere. One of the great gains the savage soul makes on the mental plane is that of the development of comradeship. This is caused by reunion of the soul with its friends of earth-life and hence the resulting joy. The animosities of earth life are softened by nature of life on the mental plane since there is abundant supply of all that the savage craves for. This results in far less opportunity for jealousy and rivalry that would be normal on the physical plane. Accordingly, hatred is removed and elementary friendship (the budding of universal love) is encouraged. Each trip to the mental plane burns out a little more of the lower nature and awakens a little more of the higher, otherwise there would be no progress for the race in repeated lives. Each soul, no matter how undeveloped it may be, learns a little more of that feeling of unity and oneness. Thus it can be observed that even in these crude heavens of the primitive people, there is the opportunity and certainty of progress.

The moral and spiritual qualities have to find a field in which their energies can expand themselves. The mental plane is one such field. Hence, the great plane of moral reform and intellectual research into abstract principles of nature, the divine and spiritual aspirations that fill the brightest part of life on earth, bear fruit in the mental plane. The soul occupies itself in this inner world enjoying the effects of the many beneficial spiritual causes sown the physical plane.

On the mental plane the soul lives a pure and spiritually conscious existence, a dream of realistic vividness, until karma being satisfied in that direction causes the individual soul to move into its next stage of causes either in this same world or another, according to its level of progress. The dream like life one spends on the mental plane is the fruit one reaps for those psychic germs sown during physical existence. All unrealized hopes and aspirations become fully realized, on the mental plane. Yet so grounded in materialism is the world of humans, that they would speak of the heaven world as a mirage or a mere dream, They consider nothing real unless it is on the physical plane and exhibit their ignorance to the fact that in it there is absolutely no permanence, The mind itself is not quick enough to catch a glimpse of material reality, for before the mind can grasp a material fact, the fact has merged into something else. The world of mind which seems true is far less true than the world of spirit. From the spiritual point of view there is nothing at all real but Spirit. Matter is regarded as the most fleeting and unreal of all-illusory appearances. From the same viewpoint, the higher in scale one rises above the material plane, the more real becomes the phenomenon experienced. Therefore, it follows that the experiences of the soul on the mental plane are not only unreal in nature, but by comparison, are far more real than the experiences of life on the physical plane.

Upon entry into the mental plane each individual soul shuts itself up in its own shell of mental matter. During the initial stages of its life on the mental plane, the soul does not actively participate in the life of the mental plane at all. It does not move about freely and interact with other entities as one does on the astral plane. The final separation of the mental body from the astral does not involve any pain or suffering; one simply feels one to be sinking gently into a delightful repose. There is however a period of blank unconsciousness, similar to that which usually follows physical death. This period may vary within wide limits and from it one awakens gradually. It appears that this period of unconsciousness corresponding to the pre-natal physical life is necessary for the building up of the devachan ego for the life on the mental plane. Part of it appears to be occupied in the recording and absorption of all events, characteristics developed and activities carried out on the astral plane. They are recorded into the memory banks, which are required to be carried forward to the future. Also part of this period of unconsciousness is involved in vivifying the matter of the mental body for its coming separate life.

During one's purgatorial life on thc astral plane the lower part of one's nature burns itself away. Now only the higher and more refined thoughts, the noble and unselfish aspirations which one entertained during one's life on the physical plane remain. On the astral plane one may have a comparatively pleasant life though distinctly limited as compared to the mental plane. However on the mental plane one reaps the result only of such thoughts and feelings which have been entirely unselfish; hence the life on the mental plane is blissful.

As a spiritual master described the mental plane – 'It is the land where there are no tears, no sighs, where there is neither marrying nor giving in marriage, and where the just realize their full perfection.' The thoughts which cluster around the soul make a sort of shell through the medium of which it is able to respond to certain types of vibrations in this refined matter. These thoughts are the power by which it draws on the infinite wealth of the mental plane. They serve as windows through which the soul can look out upon the glory and beauty of the mental plane. Every human must have had some touch of pure unselfish feelings, even if they were only once in one's life time and these will now serve as a window for the soul on the mental plane. It will be an error to regard the shell of thought which surrounds the soul upon entry into the mental plane as a limitation. Its function is not to shut the individual life force from the vibrations of the plane, but rather to enable it to respond to such influences. The mental plane is a reflection of the divine mind from which the person enjoying it is able to draw in accordance to the power of one's own thoughts and aspirations generated during one's physical and astral life. Each individual is able to draw upon the mental plane and to cognize only so much of it as one has by previous effort prepared oneself to take. As the Eastern saying goes, everyone brings a cup; some of the cups are large while some are small. Whether large or small, every cup is filled to its utmost capacity; the sea of bliss is far more than enough for all.

According to the law of karma no force can ever be lost or robbed of its due effect and until its opportunity arises it remains as stored-up energy. In other words, much of the higher spiritual energy of the individual life force cannot bring about its due result on the physical plane. On the mental plane for the first time, all this hindrance is removed and the accumulated energy pours forth in accordance with the law of karma. So perfect justice is done and nothing is ever lost, although on the physical plane it may seem that much has not come to fruition. The mental plane is thus by no means a dream but on the contrary, it is a condition of existence, where the mind and the heart develop, unhindered by gross matter.

The mental plane, being that of thought itself is far nearer to reality than any lower plane. The materials of the mental plane are capable of combining under the impulse of thought-vibrations, to give rise to any combination which thought can construct. Just as iron can be made into a spade or a sword, so can mental matter be shaped into thought-forms? In this region, thought and action is thus one and the same thing. In the case of the astral plane, it is possible to give some account of its scenery, but this cannot be done for the mental plane since it has no inherent scenery except that of each individual life force chooses to make for itself by its thought.

But out of this splendor of living reality each individual soul sees only that which its development can enable it to perceive. Awareness of objects, the aspect of intelligence is the dominant point of the mental plane. Desire to attain objects is the dominant point of the astral plane while the aspect of activity is the dominant point of the physical plane. Each of these aspects is present all the time. For purposes of understanding, the mental plane can be considered to be divided into seven sub-planes. The first three belong to the higher mental or the causal plane, the home of abstract thinking and the lower four sub-planes belong to the lower mental plane which is the home of concrete thinking. Abstract thinking is a function of the individual life force expressing itself through the higher mental or causal body, on the other hand concrete thinking is performed by the working of the individual life force in the mental body or the lower mental body as it is sometimes called. The act of concrete thinking sets in vibration the matter of the mental body. This vibration is transferred an octave lower to the grosser matter of the individual life force's astral body, from that in turn the etheric particles of the brain are affected. Through them finally the denser grey matter of the physical body is brought into action. Thus before a thought can be translated into active consciousness on the physical brain all these successive steps must be taken. The sympathetic nervous system is mostly connected with the astral body, while the cerebro-spinal system is more under the influence of the ego working through the mental body.

The first impressions of one who enters the mental plane in full consciousness will be of intense bliss, enormously increased power and perfect confidence which flow from these. One finds oneself in the midst of what seems to be a whole universe of ever-changing light, color and sound. It appears as though one is in a sea of living light, surrounded by every possible conceivable variety of loveliness in color and form, everything changing with every single wave of thought that one sends out and being indeed, as one will discover only the expression of one's thought in the matter of the lower mental plane and its elemental essence. Concrete thoughts, as described previously, take the shapes of their objects while abstract ideas usually represent themselves by all kinds of perfect and most beautiful geometrical forms. In this connection it should be remembered that many thoughts, which to us on the physical plane are little more than mere abstractions, are on the mental plane concrete thoughts. The feeling of freedom on the mental plane is so great that in comparison to it life on the astral plane appears to be a state of bondage. If one wishes to abstract oneself from one's surroundings on the mental plane and devote oneself to the quiet thought, one May live-in a world of one's own without any possibility of interruption. One will have the additional advantage of seeing all of one's ideas and their consequences fully worked out and passing before one giving a sort of panoramic view. If however one wishes instead to observe the plane upon which one is, one must carefully suspend one's own thought for the time so that one may not influence the readily impressible matter around oneself. One will perceive that one is seeing the color-language of devas, the expression of the thought on conversation of beings far higher than oneself in the scale of evolution. By experiment and practice one will also find that one can also use this mode of expression and thus hold conversation and learn from these lofty non-human entities. As was described previously such conversations with devas are possible as a thought form of rapidly vibrating particles of mental matter. These set up vibrations all around it and give rise to sensations of sound and colour in any entities adapted to comprehend them. It is also possible for a visitor to the mental plane to form around oneself a huge shell through which none of the thought or conversation of other entities can penetrate. Then holding one's own mind perfectly still one can examine the conditions inside the shell.

On the mental plane one may circle the world with the speed of thought; one is at the other side of it even as one formulates the wish to be there. The response of mental matter to thought is immediate and is readily controlled by will. On the mental plane there is no alternation of day and night and nothing to correspond to sleeping or waking, except of course on first entering the plane and on finally leaving it. Between those who are fully conscious on the mental plane there is a far closer union than is possible at any lower level. One can no longer deceive another with regard to what one thinks, for all mental operations lie open for everyone to see. Opinions or impressions can now be exchanged not only with the quickness of thought but also with perfect accuracy. Each now receives the precise idea of the other deal without the clutter caused by words. On the mental plane one communicates directly by thought-transference. Space is no barrier, as one can come into contact with any other soul merely by directing one's attention to that soul. The real barriers between souls are caused by their varying degrees of evolution. The less evolved can know only as much of the more evolved as one is able to respond to and such limitation can obviously be felt only by the more evolved.

An ordinary soul is not capable of any great activity in the mental world, its condition is chiefly receptive, and its vision of anything outside its own shell of thoughts is of a very limited nature. It cannot suddenly form new thoughts, as a result it can profit very little from the living forces which surround it, or the angelic inhabitants of the mental world despite the fact that many of them readily respond to certain aspirations of that particular soul. Hence one, who during earth-life has given great importance only to physical things, has made only a few windows through which one may contact the world in which one now finds oneself. However, one whose interest lay in art, music or philosophy will find measureless enjoyment and unlimited instructions waiting on the mental plane. The extent to which one can benefit from these depends solely upon one's own power of perception. During the devachanic period the ego reviews its store of experiences, separating and classifying them. Thus devachan except for a very few is an absolute necessity in the scheme of things. An important point of difference to be noted between the astral and the mental life is that on the mental plane one does not pass through the various levels in a certain order but is drawn directly to the level which best corresponds to one's degree of development. On that level one spends the whole of one's life in the mental body. The varieties of that life are infinite, as each individual life force makes its own for itself.

An ordinary individual life force on the mental plane is filled with bliss to the very utmost of which it is capable, and there can be no greater joy than what it is experiencing. It surrounds itself with images of its friends, and through those images it is actually in closer contact with its friends than it has ever been on any other plane. The individual life force on the mental plane by no means forgets that there is such a thing as suffering, because it remembers clearly its past life. It now understands many things that were not clear when it was on the physical plane, and the bliss of the present is so great that sorrow seems to be almost a dream. The shell on the mental plane may be compared to the shell of an egg on the physical plane. The only way to get anything into the shell of the egg, without breaking it, would be to pour it from a higher dimension, or find a force whose vibrations are sufficiently fine to penetrate between the particles of the shell without disturbing them. The same is true of the mental shell; it cannot be penetrated by any other vibrations of matter of its own level, but the finer vibrations from higher levels.

The mental body is the vehicle through which the individual life force manifests and expresses itself as the concrete intellect. The senses of the mental body differ greatly from the senses of the physical body. The mental body comes into contact with the things of the mental world as it were directly, becoming conscious of everything which it is able to impress. There are no distinct organs for sight, hearing, touch, taste and smell in the mental body. The word senses is in fact a misnomer and it is more accurate to speak of the mental sense. From this it is clear that being able to communicate directly by thought transference, without even having to formulate the thought in words, the barrier of language no longer exists on the mental plane, as it does on the astral plane. If a trained student passes onto the mental plane and communicates with another student, his mind in 'speaking', speaks at once by color, sound and form. The complete thought is conveyed as a coloured musical picture as opposed to only a fragment of it being shown, as is the case on the physical plane, by the symbol we call words. It is not that the mind thinks a color, a sound or a form, it thinks a thought which is a complex vibration in mental matter, and that thought expresses itself in all these ways by the vibrations it sets up. In the mental body, one is freed from the limitations of one's separate sense organs and is receptive at every point to every vibration which in the physical world would present itself as separate and different. An ordinary individual life force uses matter of the seventh or lowest mental sub-plane only, that being very near to the astral plane. All thoughts of the individual life force are colored by reflections from the astral or emotional world. Very few can as yet deal with the sixth sub-plane. Great scientists certainly use it a good deal but unfortunately they often mingle with it the matter of the lowest sub-plane, and then they become jealous of other people's discoveries and inventions. The matter of the fifth sub-plane is much freer from the possibility of astral entanglement. The fourth sub-plane being next to the causal plane is far away from the possibility of entanglement with astral vibrations.

The matter of the mental plane is divided into seven grades of fineness, precisely the same as that of the astral and physical planes. The three higher grades of mental matter are called arupa or formless; the four lower grades are termed rupa or having form. The distinction is a real one, being related to the divisions of the mind itself. In the rupa levels the vibrations of consciousness give rise to images or pictures, every thought appearing as a living shape. In the arupa levels, consciousness seems rather to send out streams of living energy, which does not blend itself into distinct images. In other words, the arupa levels are concerned with the expression of abstract thoughts, ideas, principles, and the rupa levels with concrete thoughts and particular ideas. Words being largely symbols of images, and belonging to the workings of the lower mind in the brain, it follows that it is almost impossible to describe in words the workings of abstract thought. For the arupa levels pertain to pure reason, which does not work within the narrow limits of language. Another broad distinction between the rupa and arupa levels of the mental plane is that on the rupa levels an individual life force lives in its own thoughts, and fully identifies itself with its personality in the life which it has recently quitted. On the arupa levels the individual life force is simply the reincarnating ego, who if sufficiently developed on that level, at least understands to some extent of its evolution. Since mental matter is so much finer than either astral or physical matter, it follows that the life forces on the mental plane are enormously increased in activity. Mental matter is in constant ceaseless motion, taking form under every stimulus of life and readily adapting itself to every change of motion. Even astral matter seems relatively heavy and lusterless. The vibrations of mental matter when compared to physical vibrations are what vibrations of light are to those of sound.

On the four levels i.e., level 4 to level 7 of the mental plane, some degree of illusion is still possible. It appears less for the individual life force which can function there in full consciousness during the physical life than for an undeveloped individual life force after death, as explained previously. The lower mental plane is thus still a region of possibility and error while on the higher mental plane, there is much that the ego or the individual life force does not know, but what it does know, it knows correctly. The life of the individual life force in the causal body on the causal plane will be discussed in detail later. There is a radical difference between the lower and the higher mental planes. In the lower mental plane, matter is dominant while on the higher planes, life is the prominent thing. The difficulty in the lower planes is to give life expression in the forms, but in the higher it is quite the reverse, to hold and give form to the flood of life.

It is said to be difficult to describe the difference between the matters of various sub-planes of the mental world, because there are no adjectives to describe the lowest sub-plane and thus none for the higher sub-planes. All that can be said is that as one ascends, the material becomes finer, the light more living and transparent. There are more overtones in the sound, more delicate shades in the colors, newer colors appear as one rises through the sub-planes. It has been said poetically and truly, that the light of a lower plane is darkness to the one above it. On the highest sub-plane, the matter is vivified by an energy which flows like light from above and this comes from the buddhic plane. As one descends through each sub-plane, the matter of each sub-plane becomes the energy of the sub-plane immediately below. The original energy, plus the matter of the higher sub-planes becomes the vivifying energy of the next lower sub-plane. Thus the seventh or the lowest sub-plane consists of the original energy six times enclosed or veiled, and is therefore so much weaker or less active as compared to the first sub-plane.

There are a large number of people whose only higher thoughts are those which are only connected with affection and devotion. One who loves another deeply, or feels strong devotion to a personal deity, makes a strong mental image of that friend or of the deity and inevitably takes that mental image into the mental world. This is because it is to that level of matter that it naturally belongs. These results in the following: the love that forms and retains the image is a very powerful force and is strong enough to act upon the ego of the friend which exists on the causal plane, for it is the ego that is the individual life force loved, not the physical body which was only a partial representation of it. The ego of the friend, eagerly responds to the vibration, and pours itself into the thought form which has been made for it. The friend is therefore truly present with the individual more vividly than ever before. The key point to note is that it makes no difference whether the friend is what we call living or dead, because the appeal is made to the ego itself on its own true level. The ego always responds and if one has a hundred friends, one can simultaneously respond to the affection of every one of them. Hence one can express oneself in the heavens to an indefinite number of people. In the limited physical world one is accustomed to thinking of one's friends as only the limited manifestation which one knows on the physical plane. In the heaven world on the other hand, one is clearly much nearer to the reality in one's friend than one was ever on earth, as one is now two stages or planes (physical and astral) nearer to the home of the ego itself.

During one's life on the mental plane one is not conscious of the personal lives of one's friends on the physical plane as it would obviously be impossible to be happy, if one looked back and saw those loved ones in sorrow or suffering. On the mental plane there is no barrier between souls. The soul of one's friend lives in the form one has created of it to the extent that the two can throb in sympathetic vibration to each other. One can have no touch with those with whom on earth one had any difference in the inner life or the ties were only of a physical or astral nature. Hence on the mental plane no enemy can enter for only sympathetic accord of mind and heart can draw individuals together. With those who are more advanced in evolution one comes in contact only to the extent one can respond to them.

There is an important difference between life on the mental plane and life on the astral plane. On the astral plane one meets one's friends (during the sleep of their physical bodies) in their astral bodies, i.e., one is still dealing with their personalities. On the mental plane however, one does not meet one's friends in the mental bodies which they use on earth. On the contrary, their egos build for themselves entirely new and separate mental vehicles. Instead of the consciousness of the personalities, the consciousness of the egos works through their mental vehicles. The mental plane activities of one's friends are thus entirely separate in every way from the personalities of their physical lives. Hence any sorrow or trouble which may fall upon the personality of a living individual cannot in the least affect the thought form of which that person's ego is using as an additional mental body. If in that manifestation one does not know of the sorrow of that personality, it would not cause any trouble at all because one would regard it from the point of view of the ego in the causal body i.e., as a lesson to be learnt, or karma to be worked out. In this point of view there is no delusion. On the contrary, it is the view of the lower personality which is the deluded one, for what the personality sees as troubles and sorrows are to soul in the causal body mere steps on the upward path of evolution. On the mental plane, all that was valuable in the moral and mental experiences of the individual during the life just ended is worked out. These are gradually transmuted into definite moral and mental faculties which one will take with one to one's next incarnation.

One does not work into the mental body the actual memory of the past, for the mental body in due course disintegrates. The memory of the past abides only in the individual life force itself, which has lived through it. However, the facts of past experience are worked into specific mental characteristics. For example if one has studied some subject deeply, the effect of that study will be the creation of a special faculty to acquire and master that subject when it is first presented to the individual in another incarnation. One will be born with a special aptitude for that line of study and will absorb it easily. Everything thought upon the physical plane is thus utilized on the mental plane. Every aspiration is worked into a power; all frustrated efforts become faculties and abilities. As a master has said that on the mental plane the ego collects only the nectar of the moral qualities of consciousness from every terrestrial personality. One must strive to realize that the mental plane is a vast and splendid world of vivid life in which one is living now, as well as in the periods between physical incarnations. It is only one's lack of development, the limitations imposed by the physical body that prevent one from fully realizing that all the glory of the highest heaven is here and now.

Another interesting function to note on the mental plane is the creation of the Mayavirupa, which literally means the body of illusion. It is a temporary astral body made by one who is in the mental body. It may not necessarily be similar to or resemble the physical body. This form is made at will and is best suited for the purposes for which it is projected. The advantage of using the Mayavirupa is that it is not subject to glamour the astral body has to deal with on the astral plane. No astral glamour can overpower the Mayavirupa, nor can astral illusion deceive it. With the power to form the Mayavirupa, one is able to pass instantly from the mental plane to the astral and back. The Mayavirupa may or may not be visible to entities on the astral plane. It is necessary to form the astral materialisation only when one wishes to become visible to entities in the astral world. When one has finished one's work on the astral plane one withdraws to the mental plane again, and the Mayavirupa vanishes.

The apportionment of time that one spends on the physical, astral and mental planes varies considerably as one evolves. The primitive soul relating to the primitive human being lives almost exclusively on the physical plane spending only a few years on the astral plane after death. As one develops, one's astral life becomes longer and as one's intellect unfolds, one begins to spend a little time on the mental plane as well. An ordinary soul belonging to a civilised race remains longer on the mental plane than on the physical and astral. In fact the more it evolves, the shorter becomes its astral and the longer its mental life. Hence, except in the earliest stages of one's evolution, one spends by far the greater part of time on the mental plane. This period can be twice or thrice of the span of one's physical life and largely depends upon how long takes the soul to work out its desires of the earthly life on the astral plane. One's life on the astral plane decreases and correspondingly the span of one's life on the mental plane increases.

One must bear in mind that the true home of the ego is the mental plane; each descent into incarnation is merely a short, though important episode in its evolution. The devotion of the religious devotee whose main thought is not the glory of the deity, but more on the lines of redemption of one's own soul, cannot lead to a prolonged life on the mental plane. However if one never thinks selfishly of oneself only but only of love and gratitude towards the deity or leader often leads to a prolonged heaven-life of a comparatively exalted type. This would include followers of Buddha, Krishna, Ormuzd, Allah or Christ. They would all equally attain their need for celestial bliss and its length and quality would depend primarily on the intensity and purity of the feeling.

The mental plane is a world of effects, not of causes. Each soul is limited to its own individual shades of perception and its capacity to appreciate. The more points of contact it has with the outer world, the more will be the starting points for development on the mental plane. On the other hand, the mental plane from the point of view of the next life is essentially a world of causes, because in it all experiences are worked up into the character which is brought forward when one returns into incarnation. The mental plane is thus the direct result of one's life on physical plane and prepares the way for the next life on the physical plane.

No one is permitted to renounce blindly due to sheer ignorance or to depart from the ordinary course of evolution unless and until it is certain that this will benefit the individual. The general rule is that one may not renounce the mental plane until one has experienced it on the physical plane i.e., until one is sufficiently developed to be able to raise one's consciousness to that plane and bring back a clear memory of its glory. The reason for this is that it is the life of the personality with all its familiar personal surroundings, which is carried on t the lower heaven-worlds, and therefore before the renunciation can take place, the personality must realise clearly what it is that is being given up.

There are people who speculate about life on the 'other side' and the key question is related to meeting loved ones there. This question is rooted in the very heart of human love and affection. Heaven, even if it provided every joy except the joy of being with loved ones would not be heaven to the average person. Without this assurance of continued companionship and association, heaven would seem a very bleak and cold place to the average human soul. This hope and desire of the human heart has a full realization in the facts of life on the mental plane. Not only do we know each other there, but we are naturally bound by bonds of attraction to those whom we love and to those with who we are in sympathy even though we have never known them in earth life. Also there is the possibility of a far nearer and closer companionship between kindred souls than was possible during life on earth. With the discarding of the sheath of the physical body, the soul becomes capable of a far closer relation to kindred souls than it ever experienced on the physical plane. The astral fires having burnt up the gross lower attractions, the soul is able to function on much higher planes of association i.e., the four sub-planes of the lower mental plane. On the mental plane soul may meet soul in close communion and the dreams and longings of earth-life, which were found impossible to realize now become ordinary incidents in the new life of the soul. That for which the soul has longed for in vain on earth, now is found in its richest fruition. To realise what this means, it is necessary to think of the highest ideals entertained by the soul during earth-life regarding the relationships between human beings. Though these ideals are seldom lived out during earth-life, nevertheless they abide with the soul constantly, and it is one of the tragedies of earth-life that these ideals always seem too good to be true. The love of man and woman of the right kind always has as its background this ideal affection and yet how seldom does this ideal manifest. The relationships between parent and child, brothers and sisters and friends, seldom is found to approach the ideal which dwells ever in the human heart. So true is this ideal, so constant is its presence that during earth-life, when we see a companionship which seems to even partially comply with the ideal, our deepest feelings are touched. This results in deep emotion and sympathy which lift us up to higher planes of thought and life. What then must be the joy and bliss of life on this plane on which this expression is natural and where the ideal becomes the real? Those who are bound together by the bond of true love and friendship on the physical plane are presented with the full opportunity to manifest their mutual affection on the mental plane.

The highest that human imagination can picture as possible in such a companionship pales in comparison to the actual reality of the experience. It is futile to attempt to paint a picture of these scenes and relationships, for there are no words that can express the truth. The answer to the inquiry requires each soul to turn its mental gaze inward, and find the picture painted in its imagination of the highest possible bliss. Even this imaginary picture pales in comparison to the reality. It is only in the harmony of music, or the rhythmic cadences of the best poetry, or the lines of some great work of art, that the earth-dwelling soul may catch a glimpse of the truth of love on the mental plane. These things at times cause to rise in the soul faint hints of what the soul actually experiences on those higher planes of being. This is one of the reasons why music, art, and poetry are able at times to lift us above the material environment in which we are dwelling. In the flashes of Cosmic Conscience which occasionally come to souls of spiritual enlightenment, there is included a realization of this feature of the association of souls on the mental plane.

The difficulty in explaining to somebody on the physical plane about the nature and character of the companionship that exists on the mental plane is that the earthly dweller insists upon thinking in terms of a place, whereas there is no place as such on the mental plane but merely conditions and states. To dwell in the same place as the loved one on the mental plane, means simply to dwell in the same state or condition of being. This closeness surpasses the constraint created by space which is felt on the physical plane. Only an advanced soul can begin to comprehend this mystery of the mental plane. A question may arise related to the issue of souls enjoying this sort of companionship but dwelling on different sub-planes belonging to the astral or mental planes, but still being in the same state in which the experience is rendered possible. The answer to this is simple to one who is familiar with certain occult truths. As explained previously, this is brought about as the soul on the higher sub- plane feels the sympathetic attraction of the soul on the lower sub-plane and in answering this it establishes a psychic connection (akin to a highly exalted form of telepathy) between the two.This renders possible the experience of the closest mental, spiritual relationship and companionship; the experience of which far transcends the companionship of two souls in the flesh. Also, as explained before, the soul on the higher sub-plane may actually visit another soul on a sub-plane lower than itself. In this way companionship between disembodied souls of the mental plane is manifested. There is no loneliness for souls who crave for sympathy on the mental plane. There is nothing that is noble in earth-life that does not have its magnified correspondence on the mental plane. There is a natural law which operates on the mental, physical and astral planes. This law regulates and controls everything on the particular plane. The disembodied soul does not part with Nature when it leaves the earthly or astral life but rather it rises to a plane of Nature which is fuller, and richer in every way than the best of which the earth dwelling soul dreams of. Since the baggage of materiality has been burned away by the astral vibrations, the soul blossoms and bears spiritual fruit in the new life on the mental plane.

Metaphysically speaking, all that is conditioned is illusory. The more material and solid the appearance, the further it is from reality and therefore more illusory. In more general terms, the truth is that the higher one rises through the planes of being, the closer one is to reality. Paradoxically, spiritual beings are relatively real and enduring while material things are illusory and transitory. In truth, it is the thought – world that is the closest to reality, and things become more illusory as they take on more of a phenomenal character. However, the true importance of earth-life lies in the fact that it is the place where experience is to be gathered. It conditions, regulates and limits the growth of the soul. The experienced soul on the mental plane will make for itself a splendid instrument for its next earth-life while the inexperienced one will not though in each case, the only material available is that brought from the physical plane. Thus, noble aspiration is a seed which the soul would work out into splendid realisation on the mental plane and bring back with it to the physical plane for its next incarnation. It carries the mental image which is to be materialised on the physical plane when opportunity and suitable environment presents itself. For the mind the mental plane is the sphere of creation and the physical plane is only the place for materialising the pre-existing thought.

The soul is an architect that works out its plans in silence and deep meditation and then brings them forth into the outer world where its edifice is to be built, out of knowledge gained in past life. The objective manifestation follows the mental meditation, first idea then form. This brings to an end a brief overview of life on the mental plane undertaken in this section.

SUBPLANES OF THE MENTAL PLANE

Seventh Heaven	1st Sub plane
Sixth Heaven	2nd Sub plane
Fifth Heaven	3rd Sub plane
Fourth Heaven	4th Sub plane
Third Heaven	5th Sub plane
Second Heaven	6th Sub plane
First Heaven	7th Sub plane

Figure 1 - Symbolic representation of the 7 Sub-planes of the Mental Plane

Characteristically the mental plane has been described as being divided into seven sub-planes, the seventh being the lowest and the first being the highest. Consequently the 7th, 6th, 5th and 4th i.e., the first four sub-planes belong to the lower mental or rupa i.e., form levels. The

3rd, 2nd and 1st i.e., the three higher sub-planes belong to the causal or arupa i.e., formless levels. Although each of the four lower heavens has their own peculiar characteristics, it must not be assumed that the soul divides its life on the mental plane between the various levels. On the contrary, the soul awakens to consciousness on the mental plane at that level which best corresponds to its degree of development. It is on that level it spends the whole of its life in the mental body. The reason for this is that the higher level may always include the qualities of the lower, as well as those peculiar to itself; its inhabitants almost invariably have these qualities in fuller measure than the souls on a lower level.

A brief description about the nature and type of life prevailing on these lower planes i.e., 4th, 5th, 6th and 7th sub-planes is as follows, the 1st, 2nd and 3rd sub-planes which belong to the upper mental or the causal plane will be covered in detail in the next chapter.

1. The Seventh Sub-Plane or the Lowest Heaven

The lowest heaven i.e., the seventh sub-plane has affection for family or friends as its main characteristic. This affection must be unselfish but is usually somewhat narrow in its nature. It must not be assumed that this love is confined to the lowest heaven, but rather that this form of affection is the highest of which those who find themselves on the seventh level are capable of. On the higher levels love of a far nobler type is to be found. A few interesting cases have been studied which can throw some light on the characteristics and life in general on the seventh sub-plane. In this regard it may be useful to describe a few typical examples of the inhabitants of the seventh sub-plane. One was that of an ordinary man, honest and respectable, but of no intellectual development or religious feeling. Although he had probably attended church regularly, he hardly understood religion since it had no connection with the business of everyday life. Hence while he had no depth of devotion, nevertheless he had affection for his family. They were constantly on his mind and he always put them ahead of himself. His surroundings on the mental plane wouldn't be of a very refined type, but nevertheless he would be as intensely happy as he would be capable of developing unselfish characteristics which would be built into his soul as permanent qualities.

Case studies have shown that a large number of western people are found on this sub-plane due to the fact that the principal unselfish activity found its outlet through family affection. Comparatively few eastern people especially among the Hindus or Buddhists were found on this sub-plane, because in their case real religious feeling usually enters more immediately into their daily lives, and consequently takes them to a higher level. For those on this lowest level of the mental plane there is not much material out of which a particular faculty can be molded and progress is very limited. The inhabitants on this level find their family affections nourished and they are re-born with an improved emotional nature which will help them to recognize and respond to a higher ideal.

2. The Sixth Sub-Plane Or The Second Heaven

During the soul's life on the mental plane it is able to witness the various prophets, sages and founders of various religions. However it must be understood, that this environment which the soul witnesses is of the nature of a mirage as partly it is a product of human thought. The thought-forms of a particular form of religious thought gather great strength on the mental plane and endure with all the appearance of reality to the believer and devotee, although entirely invisible to those of a different faith. The presence of prophets and sages remain with the environment though the souls of these individuals have long since passed on to other planes. The mental plane is a realm of ideals and each soul finds its ideals realised on this plane. The good Christian finds a manifestation of the best of one's own creed and beliefs and rests fully assured that one has had the true faith and has reaped the reward that one had expected. The same holds good for the Hindu, Muslim or Buddhist. Moreover, each particular sect of religious belief finds a corroboration of its own beliefs on the mental plane and there is no conflict of sects or religions. Each soul finds its own, and is oblivious of the rest. The only apparent exception is the soul which has advanced far enough to realise the fundamental truth in all religious beliefs which is allowed to see the joy of the blessed of all religious faiths. However it must be remembered that these mental representations of the various religious faiths comprise only the best of each particular form of belief. Thus the soul witnesses the highest conception and ideal of which it is capable of regarding its favourite religion. This naturally has the effect and result of developing the highest religious conceptions in the soul and inhibiting the lower ones. This enables the soul to carry with it only the highest in its religion when it undertakes its next journey to the physical plane. Sometimes a soul will evolve from one form of religious conception during its mental life and upon its reincarnation will be ready for one higher.

The principal characteristic of the sixth sub-plane or the second heaven of the mental plane may be described as anthropomorphic religious devotion. There appears to be some correspondence between this level of the heaven-world and the second astral sub-plane, the difference being that on the astral there is invariably an element of selfishness whereas in the heaven-world the devotion is entirely free from any such taint. This phase of devotion, which consists essentially in the perpetual adoration of a personal deity, must be distinguished from those still higher forms which find their expression in performing some definite work for the sake of the deity.

A few examples will show these distinctions. A fairly large number of entities on this level are drawn from oriental religions whose devotion is pure. Worshippers of Vishnu and Shiva are found here, each wrapped up in a shell of one's own thoughts and oblivious of the rest of mankind. An exception would be related to one's affections associated with those whom one loved on earth.

Women form a very large majority of the inhabitants of this sub-plane and example to illustrate this follows. There was a Hindu woman who had glorified her husband into a divine being and who also thought of the child Krishna as playing with her own children. While these children were thoroughly human and real, the child Krishna was obviously nothing but an image. Krishna also appeared in her heaven as an effeminate young man playing a flute but she was not in the least confused by this double manifestation. Among other examples of inhabitants of this sub-plane was an Irish peasant who was absorbed in the deepest adoration of the Virgin Mary, whom he imaged as standing on the moon but holding out her hands and speaking to him

Even if one is a materialist and agnostic, one will still have a heaven-life, provided that one had been capable of devotion. For deep unselfish family affection, as well as earnest philanthropic activity must produce their result and can manifest nowhere but on the mental plane. It will be seen that blind unreasoning devotion does not at any time raise its votary's to any great spiritual heights but does result in happiness and satisfaction. Nor is such a heaven-life without a very good affect on their future journey. For although no amount of mere devotion will ever develop intellect, yet it does produce an increased capacity for a higher form of devotion and in most cases it leads to purity of life. One who enjoys a heaven such as the one described is not likely to make rapid spiritual progress but is at least guarded from many dangers. It is improbable that in the next birth such a person will fall into any of the grosser sins or be drawn away from one's devotional aspirations.

3. The Fifth Sub-Plane Or The Third Heaven

The principal characteristic of this level of the heaven-world may be described as devotion expressing itself in active work. It is especially the plane for the working out of great schemes and designs unrealized on earth, of great organizations inspired by religious devotion and usually having for their object some philanthropic purpose. It must however be noted that as we rise higher, greater complexity and variety are introduced. A few examples will clearly explain the nature and life on the third heaven or the fifth sub-plane. A typical case was that of a deeply religious man who was found carrying out a grand scheme devised by himself for the better condition of the poorer classes. The scheme comprised amalgamation of businesses in order to affect economies, high wages, the provision of cottages and profit sharing. He hoped that this demonstration of the practical side of Christianity would win over many to his own faith out of gratitude for the material benefits they had received.

A curious case of personal religious work was that of a nun. In her heaven, she was constantly occupied in feeding the hungry, healing the sick and helping the poor. The peculiarity of each case being each person treated by her got changed into Christ, whom she then worshipped with fervent adoration.

On this plane are found the higher type of sincere and devoted missionaries, engaged in the congenial occupation of converting multitudes of people to the particular religion which they advocated. Also on this plane are found devotees of art, who follow it for its own sake or regard it as an offering to their deity. Artists, who pursued art for the sake of fame and self-gratification, would of course not find their way to this plane at all. On the other hand, those who regarded their faculty as a great power entrusted to them for the spiritual elevation of others would reach a heaven even higher than the present one.

One will perceive that the three lower heavens i.e., the first, second and third heavens are concerned with the working out of devotion to personalities, either to one's family and friends,

or a personal deity rather than the wider devotion to humanity for its own sake,. This as we shall see, finds its expression on the next sub-plane.

4. The Fourth Sub-Plane Or The Fourth Heaven

THE fourth heaven, or the fourth sub-plane, is the highest sub-plane of the lower mental plane. Its activities are so varied that it is difficult to group them under a single characteristic. They are best explained by arranging them into four main divisions –

(1) Unselfish pursuit of spiritual knowledge.

(2) High philosophic or scientific thought.

(3) Literary or artistic ability, exercised unselfishly.

(4) Service for the sake of service.

A few examples of each of these classes will make them more readily comprehensible.

(1) Unselfish Pursuit of Spiritual Knowledge -

Most of the inhabitants of this class are drawn from those religions in which the necessity of obtaining spiritual knowledge is recognized. Thus, of Buddhists, there are found here those more intelligent followers who looked upon Buddha as a teacher rather than as a being to be adored and whose supreme aspiration was to sit at his feet and learn. In their heaven-life their wish is fulfilled for the thought-image which they have made of Buddha is no mere empty form; through it shines the wonderful wisdom, power and love of one of the greatest of earth's teachers. They are therefore acquiring fresh knowledge and wider views, the effect of which will greatly influence their next life. They will not remember any individual facts, but when such facts are presented to them in a subsequent life they will grasp them readily and intuitively recognize their truth. Furthermore, the result of the teaching will be to build into the ego a strong tendency to take broader and more philosophical views on all such subjects. The effect of such a heaven-life is to hasten considerably the evolution of the ego. Hence we can see the enormous advantage gained by those who accepted the guidance of living and powerful spiritual teachers. A similar result though to a lesser degree, accrues to one who has followed the teachings of a great and spiritual writer. The ego of the writer will enter into the student's heaven-life and by virtue of its own developed power, vivify the mental image, and thus further illuminate the written teachings.

(1) Highly Philosophic or Scientific Thought.

This class does not include those philosophers who spend their time in verbal argument and discussion which has its roots in selfishness and conceit. This can never help towards a real understanding of the facts of the universe, nor produce results that can work them out on the mental plane. One finds here those noble and unselfish thinkers who seek insight and knowledge only for the purpose of enlightening and helping others.

A typical example was that of an astronomer whose studies had led him to Pantheism. He was still pursuing his studies with reverence and was gaining knowledge from those orders of devas. He was lost in contemplation of a vast panorama of whirling nebula and gradually forming systems and worlds striving to form some idea of the shape of the universe. Scientists such as this astronomer would return to earth as great discoverers, with unerring intuition of the mysterious ways of nature.

(2) Literary or Artistic effort, exercised unselfishly-

On this level are found the greatest musicians like Mozart, Beethoven, Bach, Wagner and others. They are still flooding the heaven-world with harmony far more glorious than they were able to produce when on earth. Streams of divine music pour into them from higher regions. Both those who are functioning in full consciousness on this plane as well as disembodied entities of this level, each of whom is wrapped up in one's own thought-cloud, are deeply affected by the influence of this music. An example was that of a man who had on earth refused to use his literary power merely to earn a living for himself but had instead written a book which none would read. He had been alone all his life and eventually had died of sorrow and starvation. In his heaven-life he was also in solitude but he saw stretching before him the Utopia of which he had dreamed and the vast impersonal multitudes whom he had longed to serve. The bliss of their joy surged back to him and made his solitude a heaven.

(3) Service for the sake of service –

On this level are found many who have rendered service for the sake of service, rather than because they desired to please any particular deity. It should be noted that the various examples given above are for the sole purpose of explaining in more simple and clear terms the characteristics and life activities on the various sub-planes. These examples are the outcome of spiritual experiences of those spiritual masters, who while living in the physical body were able to visit the mental plane in altered and deep states of meditation.

MENTAL PLANE INHABITANTS

In this section, a brief overview of the more common entities that inhabit the mental plane has been undertaken. One important difference between the entities inhabiting the mental plane and those on the astral plane is that the products of evil passion cannot exist on the mental plane. As a result the sub-divisions are far fewer than in the case of astral entities. Some of the common entities belonging to the mental plane are –

1. Highly spiritually advanced humans still living in the physical body -

Certain highly spirituals advanced human beings who while still present in the physical body and living on earth, are able to move in full consciousness on the mental plane. These are either adepts or their initiated pupils. Until one has been taught by one's master how to use one's mental body, it will be difficult to move with freedom even upon its lower levels. One question which comes to mind is related to travel to the mental plane while still on the physical plane. In very high and altered states of meditation, cosmic currents arise and travel via the spinal cord through the nerves to the brain, where they fall as cosmic irradiations. These currents travel to higher centers in the brain namely the Pituitary, Thalamus, Hypothalamus and the Pineal glands, which is the highest gland or centre. When the cosmic currents reach the Pineal gland then contact with entities of the mental plane and travel in it is possible. Adepts and Initiates appear as splendid globes of living color, driving away all evil influence wherever they go. It is here in the mental world that most of their important work is done, particularly on the higher levels, where it is possible to act directly on the individuality or the ego. It is from this plane that they are able to shower the highest spiritual influences upon the world of thought and also initiate great movements of all kinds. Here also, direct teaching is given to those who are sufficiently advanced to receive it, as it is possible to impart it far more readily here as compared to the astral plane. They also have a great field of work in connection with those whom we term as the dead. Adepts or masters for the most part of their work generally reside on the highest level of the mental plane.

In order to gain a better understanding of the conditions of the mental plane and its inhabitants, it is essential to know those who are not present on the plane. The characteristics of the mental plane being unselfishness and spirituality, it follows that the black magician and his pupils can find no place there. In spite of the fact that in many of them the intellect is very highly developed, and consequently the matter of their mental bodies is extremely active and sensitive along certain lines, yet in every case those lines are connected with personal desire of some sort. They can, therefore find expression only through that lower part of the mental body, which is inextricably entangled with astral matter. As a consequence of this limitation, their activities are practically confined to the astral and physical planes. One whose whole life has been evil and selfish, may have periods of purely abstract thought during which one may utilize one's mental body, provided one knows how to do so. One might therefore say that an ordinary human could function on the mental plane only if one forgot about one's evil and selfish motives. For ordinary people during sleep or for psychically developed persons in trance, to penetrate the mental plane is possible though extremely rare. Purity of life and purpose are absolute pre-requisites to enter this plane.

2. The ordinary human after death –

This class comprises persons in varying degrees and conditions of consciousness found on the various sub-planes of the mental plane, as described in some detail in the previous section of this chapter.

3. Second Elemental Kingdom-

The genesis of mental elemental essence has already been described under the heading 'Elemental Essence' in the sub-section 'Some Astral Entities' in the previous chapter 'The Astral Plane' There are three Elemental Kingdoms, the first ensouls matter of the higher mental or causal sub-planes, the second ensouls the matter of the four lower levels of the mental plane, and the third ensouls astral matter. In the Second Kingdom the highest subdivision exists on the fourth sub-plane, whilst there are two classes on each of the three lower sub-planes, thus making in all seven sub-divisions on these four sub-planes.

As described in the previous chapter the mental essence is on the downward arc of evolution i.e., progress for it means descent into matter, and hence is less evolved than astral essence or any of the later kingdoms such as the mineral kingdom. Mental essence is much more instantaneously sensitive to thought-action than astral essence. It is in this response that its very life consists of its progress through usage by thinking entities. If it could be imagined as being entirely free say for a moment from the action of thought, it would appear as a formless conglomeration of dancing infinitesimal atoms but probably making very little progress on the downward path of evolution into matter. However, the moment thought works on it and stirs it into activity, throwing it on the rupa or form levels into all kinds of lovely forms, it receives a distinct additional impulse which when often repeated, helps it progress forward. When a thought is directed from higher levels to the affairs of earth, it sweeps downwards and takes upon itself the matter of the lower planes. In doing so it brings the elemental essence of which its first veil was formed, into contact with that lower matter; thus by degrees the essence becomes accustomed to answer to lower vibrations, and so progresses in its downward evolution into matter.

There is a vast difference between the power of thought on its own plane and the comparatively feeble effort we know as thought on the physical plane. Ordinary thought originates in the mental body (inter-related to the mental plane) and as it descends it envelops itself in astral essence. If one can make use of one's causal body then one can generate one's thoughts at that level. These thoughts then envelop themselves in lower mental essence and are infinitely finer and more effective in every manner. If thoughts are directed exclusively to higher objects, their vibrations may be too fine to find expression in astral matter. When they do affect this lower matter their effect is far greater than what can be possibly generated on a level which is much nearer to the level of that lower matter. Following this idea further, the thoughts of an initiate are generated on the buddhic plane, and envelop themselves in causal matter; the thoughts of a master are generated on the atmic plane, thus wielding the incalculable powers of a region of matter even beyond the buddhic and causal planes.

4. Artificial Elementals–

Mental elementals, or thought-forms, have already been discussed in detail previously, hence only a brief description about them is needed here. The mental plane has far more artificial elementals inhabiting it than the astral plane and they play a vital role among those who live and function on it. These thought forms are more radiant and stronger than astral elementals. The importance and influence of such artificial entities can scarcely be exaggerated when one looks at the fact that thought is much grander and more powerful on the mental plane and its forces are being utilised not only by human entities, but by beings like devas, and by visitors from higher planes. Masters and initiates make great use of these mental elementals and the elementals which they create have a much longer existence and proportionately greater power than any of those which were described in dealing with the astral plane.

5. Animal Group-Souls-

The group-souls, to which the vast majority of animals are attached, are found on the lower mental plane. These have already been described in detail under the heading 'Group Souls' in the previous chapter 'The Astral Plane'.

6. Individualised Animals –

Individualisation, by means of which an animal rises to the human kingdom, is attained by association with humans. The intelligence and affection of the animal is developed to the degree necessary by its close relationship with its human friend. An animal that has attained individualisation after death on the physical and astral planes has usually a very prolonged, though often somewhat a dreamy life in the lower heaven world. Its condition is sometimes called 'dosing' consciousness and is analogous to that of a human on the same level, though with far less mental activity. It is surrounded by its own thought-images; even though it may be only dreamily conscious of them and these will of-course include images of its earth-friends in the very best moods. These images will of course awaken response from the egos of its friends in the usual way. The animal will remain in the condition described until in some distant future it assumes the human form.

7. Cosmic entities from other planes -

It was mentioned in the chapter 'The Astral Plane' that there are occasionally found on this plane certain cosmic entities and visitors from other higher planes and systems. Such visitors are found in much greater number on the mental plane. Not a lot has been written about these entities in esoteric literature; however they are very lofty beings and are not so much concerned with individuals, but with great cosmic processes.

8. Rupadevas or Gods of Form -

Rupa means form and deva means God. These beings known to the Hindus as Devas, to Christians as Angels, and elsewhere as Sons of God, etc., belong to an evolution distinct from that of humanity. This may be regarded as a kingdom just above humanity, similar to humanity being just above the animal kingdom. There is however an important difference; while an animal can only pass into the human kingdom, a human being having attained a certain level of spiritual development has several choices of which the deva line is one. Though at present it is not possible for us to understand a lot about them, it is quite clear that the aim of their evolution is considerably higher than ours.

There are at least as many types of angels or devas as there are races of humans on earth and in each type there are many grades of power, intellect, and general development. None of devas have physical bodies such as we have. The lowest kind are Kamadevas, who have as their lowest body the astral (Kama is a Sanskrit word meaning desire), the next class is that of the Rupdevas who have bodies of lower mental matter, and who have their habitat on the four lower or rupa levels of the mental plane. The third class is that of the Arupadevas, who live in bodies of higher mental or causal matter, and who have their habitat on the three higher or arupa levels of the mental plane known as the causal plane. Above these are four other great classes inhabiting the other higher planes and above and beyond the deva kingdom stand the great host of the planetary spirits. The relationship of devas to nature-spirits (entities of the astral plane which assist in the running of various phenomena of nature) somewhat resembles at a higher level, that of humans to animals. Just as an animal can attain individualization only by association with a human being, so also it appears that a nature-spirit can normally acquire a permanent reincarnating individuality only by an attachment of a somewhat similar character to devas. Devas will never be human, as most of them are already beyond that stage though there are some who have been human beings in the past.

The bodies of devas are more fluidic than those of humans, being capable of far greater expansion and contraction. They have also a certain fiery quality which clearly distinguishes them from human beings. The fluctuation in the aura of a deva is also much greater than that of a human being. The colors in the aura of a deva are more of the nature of flame than of cloud. They are described as radiant, embodiments of strength, possessing vast knowledge, great power and are most splendid in appearance. They guide natural order, their cohorts carrying on ceaselessly the processes of nature with regularity and accuracy. Not much is known of any rule or limit for the work of devas. They have more lines of activity than one can imagine. In general, devas unreservedly co-operate with the great plan of the universe and as a direct result of that is the perfect order that one finds in nature.

DEATH OF THE MENTAL BODY

Life on the mental plane is finite in nature, as has been observed. Death happens when the ego has assimilated all the essence of the experiences which were gathered in the preceding physical and astral lives. All the mental faculties which were expressed through the mental body, are then withdrawn within the higher mental or causal body and remain there in a latent condition until the time comes for re-birth. The physical, astral and mental faculties which lie in seed form. Dormant within the causal body is all that remains to the ego of its bodies in the lower worlds. The mental body itself, the last of the temporary vestures of the ego, is left behind as a mental corpse, just as the physical and astral bodies were left behind. Its materials disintegrate and return to the general matter of the mental plane.

Every human being, upon the completion of one's life on the astral and lower mental planes, obtains at least a flash of consciousness of the ego in the causal body. In this momentary flash of ego-consciousness, one sees one's last life as a whole, and gathers from it the impression of success or failure of the work which it was meant to do. Together with this, one also observes a forecast of the life that lies ahead, with the knowledge of the specific progress which one has to make in it. Only very slowly does the ego awaken to the value of these glimpses but when it comes to understand them, it naturally begins to make use of them. Eventually it arrives at the stage when this glimpse is no longer momentary, when it is able to consider the question much more fully, and to devote some time to its plans for the life which lies before it.

In a Nutshell

The Mental World

The mental plane and its principles – The mental plane is known devachan – the shining land. Lower desires cannot enter. One's life here largely depends upon one's desires and ideals that one had on earth. The lower mental planes shape themselves into each of the various heavens depicted by the various religions. In Devachan morals and true ideals now bear fruit. Experiences on the mental plane are far more real than on the physical material plane.

Pure thoughts and unselfish feelings are the window into the mental plane. Each individual is able to draw upon the heaven world and to cognize only so much of it as one has, by previous effort, prepared on earth through pure thoughts unselfish feelings and a moral life. The mental plane is composed of seven sub planes. The lower four have form (rupa) whilst the upper three are formless (arupa).

Concrete versus abstract thinking is (pure reason). Ever changing light and color is the color language of the Devas. A far closer union is possible on the mental plane.

The ordinary soul is largely receptive. A complete thought is conveyed as a color musical picture. On the arupa level the individual life force is the reincarnating ego. There is a far closer communication between soul to soul than on earth. One's ego builds a new mental vehicle in Devachan and looks at any sorrow of trouble from the true perspective of the ego as karma to be worked out. Karma is elaborated on the mental plane for a future Earth life.

One's lack of development prevents one from realizing the glory of the highest heaven world now. Primitive people spend only a few years on the astral plane after death. The true home of the ego is the mental plane. Spiritual beings are real and enduring, material things are illusionary and transitory. Earth life is a field where experiences are to be gathered.

Theseventh sub plane is characterized by being closely connected to those who are connected here on earth. The six sub plane is characterized by being connected to those who profess and practice the same faith and religion. The fifth sub plane or the heaven is characterized by those who have devotion expressed as deeds. The fourth sub plane or fourth heaven is characterized by the pursuit of spiritual philosophy and unselfish literary or artistic pursuits.

Mental Plane Inhabitants

High spiritually advanced humans in physical

incarnation. Adepts or masters generally reside on the highest mental sub plane. Ordinary human beings after death go to the second elemental kingdom. Artificial elemental and animal group soul are cosmic higher entities from the other planes Rupa Devas or God of form – also angels of the Christians guide the natural order.

Death of the Mental Body

When all experiences have been gathered in the mental plane the mental body dissolves and the seed of the experiences is taken into the causal body. One sees ones future karma and there makes plans for its implementation.

CHAPTER 4

THE CAUSAL PLANE

The ego is said to have a causal body (the state of the `I' during sleep), but how can you make it the subject of your investigation? When the ego adopts that form, you are immersed in the darkness of sleep.

Sage Sri Ramana Maharshi

CAUSAL PLANE PRINCIPLES

In the previous two chapters The Astral World and The Mental World the life of the soul on the astral plane and on the lower mental plane has been described. In this chapter the life of the soul on the causal plane will be briefly described.

In the lower mental plane matter is dominant, and consciousness shines with difficulty through the forms. In the higher planes life is the most prominent thing, and forms are there only for its purposes. The difficulty in the lower planes is to give the life expression to the forms while the reverse holds good for the higher planes. On the causal plane matter is subordinated to life, altering at every moment. An entity changes form with every change of thought. Matter is only an instrument of the soul's life. Causal consciousness thus deals with the essence of a thing, whilst the lower mind studies its details. With the mind, one talks about a subject or makes an attempt to explain it, while with the causal consciousness, one takes up the essence of the idea of the subject, and moves it as a whole. It is akin to moving a piece while playing chess. The causal plane is a world of realities; one no longer deals with emotions or conceptions, but with the thing in itself.

Life on the causal plane plays a very small part in the life of ordinary individuals because in such cases the ego is not sufficiently developed to be awake on the causal plane. Individuals with very little spiritual development and awareness, in fact, never consciously attain the heaven-world at all, while a still larger number obtain only a comparatively slight touch of some of the lower sub-planes. However in the case of one who is spiritually developed, life on the causal plane is glorious and fully satisfying. Nevertheless, consciously or unconsciously, every human being must touch the higher levels of the mental plane before reincarnation can take place. As further evolution proceeds, this touch becomes more definite and real. As one progress, not only is one more conscious on the causal plane but the period one passes there becomes longer.

As evolution proceeds, the principle governing the life after death on the lower levels, both of the astral and the mental planes gradually shortens, while the higher life becomes steadily longer and fuller. Eventually the time arrives when the consciousness is unified, i.e., when the higher and the lower selves are united and realizes the possibilities of one's life on the causal plane.

The time spent on the causal plane varies according to the stage of development. This ranges from 2-3 days of unconsciousness for an undeveloped person to a long period of years of conscious and glorious life in the case of advanced individual.

It is only when consciousness has withdrawn from the lower bodies and is once more centered in the ego, that the final result of the incarnation just concluded is known. Then one is able to observe the new qualities one has acquired in that particular cycle of one's evolution. At that time also, a glimpse of the life as a whole is obtained, the ego has for a moment a flash of clearer consciousness. These results in one seeing the results of the life just completed and a glimpse of what is to follow in its next birth. Initially one makes little use of it as one is very dimly conscious and cannot comprehend facts and their interrelationships. Gradually the power to comprehend what one sees increases. Later comes the ability to remember such flashes at the end of previous lives and to estimate the progress one is making. In addition to this activity, one will devote some time to one's plans for the life which is to come. One's consciousness gradually increases, until one has an appreciable life on the higher levels of the mental plane, each time one touches them.

The soul uses the causal body for its tenure of life on the causal plane. Though life in the heaven-worlds of the lower mental plane has been glorious, it does eventually come to an end. The mental body in turn drops away and the soul's life in its causal body begins. The personality consists of the physical, astral and the lower mental bodies while the individuality consists of the ego in the causal body. As leaves grow on a tree to last through spring, summer and autumn, so do personalities manifest in the individual to last through the life periods spent on the physical, astral and lower mental planes. Just as the leaves assimilate and pass on nutriment to the sap, which is eventually withdrawn into the parent-trunk, and then perishes so does the personality gather experience and passes it on to the parent-individuality eventually and perishing when its task is completed. All through the heaven-life, the personality of the last physical life is distinctly preserved. It is only when the consciousness is finally withdrawn into the causal body, that this feeling of personality is merged into the individuality and the soul for the first time since its descent into incarnation realizes itself as the true and comparatively permanent ego. In the causal body, one needs no windows, which were formed by one's own thoughts in the lower heavens, as the causal plane is one's true home. The causal plane is the true and relatively permanent home of the ego. Here one is free from the limitations of the personality, and is simply the reincarnating entity.

Physical, astral and mental bodies exist for one human incarnation only. i.e., are distinctly mortal, the causal body persists throughout the whole of one's evolution and is therefore relatively immortal. This is because in due course, when one has completed one's evolution on the causal plane, life on the still higher planes starting with the buddhic plane begins and actually one loses the causal body. The causal plane provides materials to clothe abstract thoughts, the lower mental plane provides materials to clothe concrete thoughts and the astral plane provides materials for the clothing of desires. The causal body owes its name to the fact that in it reside the causes which manifest themselves as effects on the lower planes. For it is the experiences of past lives, stored in the causal body, which are the cause of the general attitude towards life and the actions undertaken. In Sanskrit, the causal body is known as the Karana Sharira, Karana meaning cause. The causal body has two main functions; one is to act as a vehicle for the ego and the second is to act as a storehouse for the essence of the experiences of the ego in its various incarnations. In the causal body are stored the seeds of qualities to be carried over to the next incarnation. Hence one observes that the lower manifestation of the ego i.e., its expression in its mental, astral and physical bodies depends ultimately upon development in the causal body. This in turn, is dependent on the experiences it gains during its manifestation in the lower planes.

Thus the object of the ego is to unfold its latent powers and this it does by putting itself down in successive personalities. At its inception, the causal body is described as a delicate film of subtlest matter. This delicate, almost colorless film is the body which will last through the whole evolution process. The causal body is the storehouse of all that is noble and harmonious and in accordance with the law of the spirit; every great and noble thought's essence is worked into the substance of the causal body. Hence the condition of the causal body is a true barometer of the growth of the individual. All the other bodies (physical, astral and mental) should be regarded as casings or vehicles, enabling the ego to function on that particular plane. Relatively speaking, to the ego, all these bodies are transient, and they wear out and are renewed, time after time adapting to its various needs. A key point to bear is that as the mind is fundamentally dual in its functioning, so the ego is provided with two bodies. The mental body which serves for concrete thought while the causal body for abstract thought. In the causal body one thus has the abstract, the pure internal working, no longer confused by the senses nor in any way interfered with by the outer world. In the causal body also lies the creative power of meditation; the energies that grow out of one-pointed contemplation. The size of the causal body is many times larger than that of the physical body, and there is displayed magnificent development of the highest types of intellect, love,, devotion and spirituality. In an undeveloped individual the causal body is at first almost empty and as one develops, it gradually fills up. When it is completely filled, not only will it commence to grow in size but also produce streams of force that flow out in various directions. This in fact is one of the grandest characteristics of a spiritually developed individual; the capacity to serve as a channel for higher force. The attitude of helpfulness and readiness to give makes it possible for the divine strength to descend upon such an individual in a steady stream. This enables it to reach many who are not yet strong enough to receive it directly.

Furthermore as has been described in esoteric literature, from the upper part of the causal body there ascends a crown of brilliant sparks, indicating the activity of spiritual aspiration and adding greatly to the beauty and dignity of one's appearance. No matter how one may be occupied on the physical plane, this stream of sparks rises constantly. The reason for this is that once the ego of the individual is awakened upon its own level and begins to understand itself and its relationship to the Divine, it always looks towards the source from which it came. This happens irrespective of any activities which it may be aspiring for on lower planes. It must be remembered that even the noblest personality is but a partial expression of the ego on the causal plane. As soon as the ego or the higher self begins to look around the individual or the personality, it finds almost unlimited possibilities opening before itself unlike physical life. This very upward rushing of spiritual aspiration which is like a glorious crown for the highly spiritually advanced individual is itself the channel through which the divine power descends. The stronger the individual's aspirations become, the larger is the measure of the grace from above.

On the lower sub-planes, an elemental or thought-form, which is created hovers about and awaits a favorable opportunity of expending its energy either upon the mental, astral or even the physical body of the individual thought of. However on the causal plane the result is a kind of flash of lightning of the essence from the causal body of the thinker, direct to the causal body of the object of one's thought. While on the lower sub-planes, the thought is always directed to the mere personality; on the causal plane one influences the reincarnating ego, the real individual. If the message has any reference to the personality, it will reach that personality through the instrumentality of the causal body. It is said to be a striking sight to observe the change from an abstract or arupa idea to concrete or rupa thought, as the idea clothes itself in the matter of the four lower sub-planes. The growth and development of the causal body is greatly assisted by the work of the Masters, for they deal more with egos in their causal bodies than with the lower vehicles of individuals. They devote themselves to pouring spiritual influence upon individuals thereby evoking from them all that is noblest and best in them, hence promoting their growth. Many people are sometimes conscious of such helpful influences but are not sufficiently spiritually developed to trace them to their source.

According to the law of evolution everything that is evil has within itself the seed of its own destruction, while everything that is good has in it the seed of immortality. The secret of this lies in the fact that everything evil causes disharmony since it sets itself against the cosmic law. Hence sooner or later it faces destruction. On the other hand, everything that is good, creates harmony and hence carried forward becoming part of the stream of evolution; hence never perishes. We may conceive all the experiences of the soul as passing through a fine sieve or mesh, only that which is good can pass through. That which is evil is left behind, and rejected. The very mechanism, by which the causal body is built up, lays not only the hope but the certainty of one's final triumph. No matter how slow the growth is, or how long the journey is, it has its ending. The individual is always evolving and cannot be totally destroyed.

Most thoughts of the ordinary individual have their origin on the lower mental levels and clothe themselves as they descend with the appropriate astral elemental essence. But when one is active on the causal levels, the thoughts commence there and clothe themselves first in the elemental essence of the lower levels of the mental plane and hence are consequently infinitely finer and more penetrating. Consequently the thought of an Initiate, which rises in the Buddhic plane, will clothe itself with the elemental essence of the causal sub-planes. Similarly, the thought of an adept will pour down from the atmic plane with tremendous power that is beyond the comprehension of ordinary humans.

The ego incarnates in a personality for the sake of acquiring definiteness. Evil qualities can be expressed only in the four lower subdivisions of astral matter. These reflect their influence in the mental plane only on its four lower subdivisions; hence they cannot affect the ego at all. The only emotions that can appear in the three higher astral sub-planes are good ones, such as love, sympathy and devotion. These affect the ego in the causal body, since it resides on the corresponding sub-planes of the mental world. The ego on its own plane uses abstractions just as on the physical plane one deals with concrete thoughts. On its plane, the essence of everything is available. When a subject needs to be explained, it takes up the essence or the idea of the subject and moves it as a whole. Its world is a world of realities, where not only is deception impossible but also unthinkable. It no longer deals with emotions, ideas, or concepts but with the thing itself. On this plane, the ego has fully unrolled before it all the lives it has lived on this globe. It sees its lives as one vast whole, of which its descents into incarnation have been like the passing of days.

It sees the karmic causes which have made what it is, and also the karma still to be worked out. It thus realises with unerring certainty, its exact place in evolution.

When dealing with matters on its own plane, and those below it, all the ideas of the ego are perfect. Furthermore, anything incomplete would be unsatisfactory and could hardly be counted as an idea at all. These characteristics of the ego reflect themselves to a certain extent in its lower vehicles, and we find them appearing in various ways. For example, children always demand that fairy tales end well, that virtue be rewarded and that vice be vanquished, Those who clamor for an evil realism are those whose views of life have become corrupted because, in their myopic vision they can never see an incident as a whole but rather a fragment of it, which shows in one incarnation.

Many metaphors have been used to illustrate the relation between the ego and its personalities or incarnations. Thus, each incarnation has been compared to a day at school. In the morning of each new life the ego takes up its lessons again, at the point where it left them the night before. The time taken to complete the lesson is left entirely to one's own discretion. The wise pupil perceives that school-life is not an end in itself, but merely a preparation for a more glorious future. One co-operates intelligently with the teachers, and sets oneself to do the maximum work which is possible so that as soon as one may enter into one's kingdom as a glorified ego.

The coming down of the ego into the physical world, for brief glimpses of mortal life has been likened to the diving of a bird into the sea for fish. As a-diver plunges into the depths of the ocean to seek a pearl, so the ego plunges into the depths of the ocean of life to seek the pearl of experience. Like the diver it does not stay there long, for that is not its own element. It rises up again, into its own environment and shakes off the heavier element, which it leaves behind. Hence it is truly said that the soul that has escaped from earth has returned to its own place, for its home is the land of the Gods. Every earth-life is an opportunity carefully calculated for development in quality and quantity as is most needed by the ego. Failure to use that opportunity results in another similar incarnation and suffering probably aggravated by the additional karma incurred.

There is a link or a mode of communication between the higher self, or ego, and the lower self or personality. This link is known as the antahkarana. This Sanskrit word means the inner organ and is known as the link between the causal faculty and desire faculty during incarnation. One who can unite the two faculties through the thought faculty which belongs to the lower mental plane is known as the antahkarana.This thought faculty becomes pure and free from desire. When the ego and the personality are perfectly united then the attenuated thread of antahkarana ceases to exist. Its destruction implies that the ego no longer needs an instrument but works directly on the personality. When one does will operates the ego and the personality, and then there is no longer any need for the antahkarana. The earlier stages of one's evolution consist in the opening of this antahkarana, or line of communication, so that the ego may be able to increasingly assert itself through it. This finally results in domination of the personality so that it may have no separate thought or will, but is merely an expression of the ego on the lower planes, operating within the limitations of the lower planes.

One needs to further understand more specifically the attitude which the ego takes up towards its incarnation in a personality. Since the method for evolution of the latent qualities of the ego is by means of impact from the external environment, it is clearly necessary that the ego should descend far enough to enable it to meet such impact which can affect it. The method of achieving this result is by reincarnation; the ego putting forth part of it into the lower planes for the sake of the experience to be gained there and then withdrawing back into itself, carrying with it the results of its endeavor. It must not be misconstrued that the ego makes any movement in space. It endeavors to focus its consciousness at a lower level to obtain an expression through a denser variety of matter. This putting forth of part of itself into incarnation has often been compared with an investment. The ego expects, if all goes well, to reclaim not only the whole of its capital invested but also a considerable amount of interest. But, as with other investments, there is occasionally loss instead of gain for it is possible that some portion of that which the ego has put down may become so entangled with the lower matter that it may be impossible wholly to reclaim it. If the matter be of the lower mental plane, then it results in an individual who is completely materialistic. One may perhaps be keenly intellectual, but not spiritual, one may very likely be intolerant of spirituality, and quite unable to comprehend or appreciate it. One may probably call oneself practical but from the point of view of the ego, one is a failure as one is not making any spiritual progress. If on the other hand, the matter in which one is so fatally entangled be astral then on the physical plane one will think only of one's own gratification and will be totally ruthless in pursuit of some object which one strongly desires. An individual will be quite unprincipled and brutally selfish. Cases such as these have been spoken of as lost souls though they are not irretrievably lost. The ego, belonging as it does to a higher plane, is a much greater and grander thing than any manifestation of it can be. Its relation to its personalities is that of one dimension to another, that of a square to a line or a cube to a square. No number of squares could ever make a cube because the square has only two dimensions, while the cube has three. So no number of expressions on any lower plane can ever exhaust the fullness of the ego. For example if it could take a thousand personalities, it may not still sufficiently express all that it is. The most for which one can hope is that the personality will contain nothing which is not intended by the ego, that the personality will express as much of the ego as canbe expressed in this lower world.

Slowly the animal nature is reduced and the human increased. At a certain stage during this progress, the personalities begin to answer to the higher vibrations and dimly to sense that they are something more than isolated lives, but are attached to something immortal. They may not quite recognize their goal, but they begin to thrill and quiver under the touch of the ego. Thereafter progress becomes more swift and the rate of development increasing enormously in the later stages. The consciousness of the ego may be reached by maintaining the mind in an attitude of attention, without the attention being directed to anything; the lower mind being stilled in order that consciousness of the higher mind may be experienced. Although we have seen that the personality is part of the ego, it's only life and power being that of the ego, it nevertheless often forgets those facts and comes to regard itself as an entirely separate entity and works for its own ends. In the case of ordinary people who have never studied these matters, the personality is for all purposes the real individual, the ego manifesting itself only very rarely and partially.

The ordinary individual is hardly awake to the real and higher life at-all. If one complains that the ego takes very little notice of one, and then let one ask oneself how much notice has one taken of one's ego. If we look at many personalities around us we notice their physical bodies full of drugs and poison, their astral or desire part reeking with greed and sensuality and their mental having no interest beyond money making. It is not difficult to see why an ego, surveying them, might decide to postpone its serious effort to another incarnation. The whole course of the movement down into matter is called the pravritti marga literally meaning the path of pursuit while the nivritti margais the path of return and of renunciation. On the path of pursuit, on which are the vast majority of humans, desires are necessary and useful as these are the motives that prompt one to activity. On the nivritti marga desire must cease. What was desireon the path of pursuit becomes willon the path of return.

As soon as an ego becomes at least partially conscious of its surroundings and of other egos, it leads a life that has interests and activities of its own plane. But even then, one must remember that it puts down into the personality only a very small part of itself and that part constantly become entangled in interests which are often different from the general activities of the ego itself. The ego consequently does not pay any particular attention to the lower life of the personality unless something rather unusual happens to it. When this stage is reached, the ego usually comes under the influence of a Master. In fact, often its first clear consciousness of anything outside itself is its touch with that Master. The tremendous power of the Master's influence magnetises it, draws the individual's vibrations into harmony with those of the Master, and multiplies manifold the rate of its development. It radiates upon the individual like sunshine upon a flower and one evolves rapidly under its influence. While the earlier stages of progress are so slow, when the Master's attention is turned towards the individual the speed of advancement increases dramatically. Also it is on the causal plane that most of the important work of the Masters is done as the individuality can be acted upon directly. Here also direct teaching is given to those pupils who are sufficiently advanced to receive it in this way, since it can be imparted far more completely here than on the lower planes.

No description of the causal and the lower mental plane would be complete without an account of what are known as the Akashic Records. They constitute the only reliable history of the world and also as the true Karmic Records.

The word akashic is somewhat of a misnomer, for, though the records are read from the akasha or matter of the mental plane, yet they do not really belong to that plane. A still worse name, which was often used in the earlier literature on the subject, was 'records of the astral light'. This is incorrect for they lie far beyond the astral plane, only broken glimpses of them being found on the astral plane. The word akashic is suitable only because it is on the mental plane that one definitely first comes in contact with the records and finds it possible to do reliable work with them.

On the astral plane the reflection is exceedingly imperfect, such records which can be seen there are fragmentary and often seriously distorted. The analogy overwater, which is so often used as a symbol of the astral world, is apt in this case. A clear reflection in still water is at best only a reflection, representing in two dimensions objects which are three-dimensional, and showing only their shape and color also the objects are inverted. If the surface of the water be disturbed, the reflection is so distorted that it is rendered useless. Now on the astral plane, one can never have anything close to a still surface and hence one cannot depend upon getting a clear and definite reflection. Thus a clairvoyant possessing only the faculty of astral sight can never rely upon accurate picture of the past that comes before him as being accurate and perfect.

On the mental plane, conditions are very different. There the record is full and accurate; also it is impossible to make any mistake in reading. That is to say, any number of clairvoyants, using mental sight and examining a certain record, would all see precisely the same reflection resulting in a correct impression from reading it. With the faculties of the causal body, the task of reading the records is still easier. It appears in fact, that for perfection in reading (as far as is possible on the mental plane) the ego must be fully awakened. It is well known that if a number of persons witness a given event on the physical plane, their accounts of the same will often vary considerably. This is because of faulty observation as each will observe only those features of the event which most appealed to that individual. This personal equation would not appreciably affect the impressions received in the case of an observation on the mental plane. Each observer would thoroughly grasp the entire subject. Error, however, may easily occur in transferring the impressions received to the lower planes.

The appearance of the records varies to a certain extent, according to the conditions under which they are seen. Upon the astral plane, the reflection is usually a simple picture, though occasionally the figures seen would be endowed with motion. On the mental plane they have two widely different aspects. Firstly if the observer is not thinking specially of them, the records simply form a background to whatever is going on. Under such conditions they are merely reflections from the ceaseless activity of a great Consciousness upon a far higher plane and have very much the appearance of cinematograph pictures. The action of the reflected figures constantly goes on as though one was watching the actors on a distant stage. Secondly if one is a trained observer and one's attention is turned especially to any one scene, then, this being the plane of unhampered thought, it is instantly brought before the observer. Thus, if one wished to see the landing in Britain of Julius Caesar, in a moment one finds oneself, not looking at a picture, but actually standing on the shore among the legionaries, with the whole scene being enacted around oneself, precisely as one would have seen it had once been there when it occurred in 55 BC. The actors are of course entirely unconscious of the observer, as they are but reflections and nor can any effort on one's part change the course of their action in any way. But one has the power of controlling the rate at which the drama shall pass before one. One may thus have the events of a year take place before one in an hour. One could also stop the movement at any moment and hold any particular scene in view as long as one chooses. Not only does one see all that one would have seen physically, had once been present when the events occurred, but one hears and understands what the people say and one is conscious of their thoughts and motives.

There is one special case where an investigator can enter into an even closer sympathy with the records. If one is observing a scene in which one had taken part in a previous life, there are two possibilities open to the observer. One may regard it in the usual manner, just as a spectator, though (as indicated above) a spectator whose insight and sympathy are perfect. One may once again identify oneself with that long-dead personality of one and experience again the thought and emotions of that time. In fact one recovers from the universal consciousness that portion with which one had been associated. Thus one can readily perceive the wonderful possibilities that open up before an individual who is in full possession of the power to read the akashic records at will.

The akashic records must not be confused with mere, human-made thought-forms which exist in abundance on both the mental and the astral planes. To see thought-forms needs nothing but a glimpse of the mental plane. Hence many visions of saints, seers, etc., are not of the true records but merely of thought-forms. The records, referred to as the memory of nature, are on the plane of buddhi and are much more than just memory in the ordinary sense of the word. On this plane time and space are no longer limitations. The observer no longer needs to pass through a series of events to review an event , for past, present, as well as future, are all simultaneously present for the observer.

Also related to past lives it is obvious that the physical body can have neither a memory nor a record of a past incarnation in which it itself did not participate. Precisely the same consideration applies to the astral and mental since all these vehicles are new for each incarnation. As the causal body is the only one that persists from one incarnation to another, the lowest level at which one can hope to get reliable information about past lives is that of the causal body. In these past lives, the ego in its causal body was present so it is an actual witness. All the lower vehicles not being witnesses, can report only what they receive from the ego. Consequently, when one bears in mind how imperfect is the communication between the ego and the personality in an ordinary individual one shall see at once how entirely unreliable such information is likely to be.

When the consciousness is centered in the heart, during meditation, it is most susceptible to the influence of the ego. The head is the seat of mental activities. One who in concentration can take the consciousness from the brain to the heart is able to unite the desire or the thought element with the higher or divine element. One is then in a position to catch some of the messages of the ego. One, who is absolutely untrained, has practically no communication with the ego. An Initiate on the other hand, has full communication. Consequently one finds, that there are individuals at all stages between these two extremes. A key point to bear in mind is that there is only one consciousness, yet one often feels there are two, so one is led to wonder whether the ego is entirely dissociated from the physical body. The apparent difference is caused only by the limitations of the various vehicles. One should not therefore imagine that there are two entities in an individual. There never is any lower self as a separate being, but as previously explained, the ego puts down a tiny portion of itself into the personality, in order to experience the vibrations of the lower planes. The ego is never likely to be wrong. It is apparently not deceived by anything, but the personality is ignorant of certain matters and the very purpose of incarnation is to remove that ignorance. What is needed is the purification of the personality and also the channel between it and the ego must be opened. Until this is done, the personality sees everything from its own very limited point of view. Under the more peaceful conditions of the causal plane all previous experiences are examined with clear vision and hence all the unwanted experiences can be thrown away; the treasure being preserved.

When an ego becomes sufficiently developed to come under the direct influence of a Master, the amount of that influence, which can be passed on to the personality, depends upon the connection between that personality and the ego. This aspect has an infinite variety in human life. One must also bear in mind that while the ego tends to exclude the material, and receive the spiritual, the general tendency of the personality at least in the earlier stages is to exclude the spiritual and receive the material. Meditation and the study of spiritual subjects in this earthly life undoubtedly make a great difference in the life of the ego.

Since selfishness is the intensification of the personality, the first step should be to rid oneself of that vice. Next, the mind should be kept filled with high thoughts, for if it is continually occupied with lower matter, the ego cannot readily use it as a channel of expression. In the savage, the personality expresses itself in all kinds of emotions and passions, of which the ego could not possibly approve. In an evolved individual, there are no emotions but such as one chooses to have. Instead of being swayed by emotions one simply selects them. For example, one could say love, devotion and sympathy are good things, so I'll allow myself to feel them. The emotions are thus under the dominion of the individual mind, which is an expression of the causal body. At this stage one is very near to the condition of almost complete unity of the higher and lower self. Even if one falls many times, there is no reason to be disheartened as even failure is to a certain extent success. By failure one learns, and becomes wiser to meet the next problem.

The great danger lies in undisciplined imagination. Were it not for the imagination, external objects of desire would have no power over us. The ego should therefore acquire full control over imagination. One who grasps the fact that one is the Immortal Ruler gains expression of dignity and power which grow even stronger and more compelling on the lower nature? The knowledge of truth sets one free. One who has succeeded in raising one's consciousness to the level of the causal body and thereby unifying the consciousness of the lower and higher selves, i.e. of the personality with the ego has of course the consciousness of the ego at one's disposal during the whole of one's physical life. This will not be affected by the death of the physical body, or even by the second and third deaths in which one leaves behind one's astral and mental bodies respectively. One's consciousness in fact resides in the ego all the time and plays through whatever vehicle one may happen to be using at any given moment. For such an individual, the whole series of one's incarnations is only one long life. All through human evolution, one's consciousness is fully active. It may be noted that one is generating karma just as much at one period as another. While one's condition at any given moment is the result of the causes one has set in motion in the past, yet there is not an instant during which one is not modifying one's condition by the exercise of thought and will. While this consideration applies to everyone, yet it is clear that one who possesses the ego consciousness is in a position to modify one's karma more deliberately and with more calculated effect, than one who has not achieved continuous ego-consciousness.

The ego is concerned solely with purely unselfish feelings and thoughts. Two simple but excellent rules may be given for differentiating between a true intuition and mere impulse. Firstly if the matter is set aside and one forgets about it then the impulse will probably die away while a genuine intuition will remain as strong as ever. Secondly, intuition is always connected with something unselfish. If there is any touch of selfishness, it may be taken for certain that it is only an astral impulse. For example it is far easier to affect the physical body with a barbaric thought as compared to a subtle point by a philosopher.

One means the ego uses for communication with the personality is that it impresses its ideas upon the personality in dreams, using sets of symbols. Prophetic dreams must be attributed exclusively to the action of the ego, who either foresees some future event for which it wishes to prepare its lower consciousness. This may be of any degree of accuracy and depends on the power of the ego to assimilate it and then to impress it upon the waking brain. Sometimes the event is one of a serious nature, such as death or disaster, so the motive of the ego is obvious. Stories of such prophetic dreams are quite common. In order to bring through, into the physical brain, impressions from the ego, it is obvious that the brain must be calm. Everything from the ego on the causal plane must pass through the mental and astral levels and if either of these is disturbed, it reflects imperfectly.

The will, is undoubtedly a quality of the ego and must not be confused with the desires of the personality in the lower vehicles. Desire is the outgoing energy determined by the attraction to external objects. In the early stages of evolution desire has complete sovereignty and one is ruled by one's astral body. In the middle stages of evolution, there is continual conflict between desire and will. One struggles with the desire-thought element. In the later stages of evolution desire dies and will rules unopposed; the ego is in command. To summarize, one may say that the voice of the ego or higher self speaking from atmic level, is true conscience; from the buddhic level, is intuitive knowledge between right and wrong and from the causal level is inspiration. God in every one is the monad, and as the ego is to the monad, so is the personality to the ego. It has been suggested that the higher self ought to take more interest in the unfortunate personality struggling on its behalf on the lower planes. Gradually one should come to realise that the personality that is seen on the lower planes is but a very small part of the individual and that the higher self is the real individual. For there is only one consciousness, the lower being an imperfect representation of the higher, in no way separate from it. Thus, instead of thinking of raising oneself till one can unite with the glorified higher self, one should realise that the higher is the true self. To unite the higher with the lower really means to open out the lower so that the higher may work more freely and fully through it. One should thus endeavour to become certain beyond the possibility of doubt, that one is the spirit or the higher self; One should develop confidence in one's own powers as the ego and have courage to use those powers freely. Instead of looking upon one's usual state of consciousness as normal and looking upwards towards the ego as a lofty being to be reached by continuous and tremendous effort, one should learn to look upon one's ordinary state of consciousness as abnormal and unnatural and upon the life of the spirit as one's own true life, from which by continuous effort one keeps oneself estranged.

SUBPLANES OF THE CAUSAL PLANE

As explained in the previous chapter the mental plane has been characteristically described as being divided into seven sub-planes. The seventh being the lowest and the first being the highest. Consequently the 7th, 6th, 5th and 4th i.e., the first four sub-planes belong to the lower mental or rupa i.e., form level. The 3rd, 2nd and 1st i.e., the three higher sub-planes belong to the causal or arupa i.e., formless level, these constitute what is known as the causal plane. A brief description about the geographical nature and type of life prevailing on these higher i.e., 1st, 2nd and 3rd sub-planes is as follows –

1. Third Sub-Plane Or The Fifth Heaven

This is the lowest of the formless mental sub-planes. It is also the most populous of all the regions because here are present almost all the souls who are said to be engaged in the present human evolution, Each soul may be pictured as being represented by an ovoid form, which at first is a mere colorless film, but which later, as the ego develops, begins to show a shimmering iridescence like a soap-bubble. Those who are connected with a physical body i.e., still in the physical body but may be able to travel to the causal plane in altered states like in meditation, are distinguishable from those in the disembodied state by a difference in the types of vibrations set up on the surface of their causal bodies. It is therefore easy on this plane to see at a glance whether an individual is or is not in incarnation at the time. The immense majority, whether in or out of the body, are but dreamily semi-conscious, though few are now in the condition of mere colorless films. Those who are fully awake are marked and brilliant exceptions, standing out amid the less radiant crowds like stars of the first magnitude. Between these and the least-developed are ranged every variety of size and beauty, each thus representing the exact stage of evolution at which one has arrived.

The majority are not yet sufficiently developed to understand the purpose of the laws of the evolution in which they are engaged. They seek incarnation in obedience to the impulse of the Cosmic Will and alsothe blind thirst for manifested life. In their earlier stages, such entities cannot feel the intensely rapid and piercing vibrations of the highly refined matter of their own plane (the causal plane,). The strong and coarse but comparatively slow movements of the heavier matter of the physical plane are the only ones that can evoke any response from them. Hence it is only on the physical plane that they feel themselves to be alive at all and this explains their strong craving for re-birth into earth-life. Thus for a certain period of time, their desire matches exactly with the law of evolution. Slowly their power of response increases and is awakened first to the higher and finer physical vibrations and still more slowly to those of the astral plane. Next, their consciousness begins to be centred on the astral plane i.e., consciousness begins to be centred in their emotions than in mere physical sensation. At a later stage but always by the same process of learning one learns to centre one's consciousness on the mental plane, to live according to the mental images which one has formed for oneself and so to govern one's emotions by the mind. Yet further along the long road of evolution, the centre moves up to the causal body and the ego realizes it's true life. When that stage is reached, one will be found upon a higher sub-plane than the third, and the lower earthly existence will be no longer necessary.

As previously explained, the most advanced egos of this sub-plane develop to a point at which they are engaged in studying their past and learning a lot from retrospection, so that the impulses sent downwards become clearer and more definite, and translate themselves, in the lower consciousness, as imperative intuitions. On this third sub-plane are also to be found the causal bodies of the comparatively few members of the animal kingdom who are individualized. Strictly speaking, these are not animals any longer. They are practically the only examples now to be seen of the quite primitive causal body, undeveloped in size, and colored only very faintly by the first vibrations of newly born qualities. When the individualized animal retires into its causal body, to await its turn of evolution which will give it the opportunity of a primitive human incarnation, it seems to spend the time in a sort of delightful trance of the deepest peace and contentment. Even then, interior development of some sort is taking place though its nature is difficult for us to comprehend. In any case, it is enjoying the highest bliss it is capable of at that level.

2. The Second Sub-Plane Or The Sixth Heaven

From the densely populated Fifth Heaven, one passes into a more thinly populated world. Only a few have risen to this where even the least advanced is definitely self-conscious, and also conscious of its surroundings. One is to some extent able to review the past through which one has come, and is aware of the purpose and method of evolution. One knows that one is engaged in self-development and recognises the stages through which one passes in one's lower vehicles. The personality, with which one is connected, is seen by one as a part of oneself. One endeavors to guide it, using one's past experience from which one formulates the principles of conduct. These are sent down into the lower mind directing its activities. In the earlier part of one's life on this sub-plane, one may continually fail to make the lower mind understand logically the foundations of the principles one impresses upon it. Nevertheless, one succeeds in making the impression, so that such abstract ideas as truth, justice and honor, become ruling conceptions in the lower mental life. So firmly are such principles wrought into the very core of one's being, that no matter what may be the circumstances or temptations; to act against them becomes impossibility. For these principles is the life of the ego. Part of one's evolution on this sub-plane consists of increasing conscious direct touch with the personality, which so imperfectly represents one in the lower levels.

Only such individuals who deliberately aim at spiritual growth live on this sub-plane, and in consequence, become largely receptive to the influences from the planes above them. The communication grows and under this influence, the thought takes on a singularly clear and piercing quality, even in the less developed. This effect manifests itself in the lower mind as a tendency towards philosophic and abstract thinking. In the more highly evolved, the vision gives a clear insight of the past, recognising the causes set up, their working out, and what remains of their effects still not exhausted. Egos, living on this plane, have tremendous opportunities for growth for here they may receive instruction from more advanced entities and coming into direct contact with their teachers. No longer by thought-pictures, but by a flashing luminousness impossible to describe, the very essence of the idea flies like a star from one ego to another. A thought here is like a light placed in a room; it shows all things around but requires no words to describe them. In this sixth heaven one also views the vast treasures of the Divine Mind in creative activity and can study the archetypes of all the forms that are being gradually evolved in the lower worlds. A broader outlook of this level lets one understand phenomena and one sees the justification of the divine ways, so far as they are concerned with the evolution of the lower worlds.

3. First Sub-Plane Or The Seventh Heaven

This is the most glorious level of the heaven-world. It has but only a few inhabitants from our humanity. Here dwell only few other than the masters of wisdom and compassion, and their initiated pupils. No words can fully describe the beauty of form, colour and sound on this causal plane. In touching the seventh heaven, one comes in contact for the first time with a plane, which is cosmic in its extent; hence on this level one may be met by many an entity which mere human language has no words to portray. Those who are on this sub-plane have accomplished their mental evolution. From them, the illusive veil of the personality has been lifted, and they know and realise that they are not the lower nature, but use it only as a vehicle of experience. On this sub-plane, the ego is conscious of the lower heaven-world, as well as of its own.

From this highest level of the mental plane come down most of the influences poured out by the masters of wisdom, as they work for the evolution of the human race. They act directly on the souls, or egos, of individuals, shedding upon them the inspiring energies which stimulate spiritual growth. This helps enlighten the intellect and purify emotions. From here genius receives its illumination and all effort towards upliftment find their guidance. From the elders of the race light falls on everyone and each uses as much as one can assimilate, and thereby evolve. Thus, the highest glory of the heaven-world is found in the glory of service, and those who have accomplished their mental evolution are the fountains from which flows the strength for others who are climbing.

IN A NUTSHELL

The Causal Plane

The causal plane principles – In the rupa levels of the mental plane, an entity changes form with every change of thought. Causal consciousness deals with the essence of a thing. The causal plane deals with the thing in itself. Every human being must touch the higher levels of the mental plane before reincarnation can take place. One will devote some time to plan ones future life on Earth.

The Personality which is transitory is the physical, astral and lower mental bodies whilst the individuality is the ego in the causal body – the reincarnating entity. The causal plane is one's true home. The causal body persists or one's entire evolution. The object of the ego is to unfold its latent power by putting itself down in successive personalities. The growth and development of the causal body is assisted by the masters.

The ego, on its plane, deals with realities, with the thing in itself. The ego incarnates in a personality for the sake of acquiring definiteness. The ego sees what karma lies in front of it and perceives the great scheme of evolution. The ego's true home is the land of the gods.

It is intended that the personality will eventually be the true expression of the ego and is achieved through the culmination of experience in fruits through incarnation in the personality. The ego can become more perfect or less perfect after each incarnation. The task of the personality is to lessen the animal and to increase the human.

The akashic record provides an account of the history of the world. The majorities of human desires are necessary and prompt one to activity. The speed of advancement can increase in a geometrical fashion under the influence of a master. Difficulties in reliable accounts of past lives, the purpose of incarnation is to remove ignorance. One's consciousness resides in one's ego and plays through the various vehicles.

The ego is only concerned with unselfish thoughts and feelings. Prophecy forecasts from causes in existence but can fail with an individual as the individual can be, to a large extent, the master of circumstances. The ego or higher self speaking from atmic level is the true conscience. God in everyone is the monad. The ego is a lofty being to be reached by continuous and tremendous effort.

Sub Planes of the Causal Plane

The upper level of the mental plane is the causal plane.

The third sub plane or fifth sub heaven – The majority of souls are but dreamily semiconscious. They seek incarnation in obedience to the cosmic will. The center of consciousness moves in its evolutionary past from the physical astral, mental and to the causal plane, after which there is no debate to reincarnate.

The second sub plane or the sixth heaven – Only a small minority have risen to this level – these are individuals who deliberately aim at spiritual growth live on this sub plane. One sees the justification for the divine ways.

First sub plane or heaven world – Only a few inhabitants of humanity dwell here. Only the masters of wisdom and compassion with their pupils dwell here.

❋❋❋

CHAPTER 5

REINCARNATION

Real rebirth is dying from the ego into the spirit. This is the significance of the crucifixion of Jesus. Whenever identification with the body exists, a body is always available, whether this or any other one, till the body-sense disappears by merging into the source - the spirit, or Self. The stone which is projected upwards remains in constant motion till it returns to its source, the earth, and rests. Headache continues to give trouble, till the pre-headache state is regained. Thirst for life is inherent in the very nature of life, which is absolute existence - sat. Although indestructible by nature, by false identification with its destructible instrument, the body, consciousness imbibes a false apprehension of its destructibility. Because of that false identification it tries to perpetuate the body, and that results in a succession of births. But however long these bodies may last, they eventually come to an end and yield to the Self, which alone eternally exists.

Sage Sri Ramana Maharshi

REBIRTH – ITS CAUSE AND MECHANISAM

Life is a great school for the learning of lessons. It has various grades and scales of progress. One cannot escape learning the lessons and nothing once learned is ever forgotten entirely. There is an indelible imprint of the lesson on one's character, which manifests as predispositions, tastes, inclinations, etc. Our character is the working of the law of karma.

What one is in this life is the result of what one was in one's last life. What one makes of this life will reflect in the next life. One is one's own judge. It is the love of the Absolute that is forever working to lead one forward. It opens one's soul to that knowledge that burns up karma, and enables one to throw off the burden of cause and effect. Under the operation of the law of karma everyone is master of one's own destiny, one rewards oneself, one punishes oneself. It is the Absolute, which is constantly urging us towards spiritual rising and drawing the soul towards its ultimate haven of rest. One must work out one's own salvation and destiny. Under this law, every thought and action has its karmic effect upon the future incarnations of the soul. It is not exactly in the nature of punishment or rewards, but as the operation of the law of cause and effect.

The thoughts of a person are like seeds which blossom and bear fruit. Some spring into growth in this life, while others are carried over into future lives. The actions of this life may represent only the partial growth of the thought seed and future lives may be necessary for its complete fruition. Of course, one who understands the truth, and has mentally divorced oneself from the fruits of one's actions, has robbed material desire of its vital force. By seeing it as it is, and not as a part of one's real self such seed-thoughts do not blossom and bear fruit in future lives, for one has killed their germ. They have been robbed of their vitality and are unable to bear fruit.

Those who are suffering, and who see no cause for their pain, are apt to complain and rebel when they see others of no apparent merit enjoying the good things of life. That is due to the law of karma. This makes each person responsible for his or her happiness or misery. It may also be mentioned here that the fundamental objection to killing is that it interferes with the course of evolution. One has been robbed of the opportunity to use this body to progress.

The karma, which one is now acquiring and storing up by reason of one's actions, deeds, thoughts and mental and spiritual relationships, will spring into operation in future lives, when the body (and environment) appropriate for its manifestation presents itself. One does not necessarily have to wait until a future life in order to set into operation and manifestation the karma of the present life. For there come times in which there being no obstructing karma brought over from a past life, the present life karma may begin to manifest. The Karma brought over from past incarnations, which is not able to manifest at the present time owing to the opposition presented by other karma of an opposite nature, serves to hold the first in check. It is a well known physical law, which likewise manifests on the mental plane, which two opposing forces result in neutralization.

Of course, a more powerful karma may manage to operate, while a weaker is held in check by it.

There are two great principles at work in the matter of karmic law affecting the conditions of rebirth:

The first principle is that whereby the prevailing desires, aspirations, likes and dislikes, attractions and repulsions, etc., press the soul into conditions in which these characteristics may have a favorable environment for development.

The second principle is that which may be spoken of as the urge of the unfolding spirit.

It is always urging forward toward fuller expression, and the breaking down of confining sheaths, which thus exerts a pressure upon the soul awaiting reincarnation. This causes it to seek higher environments and conditions than its desires, aspirations and general characteristics would demand.

These two apparently conflicting (actually harmonious) principles acting and reacting upon each other, determine the conditions of rebirth, and have a very material effect upon the karmic law. One's life is largely a conflict between these two forces, the one tending to hold the soul to the present conditions resulting from past lives and the other ever at work seeking to uplift it to greater heights.

The desires and characteristics brought over from past lives, of course seek fuller expression and manifestation upon the lines of the past lives. These tendencies simply wish to be let alone and grow according to their own laws of development and manifestation. But the unfolding spirit, knowing that the soul's best interests are along the lines of spiritual unfolding and growth, brings a steady pressure upon the soul causing it to gradually kill the lower desires and characteristics thus enabling spiritual growth. It is that infinite love of the Absolute that is primarily responsible for the upward tendencies of the soul.

One of the greatest difficulties in the way of the seeker is the feeling that rebirth is being forced upon the individual, without any say on one's part. However this is far from being correct. The soul is attracted toward rebirth by the essence of its desires. It is reborn only because it has within itself the desire for further experience and opportunity for growth. It is true that the soul of one filled with earthly desires will by the very force of those desires be drawn back to earthly re-birth in a body best suited for the gratification of those desires. The earth-sick soul is not compelled to return unless its own desires bring it back. The sum of the desires of the soul, constitute the motivation to be reborn. Those who are reborn on earth are not reborn against their will or desire. They are carried into the current of re-birth because their desires have created longings that can be satisfied only by renewed life in the flesh. Although they are not conscious of it, they instinctively place themselves again within the operations of the law of attraction, and are swept on to re-birth, in exactly the environment best suited to enable them to live out and exhaust the force of desires. They hunger to satisfy their longings and until that hunger is appeased, the desires cannot be discarded.

This does not mean that every desire must necessarily be lived out, for it happens frequently that new insight and experience causes the soul to turn away from a former object of desire, and the desire thus dies a natural death. But so long as the desire remains alive, it tends to attract the soul toward objects and environments which are likely to satisfy it. The soul, preserving its desire for things of flesh and the material life is not able to divorce itself from these things, and naturally falls into the current of re-birth.

It is only when the soul, by means of many earth-lives, begins to see the worthlessness and illusory nature of earthly desires that it begins to get attracted to its higher nature. Escaping the flowing currents of earthly re-births, it rises above them and is carried to higher spheres. Average individuals, after years of earthly experiences, are apt to say that they have no more desire for earth life. These persons are perfectly sincere but they are not really tired of earth-life, but merely of the particular kindof earth life which they experienced during that incarnation. They have discovered the illusory nature of a certain set of earthly experiences, and feel disgusted by the same. But, they are still full of another set of desires and hunger for another set of experiences on earth.

The primary and essential reason for reincarnation is the cosmic will which impresses itself upon the ego, appearing in it as a desire for manifestation. In accordance with this, the ego copies this action by manifesting itself into the lower planes. This desire is known in Sanskrit as trishna, or thirst. It is the blind thirst for manifested life, the desire to find some region where the ego can express itself and receive those impressions from external surroundings. This is not desire for life in the ordinary sense of the word, but rather for a more perfect manifestation. If the ego did not want to come back, it would not return. As long as any desire remains for anything that the world can offer, one will want to come back. Thus an ego is not driven against its will back to this world of troubles, but its own intense hunger to fulfill certain desires drives it back. So long as one is imperfect, has not assimilated everything this world can give and utilized it to the full, one will return to re-birth.Thus karma for the individual becomes the primary cause of reincarnation, and as desire breeds other desires, this shackles one to re-birth time after time. The thirst to fulfil unfulfilled desires comes to an end when one realizes the Self.

The soul during its sojourn on the causal plane has been rested and reinvigorated. It has forgotten the weariness of life which it had experienced during the previous incarnation. It is again filled with the urge to fulfill desires and is hence led to the scene of action in which these desires may be manifested. There are many instances of this change of feeling in earth-life. One may feel tired, discouraged or even disgusted with one's earthly affairs but at the close of the day after some sleep, change of scene and the influx of new impressions, one is again filled with longing for new activities. The majorities of persons are not really tired of life but are merely experiencing an impulse towards something else like a change of scene, occupation etc and this would work a speedy cure for them. They are not world weary, but they are merely mentally and emotionally tired.

Similar is the case with the tired soul. Change its place of abode to the astral, mental and then causal planes and give it the required rest it needs and it is ready for another part to play in the drama of life.

One point which is misunderstood is related to the matter of the unconsciousness of the soul in the choice of the environment of its new birth. It is true that in souls of low development, the process is almost wholly instinctive and there is practically no conscious realization or choice in the matter. But when the soul begins to develop in spiritual knowledge, it begins to have spiritual insight into the conditions towards which it is being drawn at the time of the close of its life on the causal plane and in the state prior to rebirth and often exercises a choice. In the case of a strong personality with good spiritual development, there is often more than a dreamlike choice, such a soul does much to make circumstances for itself in its new birth within the limitations of its karma.

Another point which needs further clarification is related to the character of the desires which serve as the motive power for re-birth. It is not implied that these desires are necessarily low or unworthy desires. On the contrary, they may be of the highest character but the principle of desire is in them all. Desires, high and low, are the seeds of action, and the impulse towards action is always the distinguishing feature of desire. Love, even of the most unselfish kind, is a form of desire; so is aspiration of the noblest kind. In fact, many unselfish souls are drawn back into rebirth simply by the insistent aspirations to serve others. Whether high or low, if these desires are connected in any way with things related to earth, they are all motives of rebirth. Hence the place of birth is usually determined by the combined action of three forces; firstly the law of evolution, which causes the soul to be born under conditions which will give it an opportunity of developing exactly those qualities of which it is most in need of, secondly is the law of karma and lastly is the force of any personal ties of love or hatred that have been previously formed.

The soul may have passed a few hundred or even a thousand years of earth-time, on these planes according to its degree of development. Sooner or later, the soul feels a desire to gain new experience and to manifest in a new earth-life. For these reasons and also since the attraction to the desires which have not been cast off, the soul falls into a current sweeping it towards rebirth. To include in this are the selection of proper parents, advantageous circumstances and surroundings. Consequently, it again dies on the casual plane as it did on the physical plane hence passing towards rebirth on the physical plane.

Strictly speaking, the soul continues in a condition of partial slumber even after it has been re-born on earth-life, as it does not immediately wake up in the body of the newborn child (the form in which it has reincarnated). On the contrary, it awakens gradually during the early childhood and youth, of the child. A soul does not fully awaken from its second soul-slumber immediately upon re-birth, but exists in a dreamlike state during the days of infancy, its gradual awakening being seen as the growing intelligence of the baby, the brain of the child keeping pace with the demands made upon it. In some cases however, the awakening is premature, as we see in the cases of prodigies, child-geniuses, etc. Occasionally, the dreaming soul in the child half-wakes, and startles us by some profound observation, or mature remark or conduct. The rare instances of child geniuses are illustrations of cases in which the awakening has been more than ordinarily rapid. On the other hand, cases are known where the soul does not awaken as rapidly as compared to the average, and the result is that the person does not show signs of full intellectual activity until nearly middle-age. Cases are known where they wake up when they are forty years of age, or even older, and then take on freshened activity and energy, surprising those who had known them before.

Returning to the earlier stages of the second soul-slumber, during this period the slumbering soul undergoes a peculiar stage of spiritual digestion and assimilation. Just as, in its first soul-slumber, the soul digested the fruits of its earth-life and assimilated the lessons and experiences thereof, so in this second slumber the soul digests and assimilates the wonderful experiences of the higher planes. The period on these planes has been not only one of introspection but also a period of reconstruction and unfolding. Many things have been lived-out on these planes i.e., the astral, mental, causal planes and the soul leaves them a far different entity from that which entered it. Many undesirable characteristics have been burned away by repentance and remorse and many desirable characteristics have been unfolded in the higher planes. However there is still needed a process of stock taking, which includes readjustment of mental conditions and spiritual preparation for a new life and this is supplied during the early stages of the soul-slumber. Just as a child, or an adult, receives the energy necessary for the work of a new day, when it is wrapped in sleep at the close of the previous day, so does the sleeping soul receive energy during the early stages of soul-slumber so that it may face the new life with vigor. The soul receives a fresh impetus of energy, and is also given the psychic pattern of its new physical body, during the soul-slumber. Each soul goes to where it belongs by reason of what it is. It is not subject to the arbitrary dictates of any being in heaven or on earth, but the absolutely just and equitable law of karma which operates in every case. There is no favoritism, nor is there the slightest chance of even the faintest injustice being meted out to any soul, no matter how lowly it may be. The lowest as well as the highest comes under the purview of the same law.

When the soul is in the causal body it has within itself an imprint of the impressions of the experiences it underwent during its life on the lower planes i.e., the mental, astral and the physical planes. When the life on the higher mental sub-plane comes to an end, trishna reasserts itself and the ego once again turns its attention outwards. Desire with its army of tendencies consisting of material qualities, sensations, abstract ideas, tendencies of mind, awaits the ego as it re-emerges to assume a new incarnation. The seeds of past tendencies commence to germinate as soon as the new personality begins to form itself for the new incarnation. The process is brought about by the ego turning its attention first to the stored mental impressions, which immediately resume activity and then to the stored astral impressions. The tendencies, which had been in a condition of suspended animation, are thrown outwards by the ego as it returns to re-birth. First, it draws around itself matter from the physical world, and its elemental essence. The ego thus begins in this respect exactly where it had left off. Next, it draws round itself matter from the astral world and its elemental essence thus obtaining the materials out of which its new astral body will be built, causing re-appearance of appetites, emotions, and passions brought over from past lives. The astral matter is gathered by the ego descending to re-birth automatically. This material is an exact reproduction of the matter in the astral body at the end of its last astral life. The soul thus resumes its life in each world just where it had left it last time. Each incarnation is inevitably and automatically linked with the preceding lives, so that the whole series forms a continuous, unbroken chain.

This ego in its descent to incarnation does not receive ready-made mental and astral bodies, instead it receives material out of which these bodies will be built, in the course of the life that is to follow. Moreover the matter it receives is capable of providing it with mental and astral bodies, exactly of the same type it had at the end of its last astral and mental lives, respectively. The qualities are simply the germs of qualities, which have secured for themselves a possible field of manifestation in the matter of the new bodies. Whether they develop in this life into the same tendencies as in the last one will depend largely upon the encouragement, given to them by the surroundings of the child during its early years. Any one of them, good or bad may be readily stimulated into activity by encouragement, or, on the other hand may be starved out for lack of that encouragement. If stimulated, it becomes a more powerful factor in one's life this time than it was in one's previous existence, if starved out; it remains merely as an unfructified germ. The child cannot thus be said to have as yet a definite astral body, but the matter out of which to build it.

For example, suppose one was a drunkard in one's past life, in kamaloka or astral plane one would have burnt out the desire for drink and be definitely freed from it. But although the desire itself is dead, there still remains the same weakness of character which made it possible for one to be subjected by it. In one's next life the astral body will contain matter capable of giving expression to the same desire, but one is in no way bound to employ such matter in the same way as before. In the hands of careful and capable parents, who regard such desires as evil, one would gain control over them, repress them as they appear, and hence the astral matter will remain unverified and become atrophied from want of use. The matter of the astral body is slowly but constantly wearing away and being replaced, precisely as is that of the physical body. As atrophied matter disappears it will be replaced by matter of a more refined order. Thus are vices finally conquered and made virtually impossible for the future.

During the first few years of one's life the ego has but little hold over its vehicles, and therefore looks to its parents to help it to obtain a firmer grasp and to provide it with suitable conditions. It is impossible to exaggerate the plasticity of these unformed vehicles. Much as can be done with the physical body in its early years as in the case of children trained as acrobats for example, far more can be done with the astral and mental vehicles. They thrill in response to every vibration they encounter, and are eagerly receptive of all influences, good or evil, emanating from those around them. In early youth they are so susceptible and so easily molded, but very soon they set and stiffen and acquire habits which, once firmly established, can be altered only with great difficulty. Thus to a far larger extent than is realised by even the fondest parents, the child's future is under their control. A very striking instance is recorded where the brutality of a teacher irreparably injured the astral and mental tendencies of a child so as to make it impossible for the child in this life to make the full progress that was hoped for it. So vitally important is the early environment of child that the life in which adept ship is attained must have absolutely perfect surroundings in childhood.

Even though the majority of individuals must undergo many earthly incarnations before freedom and liberation is found, still it is equally true that when a soul reaches the stage of spiritual development in which the ties of earth no longer bind it, then it is impossible that such a soul can be held to the round of earthly incarnation. Such a soul is attracted toward other spheres, where the attractions of earth do not exist. Its karma carries it away from earth, not toward it. However, this is the condition of only very few, although little by little every soul will experience it in the aeons to come. In the next chapter a brief description of the higher planes to which this class of souls who have gone beyond reincarnation will be given. Even such souls must pass through the soul-slumber after their life on the causal plane before they can proceed further. In such cases they lose in their sleep all that is left of the confining sheaths of earth-desire, and throw aside all the fruits of earth action except that which is called liberation and freedom. Such souls never again awaken on earth, nor do they ever return there, unless, they voluntarily revisit earth as great spiritual teachers. Such souls have worn the garb of humans, now and then throughout the ages, but have always been far more than an ordinary human. There are planes of existence higher than causal plane and blessed indeed is the soul which awakens from its soul-slumber and finds itself in even the most humble of these exalted states. Even the wisest sages bow in reverence at the mention of such spheres of existence, which even transcend human imagination.

IN A NUTSHELL

Rebirth its causes and mechanism

Nothing learnt is ever forgotten. One is one's own judge, bestower and executioner. Understood and mastered desires bear no karmic fruit of future action. It is love that is at the back of all upward tendencies of the soul. The soul is reborn because of its desires for further experiences and opportunity for unfoldment. There is no force applied to an individual for rebirth. Cosmic will appears in the ego as a desire for manifestation. Many souls choose rebirth to be of service to humanity. The ego draws together all the necessary materials needed for its next birth so as to fulfill its karma. They are the germs of qualities needed. Knowledgeable parents can have a positive effect on the development of negative traits in the child. In the early years of development the child has easily molded and impressionable vehicles. There are planes higher than the causal plane where even the wisest stage bows in reverence.

CHAPTER – 6

BEYOND REBIRTH

You must distinguish between the `I', pure in itself, and the `I'-thought. The latter, being merely a thought, sees subject and object, sleeps, wakes up, eats and thinks, dies and is reborn. But the pure `I' is the pure being, eternal existence, free from ignorance and thought-illusion. If you stay as the `I', your being alone, without thought, the `I'-thought will disappear and the delusion will vanish forever. In a cinema-show you can see pictures only in a very dim light or in darkness. But when all the lights are switched on, the pictures disappear. So also in the floodlight of the supreme atman (the real Self) all objects disappear.

Sage Sri Ramana Maharshi

OVER-VIEW OF THE HIGHER PLANES

Beyond the causal plane are the Buddhic, Atmic, Anupadic and the Adi planes. These have been briefly described under the sub-heading - Realms of Life after Death – in chapter one. When the consciousness is raised to the buddhic vehicle, a very remarkable thing happens to the causal body; it vanishes. One is under no compulsion to ever to take it up again, but this cannot be done until all the karma of the lower planes is exhausted. One is not free from binding results on the lower planes, until one is perfectly selfless on those planes. If when helping another, one feels perfectly the unity with the other, then one obtains the result of one's action on the buddhic plane only and not on any of the lower planes. The buddhic consciousness gives one a realisation of the one consciousness of God, which penetrates all. Such realisation gives a sense of the utmost safety and confidence. This manifests in the form of the most tremendous stimulus imaginable though initially it might be alarming, because one may feel that one is losing oneself. When one puts aside the causal vehicle, in which one has been living for so long, then one will find the far grander and higher life. To do this needs some courage and at first it is a startling experience being totally in the buddhic vehicle, as one finds that the causal body upon which one has been depended for thousands of years, has vanished. When the experience does come, one will know with absolute certainty that the Self is one. The idea cannot be conveyed, as it has to be experienced. It must not however be assumed that when one enters the lowest sub-division of the buddhic plane, one is at once fully conscious of one's unity with all. That perfection of sense comes only as the result of much toil and trouble, when one has reached the highest sub-division of the buddhic plane. Step by step, sub-planc by sub-plane, the aspirant must win one's way for oneself, for even at that level, exertion and effort are still necessary, if progress is to be made.

One scarcely needs to be told that all description of buddhic consciousness is necessarily and essentially defective. It is impossible to describe in words what it is, as the physical brain is incapable of grasping the reality. It is difficult enough to form a concept even of lower astral plane phenomena, so trying to describe the buddhic plane is out of question. The sense of union is characteristic of the buddhic plane and on this plane all limitations begin to fall away. One's consciousness expands until one realises that the consciousness of one's fellowmen is included within one's own.

On this plane one knows by definite experience the fact that humanity is one. Though one still has a consciousness of one's own, the fact is that it has widened out into such perfect sympathy with the consciousness of others. One sees all others as oneself. While the predominant element in the causal body is knowledge, the predominant element of consciousness in the buddhic body is bliss and love. Hence the buddhic body is called by the sheath of bliss. A selfish person cannot function on the buddhic plane for the very essence of that plane is sympathy. On this plane, consciousnesses do not necessarily merge instantly at the lowest level, but they gradually grow until the highest level is reached. At this point one finds oneself consciously one with humanity. This is the lowest level at which the separateness is absolutely non-existent i.e., in its fullness, the conscious unity with all belongs to the higher atmic plane. To each ego that can reach this state of consciousness, it would seem that it has absorbed or included all others; one perceives that all are facets of a greater Consciousness. One ceases altogether to blame others for their differences with oneself. Instead, one simply notes them as other manifestations of one's own activity, for now one can see reasons which previously were hidden. Even the so called 'evil person' is seen to be part of oneself, a weak part; so one's desire is to help such an individual by pouring strength into that weak part of oneself. Thus, when one rises to the buddhic plane, one can gain the experience of others; hence it is not necessary for every ego to go through every experience as a separate individual. If one did not want to feel the suffering of another, one could withdraw, but one would choose to feel it, because one wants to help.

While the intuition of the causal body recognises the outer, the intuition of buddhic recognises the inner. Intellectual intuition enables one to realise a thing outside oneself, while with buddhic intuition, one sees a thing from inside. Thus when working in the causal body, if one wants to understand another person in order to help that individual one has to turn one's consciousness upon that individuals causal body. The particular characteristics are quite well marked but they are always seen only from the outside. If, wanting the same knowledge, one raises ones consciousness to the buddhic level, one finds the consciousness of the other person as a part of oneself. The power of identification is gained not only with regard to the consciousness of people, but with regard to everything else on the buddhic plane. That which one is examining has become a part of oneself; one examines it as a kind of symptom in oneself. This characteristic obviously constitutes a fundamental difference.

Before it can be attained, total selflessness must be acquired because so long as there is anything personal in one's point of view, one cannot make any progress with the buddhic consciousness. On the buddhic plane, past, present and future all exist simultaneously. Neither is one subject to the limitations of space such as on the physical plane. Hence, in reading the past or akashic records one no longer needs as on the mental plane, to pass a series of events in review because, past, present and future are simultaneously present.

Beyond the buddhic plane are the next three higher planes called the atmic, anupadic and the adi, adi is the highest means of the first plane; the individual Lord. It is from this plane that forming of other realms and further creative activity takes place. From here originate the Monads or units of consciousness, for whose evolution in matter, the field of a universe is prepared. The Monads reside on the anupadic plane. The term anupadic means without any vesture or without any veil i.e., the Monads are in tune with and respond to the divine vibrations of the adi plane, but do not respond to the vibrations of the lower planes. Hence each of the Monads has to go into the lower planes, so that they may respond to the vibrations of the lower planes. The fragment of Divine life known as the Monad manifests itself upon the plane of atma as the triple spirit. The spirit itself, remains upon its own plane, that of atma. The second intuition, or pure reason, as it is sometimes called puts itself down one stage and expresses itself through the matter of the plane of buddhi. The third aspect that of intelligence, resides two planes lower and expresses itself through the matter of the causal plane.

Turning first to the nature of the Monad itself, one is confronted with the difficulty that the anupadaka plane is at present beyond the reach of clairvoyant investigators. The highest which these investigators can actually know from direct observation is the manifestation of the Monad as the Triple Spirit on the Atmic plane. The best way in which one can imagine the true nature of the Monad is to think of it as a part of God which cannot really be separated. One can never be apart from God, for the very matter in which it veils itself is also a manifestation of the Divine. To take an analogy from the physical plane, it is recognized that electricity is oneall over the world though it may be active in one machine and not another but the owner ofno machine can claim it as distinctively one's own electricity. So also is the Monad one everywhere, though manifesting through apparently separate and different human beings.

All divine knowledge is in the Monad, but to express and respond to the vibrations of any lower plane of matter is the work of evolution. Hence the rationale of its evolutionary journey down and again upwards, is for the purpose of subjugating matter completely as a vehicle, until on each plane it answers to the vibrations of similar matter outside. Thus it is able to bring out moods of consciousness, which answer to those outside impressions thereby making it possible for it to be conscious of them. When manifestation begins, the Monad is thrown downwards into matter, to propel forward and force evolution. The Monad knows from the beginning what its objective is in evolution and it grasps the general trend of it. Until that portion of it, which expresses itself in the ego, has reached a fairly high stage, it is scarcely conscious of the details of the lower planes or at least it takes little interest in them. At that stage it rests in indescribable bliss without any active consciousness of its surroundings. The purpose of the descent of the Monad into matter is that through its descent it may obtain definiteness in material detail. However, it may be asked that if the Monad is the essence of divinity in the beginning, and returns to divinity at the end of its long pilgrimage, why then is it necessary for it to go through all this evolution. This includes going through much sorrow and suffering. The question is why can't it simply to return to its source in the end? This question is based on misconception of the facts. When that which we may call as the human Monad came forth from the Divine, it was not really a human Monad. It was nevertheless an all-wise Monad and it did not have the characteristics to respond to the vibrations of the lower planes. When it eventually returns after having gained the experience of these lower planes, it is in the form of thousands of millions of mighty Adepts, each capable of itself developing into a Logos or creation as described in this book. As a person who cannot swim when flung into deep water, at first is helpless, yet eventually learns to swim and move freely in the water, so is the case with the Monad. At the end of its pilgrimage of immersion in matter, it will be free and able to function in any part of the lower planes, to create at will. Every power that it unfolds through denser matter, it retains forever under all conditions, the implicit has become explicit and the potential the actual. It is its own will to live in all spheres and not in one only that draws it into manifestation. There was no developed individualization in the Monad at first; it was simply a mass of monadic essence. The difference between its state when issuing the forth, and when returning, is exactly like that between a great mass of shining nebulous matter, and the solar system which is eventually formed out of it. The nebula is beautiful, undoubtedly, but vague and, in a certain sense, useless. The sun formed from it by slow evolution pours forth life, heat and light upon many worlds and their inhabitants.

Even the ego is not the true eternal individual, as the ego had a beginning and came into existence at the moment of individualisation. Whatever has a beginning must also have an end. Therefore even the ego is also impermanent. The Monad, and the Monad alone, is the only real, permanent entity. One may look upon the ego as a manifestation of the Monad on the higher mental plane, but one must understand that it is infinitely far from being a perfect manifestation. Each descent from plane to plane means much more than a mere veiling of the spirit. It also means an actual reduction in the amount of the spirit expressed. The correspondence between the Monad in relation to the ego, and the ego's relation to the personality, will need a little further explanation. As the ego is triple, so is the Monad and the three constituents of the Monad exist on the highest three planes i.e., the adi, the anupadaka and the atmic planes. On the atmic plane the Monad takes to itself a manifestation, which we call the triple atma or triple spirit. This is for the Monad what the causal body is to the ego. Just as the ego takes on three lower bodies (mental, astral and physical), the highest of which (the mental) is on the lower part of its own plane and the lowest (the physical) two planes below. So also the Monad (the triple atma or spirit) takes on three lower manifestations (atma, buddhi and causal), the first of which is on the lower part of its own plane, and the lowest, two planes below that i.e., the causal plane. It will thus be seen that the causal body is to the Monad what the physical body is to the ego. If one thinks of the ego as the soul of the physical body, then one may consider the Monad as the soul of the ego in turn. Just as the causal body takes from the personality, whatever is of a nature to help its growth, so also the causal body passes the essence of all experiences which may have entered into it to the atma. The stay on the atmic plane is the last state, which persists before the completion of the journey of the Monad into the lower planes.

In an average individual the Monad is hardly in touch with the ego and the lower personality, although somehow both of these are expressions of it. Just as evolution for the personality is to express the ego more fully, for the ego it is to express the Monad more fully. Just as the ego in time learns to dominate the personality, so also the Monad gradually learns to dominate the ego. Just as the personality and ego eventually become one, so also the Monad and ego also become one. Thus the life on the atmic plane also comes to an end. This is the unification of the ego with the Monad, and when that is achieved one has attained the object of one's descent into matter. This brings to an end a brief overview of the life after death undertaken in this book. It must be kept in mind that this overview of life after death given in this book is only a brief blueprint to create a basic understanding of life after death, so that one may then undertake further detailed study of this subject available in esoteric literature.

IN A NUTSHELL

Overview Higher Planes

One is not free of the binding results on the lower planes until one become selfless on these planes. When one enters the buddhic plane one becomes conscious of the unity of all there is yet one still has one's own individual consciousness. The buddhic body is called the sheaf of bliss. Buddhic intuition sees things or beings as from inside as that other being/person sees it. On the Buddhic plane past, present and future exist simultaneously.

One can easily think of the monad as part of God. The purpose of the evolution of the monad is to acquire consciousness and definiteness in a material detail capable of developing into creative logos. Initially there was no individualization in the monad. The ego is not the true eternal individual. Just as the ego and personality become one so also the Monad and ego become one.

❋❋❋

CHAPTER – 7

LINK BETWEEN THELIVING AND BEYOND.

This chapter aims to give guidance and understanding, to maintain links with those who have died, to especially those every day individuals who can no longer connect with the past traditional religious rituals and practices but have not yet spiritually raised themselves to be enlightened.

Have you ever asked the question as to why there appears to be very little connection with those who have died even though our cherished spiritual philosophies claim that our departed friends are continually around us? |Through religious rituals (mainly traditions from the past) there were and are worthy attempts in achieving remembrance and service to those who have departed. For thousands of years religious rituals have felt to be appropriate up until only recently as conditions in being a human have changed. Our acceptance of formal religions and rituals has waned and thereby religious influence is now diminishing, especially in the west and as such something more is now required to add to our previous faith, rituals, prayers and ceremonies to carry us to the heights that religion once achieved with the departed. This something more is our own individual conscious effort and understanding of these processes.

Today, there sustains a wide divide of awareness between us, who are living, and the departed, hence, we easily forget about those who have crossed to the other side. In the past there was much more interaction with those who had departed although this took place in a more or less unconscious and dreamy manner. Simpler societies still maintain some connections with those who have departed through the use religious ritual and ceremonies and this will be beneficent for many years to come. Our age, because of the materialistic conceptual thought structures and individualism has created difficult conditions for us to become aware of those who have departed when we rely on methods from past. However, for the sake of humanity's future development more conscious links need to be established between the living and those on the other side.

We find it extremely difficult to recognize or to even acknowledge the possibility of the existence of another being unless this being behaves as though it is a human personality or is visible to the senses like that of the animal kingdom or presents itself as some sort of vision. However there many other beings or intelligences which surround us which are not like earthy personalities, are not visible to the senses nor appear in visionary forms and, hence these are either ignored by us, in that their effects are treated as forces of nature or, because of our current egocentric nature, they are seen as own inner impulses i.e. the effects of these non incarnated beings are generally perceived and acknowledged but the real causes of their effects is denied by being represented by concepts of inanimate mechanical chance-like forces of nature or physics or are taken to be some brilliant but unexplained unconscious operations of our inner lives. In other words the effects of the departed and the spiritual world and its beings on us have been conceptualized away with concepts that are half truths. This has had the effect of placing a veil over our eyes (maya) in preventing us from perceiving what is actually around us in its full reality. In the past when the ancients looked to the starry heavens they not only saw the physical movements of the starry realms but saw in the movements of the stars and planets the 'footprints' of the gods which had strong reverberations here on earth - today, a dim echo of this still remains in astrology. Our modern materialistic state of perceiving the world only allows us to view half the picture (Maya) but this state of being is actually a necessary requisite of our evolutionary pathway until we as individuals become sufficiently strengthened in our earthly 'I' consciousness, i.e. in our personality, so as to achieve humanity's purpose of conscious self directed activity in freedom without being controlled by the impulses and directives of hidden spiritual beings who are at all times active within our immediate environment. Further, if we are not sufficiently strengthened in our inner nature and we do prematurely become directly aware of departed souls and other entities, which surround us all the time and work within our inner lives, we can become playthings of the various psychic forces emanating from the other side and we may not develop a strong healthy self directing earthly 'I' consciousness but at the same time are continually in our presence, in fact we could become mentally unstable. Today, it is now necessary, if humanity's evolution is to move forward, to gain an awareness of the true nature of the departed and those beings which are on the other side. Only then can meaningful interactions take place. If this does not come about then the influence malevolent beings will gradually replace the beneficent influence of the departed and these influences will manifest as negative tendencies within individuals. e.g. there is a marked and rapid worldwide increase of mental illness, such as depression, and anti-social tendencies taking hold which have been caused by certain negative unconscious influences originating from the other side. However these negative influences are generally conceptualized to be of a psychological or bodily origin and it is generally thought that these influences can be cured by only a pill.

One of the major obstacles in communicating with the departed is that we are not aware how these communications can take place as we can wrongly expect that these communications should be the same or similar as they had occurred with the individuals when they were alive. There was a great deception in the recent past when mediums propagated the false notion that communications with the departed occur in the same way as they occur with personalities when, in actuality, these mediums, usually, had only accessed the discarded astral shells of departed individuals which had then become became inhabited and animated by other, usually malevolent, spiritual entities. These disguised entities then unlawfully appeared in the form of the departed personalities which worked through the medium. The real individualities, however, had already moved on to other spiritual spheres. These types of communications have given a false picture of what actually takes place with those from the other side. Hence, any communications which appear in the form of a personality, through a medium, must be treated with the utmost suspicion with respect to its genuineness as only a minority of these types of communications are actually genuine and usually with those departed souls who have recently died.

After death, as we no longer have a physical brain, we will no longer able to think but we will feel, perceive and be aware far more intensely of our spiritual environment. We will bear the fruits of understanding from what we had learnt whilst we were in a physical body. Our new environment, where we will no longer bound by the limitations of the personality, will now encompass countless higher and lower spiritual beings including those of other departed souls weaving in and amongst us and together with a myriad of living thoughts, feelings and will impulses. Some can rightly describe this in another way that we now live within GOD or SELF and from our perspective this is a simple yet appropriate description, however, although many would like to believe that after death one enters for all time into eternal bliss it is not so. Our understanding, our state of wellbeing and our interaction with these elements in our new spiritual environment will depend upon how we had lived our life on earth; whether we were moral or immoral; religious or non religious; spiritual or non spiritual. After death one special area which the departed will always be able to perceive and understand are the noble and spiritual thoughts and feelings of those friends whom they knew and who are still living.

Hence those on the physical plane can be of immense service to departed friends

The peculiarity of the departed state is that although individuals can behold the magnificence of the spiritual world they virtually can no longer understand anything new, nor initiate any new actions on their own which have not been prepared by them when they were alive. eg in an unfavorable situation it can like being born blind all ourlives and no one tells us that there are things called colors and then, if we do regain our sight we become bewildered by the perception all these colors as we have no concepts to help us to understand what we now perceive. But the situation after death is even more restrictivc in that it is not even possible for the departed to figure it out as we can still do here on earth UNLESS they have gained this ability to understand from the fruits of their deeds whilst they were alive and/or they are helped by those whom they knew who are still living. Hence life on earth is truly a special and unique place in the scheme of the universe.

If we wish to have a connection with the departed, we must be aware that instead of interacting with human personalities, with their attendant physical and intellectual characteristics responses, we now need to interact the departed souls who are now entities of awareness or consciousness and who no longer occupy any particular physical space or form but can be present everywhere in their own particular environment. Their communications to us have a similarity to forces of nature or inner psychological impulses, intuitions and feelings. There is no question of being able to chatter with the departed as we chatter with one another at five o'clock teas and in cafes. What makes it possible to put questions to the departed or to communicate something to the departed is that we unite the life of feeling with our thoughts and ideas in these communications.

Normally, when we speak, we know that the words come from us; when another person speaks to us, we know that the words come from them. The whole relationship is reversed when we are speaking with the departed. When we put a question to the departed, or say something to them, what we say comes to us from them. They inspire into our soul what we ask them, what we say to them i.e. We perceive it is as though we ourselves are asking the question or saying something. And when they answer us or say something to us, this comes out of our own soul i.e. we perceive it is as though it is the departed who answer or say something when in fact it comes from our own inner being. It is a process with which a human being in the physical world is quite unfamiliar. He feels that what he says comes out of his own being. In order to establish communications with the departed, we must adapt ourselves to hear from them what we ourselves say, and to receive from our own soul what they answer.

The moment of falling asleep is especially favorable for us to turn to the departed. Other opportunities exist, but this moment is the most favorable. One needs to create a picture memory, with feeling of the departed friend as they were when they were alive and then, also with intense feeling, work out the question that one wants answered. Your relationship with the departed must be one of the heart, of inner interest. You must remind yourself of your love for the departed when he/she was alive, and address yourself to him/her not abstractly, but with real warmth of heart. In the evening, as you are going to sleep, your departed friend will be able to receive your question without you even knowing it. Ordinary consciousness as a rule will know little of the happening, because sleep ensues immediately; but what has thus passed over often remains present in dreams. In the case of most dreams — although from the point of view of actual content they are misleading — in the case of most dreams we have of the departed, all that happens is that we interpret them incorrectly. We interpret them as messages from the departed, whereas they are nothing but the echoing of the questions or communications we have ourselves directed to the departed. We should not think that the departed is saying something to us in our dream, but we should see in the dream something that goes out from our own soul to the departed. The dream is the echo of this. If we were sufficiently developed to be conscious of our question or communication to the departed at the moment of going to sleep, it would seem to us as though the departed himself were speaking — hence the echo in the dream seems as if it were a message from the departed. In reality it comes from us. This becomes intelligible only when we understand the nature of clairvoyant connection with the departed. What the departed seems to say to us is really what we are saying to him.

The moment of waking is especially favorable for the departed to approach us. At the moment of waking, very much comes from the departed to every human being. There is no one who does not bring with him at the moment of waking countless tidings from the departed. In the unconscious region of the soul we are speaking continually with the departed. A great deal of what we undertake in life is really inspired into us by the departed and by Beings of the higher Hierarchies, although we usually attribute this to ourselves, as coming from our own soul. Hence we need to develop sensitivity for what comes from the other side in our own inner life.

Further, it is possible that those on the other side can perceive something entirely new for the world but don't have the understanding for it themselves and by passing on this perception to us we in turn can interpret it with our thinking abilities and thereby the departed soul can now understand it. This is truly a remarkable and wonderful exchange between the various planes of existence and will become more and more necessary into the future. This exchange gives meaning for our unique earthly existence in relationship to the spiritual world.

What the departed says comes in a form as though it is out of our own soul. The light of the morning draws near, the moment of waking passes quickly by, and we are seldom disposed to observe the intimate indications that arise out of our soul. And when we do observe them we are vain enough to attribute them to ourselves; Yet in all this — and in much else that comes out of our own soul — their lives what the departed have to say to us. What the departed say to us seems to arise out of our own soul. If we knew what life actually is, this knowledge would give rise to a feeling of reverence and piety towards the spiritual world in which we and our departed continually live. We should realize that in much of what we do, it is the departed and other spiritual beings who are working.

Hence after death, the departed will become aware of their loved ones and friends who they leave behind if their loved ones and friends have noble and/or spiritual thoughts. If those that are left behind are materialists the departed knows that their loved ones are here on earth but are not able to establish a connection with them but instead experiences a sad unbearable darkness where their loved ones should be. This connection with those who have remained behind on earth will be such that the departed is able to access their loved one's inner life so as to express certain intuitions, feelings (imaginations) and impulses. This, at times, can be felt as very subtle presences and we must develop sensitivity for this. Hence one must be sensitive and attentive to this experience and then it may be possible to translate these experiences into concepts. If we don't become sensitive and attentive to our inner life then, for us, it is as if our departed friends no longer exist except as memories. Further, for accurate conscious interpretations a pathway of self development is usually a pre-requisite.

Those departed souls who have led very materialistic lives or immoral lives, will after a certain period of time, experience long periods of unbearable difficulties in the form of loneliness and isolation as they are not able to 'light' up their environment in which they find themselves in and are unable to find other souls and beings to live with in community.To develop the ability to light up our way is only possible here on earth by spiritual practice, where an understanding of the spiritual world is achieved or through religious practice (formal or informal-religious practice which need not be associated with any formal religion). It is assumed that moral development goes hand in hand. However, here on earth we are also able to greatly assist and perform a valuable service to our former friends, who have died, in their current journey, especially those who had led materialistic lives and as a consequence become bewildered by their new circumstances in which they now find themselves in. We can assist them by calling to mind, in feelings and thought, how they lived and read to them, with understanding, what will be their experiences of the death or other aspects of spiritual philosophy (in religious practice:- praying, rituals and ceremonies to the dead also help). The content of this book is a good example of what can be used as reading material. It's important that the content becomes truly alive and conscious in us as the departed can only read the content of our inner life and not the actual book.

In the past, as still happens today, prayer, ritual and ceremony do much good for departed friends but this is no longer effective for many people in this current age so spiritual philosophy and enquiry are necessary and are adequate additions to the beneficent past practices which are now becoming much less effective due to the progress in evolution. Simply put, many individuals can no longer connect with the strict and unquestionable requirements of past practices and traditions of the various religious faiths but now require logical thinking and understanding. Hence, at the moment of falling asleep is the most favorable time for us to put our questions to our departed friends. At the moment of waking the departed speak with us, give us the answers but we must be alert and sensitive to this communications. During the day, by reading to the departed we are able to assist them in their new journey in preparation for their next life.

What has been communicated up until this point can be achieved by the average individual in all circumstances. However, for those who wish to proceed to a higher level of direct and conscious communication with departed individuals, need to undertake a disciplined regular and balanced pathway of self development as actual conscious direct communication with an individual who has died is very difficult. It demands scrupulous care and development on the part of the one who seeks it. Control and discipline are necessary for this kind of communication with the spiritual world, for it is connected with a very significant law. The very same thing that we recognize in men on Earth as lower impulses is, from the other, the spiritual side, higher life; and it may therefore easily happen when the human being has not attained true control of himself, that he experiences the rising of lower impulses through direct communications with the departed. It now becomes understandable why there are many cases of spiritual teachers who have fallen into deviant and damaging sexual behaviors.

It is not the departed who arouse these passions but the element in which the departed live. For consider: what we here feel as 'animal' in quality and nature is the basic element (astral substance) in which the departed live. The kingdom in which the departed live can easily be changed when it enters into us; what is higher life in yonder world can become lower when it is within us on Earth. Naturally, there can only be danger for those who have not purified their natures through discipline and control and are not aware, through thinking, what the nature of this spiritual environment is. The methods of modern spiritualism must, of course, be avoided. When the communications are not accompanied by pure thoughts it can easily lead to the stimulation of lower passions. Hence, the necessity for a disciplined and balanced pathway of self development if this advanced form of communication is to take place.

CHAPTER – 8

TRUTH – AS TAUGHT BY MASTER RAMANA

Some are born immediately after, others after some lapse of time, a few are not reborn on this earth but eventually get salvation in some higher region, and a very few get absolved here and now.

Sage Sri Ramana Maharshi

REINCARNATION AND REALITY

To the Maharshi, death, like life, is a mere thought. When one is awake, one thinks incessantly, in dream thoughts gradually reduce, but when one passes from dreamful to dreamless sleep thoughts cease, and one enjoys undisturbed peace, till one is awake and resumes thinking again, and along with it the restless, peace less awake state in which thoughts flow like waves in an ocean. When death strikes down the body, life continues in the astral, mental and causal worlds till a full awakening takes place in a new body. The daily cycle of waking and sleeping is a miniature of the cycle of life and death. To transcend birth and death one has to transcend the processes of thought, which is made possible by Self realisation

According to Sri Ramana Maharishi the entire process of rebirth is sustained by the tendency of the mind to identify itself with a body. When one realizes one's true nature of being Self-awareness, the entire super structure of the theory of reincarnation melts away. From the perspective of the Self there is no birth or death and no reincarnation.

Death, life and rebirth, formed the subject-matter of many of the questions asked by visitors visiting the maharshi. Following are some conversations with the maharshi in relation to reality and rebirth recorded by Sri. S.S.Cohen

4th January, 1937

1. A visitor asks Sri Maharshi:

Visitor - How can the terrible fear of death be overcome?

Bhagavan -When does that fear seize you? Does it come when you do not see your body, say, in dreamless sleep, or when you are under chloroform? It haunts you only when you are fully "awake" and perceive the world, including your body. If you do not see these and remain your pure self, as in dreamless sleep, no fear can touch you.

If you trace this fear to the object, the loss of which gives rise to it, you will find that that object is not the body, but the mind which functions in it and through which the environment and the attractive world is known as sights, sounds, smells, etc. Many a man would be too glad to be rid of his diseased body and all the problems and inconvenience it creates for him if continued awareness were vouchsafed to him. It is the awareness, the consciousness, and not the body, he fears to lose. Men love existence because it is eternal awareness, which is their own Self. Why not then hold on to the pure awareness right now, while in the body and be free from all fear?

2. A Mysorean, Mr. M. had read some Theosophical books and stayed here for some months trying to digest them. He wanted to know about rebirths.

M - Theosophy speaks of 50 to 10,000-year intervals between death and rebirth. Why is this so?

Bh. - There is no relation between the standard of measurements of one state of consciousness and another. All such measurements are hypothetical. It is true that some individuals take more time and some less. But it must be distinctly understood that it is not the soul that comes and goes, but the thinking mind of the individual, which makes it appear to do so. On whatever plane the mind happens to act, it creates a body for itself: in the physical world a physical body, in the dream world a dream body, which becomes wet with dream rain and sick with dream diseases. After the death of the physical body, the mind remains inactive for some time, as in dreamless sleep, when it remains wordless and therefore bodiless. But soon it becomes active again in a new world and a new body – the astral, – till it assumes another body in what is called a "rebirth". But the Jnani, the self- realised man, whose mind has already ceased to act,

Remains unaffected by death: it has dropped never to rise again to cause births and deaths. The chain of illusions has snapped forever for him.

It is now clear that there is neither real birth, nor real death. It is the mind which creates and maintains the illusion of reality in this process, till it is destroyed by Self-Realisation.

12th April, 1937

3. A Dutch lady, Mrs. Gonggrijp, a resident of Adyar, is here on a three-day visit. She wants to know the cause of the urge to live, known in the Pali scriptures by the name of Tanha is inherent in all life.

Mrs. G. - What is the cause of tanha, thirst for life, thirst for rebirth?

Bh. - Real rebirth is dying from the ego into the Spirit. This is the significance of the crucifixion of Jesus. Whenever identification with the body exists, a body is always available, whether in this or in any other one, till the body-sense disappears by merging into the Source – the Spirit, or Self. The stone which is projected upwards remains in constant motion, till it returns to its source, the earth, and rests. Headache continues to give trouble, till the pre-headache state is regained.

Thirst for life is inherent in the very nature of life, which is Absolute Existence – Sat. Although indestructible by nature, by false identification with its destructible instrument, the body, consciousness imbibes a false apprehension of its destructibility, hence it tries to perpetuate that instrument, which results in a succession of births. But however long these bodies may last, they eventually come to an end and yield to the Self, which alone eternally exists.

Mr. C. - Yes, "Give up thy life if thou wouldst live," says the "Voice of the Silence" of H. P. Blavatsky.

Bh. - Give up the false identification and, remember, the body cannot exist without the Self, whereas the Self can exist without the body; in fact it is always without it.

Mr. C. - A doubt has just now arisen in Mrs. G's mind, as she has just heard that a human being may take an animal birth in some other life, which is contrary to what Theosophy has taught her.

Bh. – The one who takes birth let him ask this question. Find out first who it is that is born, and whether there is actual birth and death. These are only of the ego, which is an illusion of the mind.

* * * *

5th May, 1943

4. Mr. B. - is a keen devotee of Sri Bhagavan. A few days ago he lost his only son, which shook his faith in the Maharshi and in God's grace. For some days he went on strike by staying away from the Ashram, but today he came in "to have it out" with Sri Bhagavan with a long list of questions which he had prepared. After receiving some answers he was satisfied.

Mr. B. - What is Faith?

Bh. - Faith, Love, Grace, are all your nature, the Self.

B. - If so, Faith and Grace are obtainable only on the Realisation of the Self. All that we call Faith etc., before then is variable and untrue.

Bh. - Quite so.

B. - Is sorrow a thought?

Bh. - All thoughts are sorrowful.

B. - Even pleasurable thoughts must be also sorrowful.

Bh. - Yes, because thoughts take one's attention away from the Self, which is undiluted Happiness.

B. - What made Bhagavan come to Arunachala?

Bh. - What made you all come?

B. - By that I want to know whether there has been any difference in Bhagavan's spiritual outlook between the day he left Madura and now.

Bh. - None at all: the same experience has prevailed throughout without change.

B. - Then where was the need for Bhagavan to write hymns in praise of Arunachala? Was that for him or for us?

Bh. - I do not know why I wrote them. It might have been for others.

B. - What is Life?

Bh. - Materially speaking Life is the body; spiritually speaking it is the Ultimate Consciousness. It depends on how you look at it.

B. - What is Death?

Bh. - It is oblivion of one's real nature.

At this stage a visitor interrupted by asking whether suicide was a wrong act.

Bh. - Killing the innocent body is certainly wrong. Suicide must be committed on the mind, where the suffering is deposited, and not on the body, which is insentient and feels nothing. The mind is the real culprit, being the creator of the anguish which tempts to suicide, but by an error of judgement, the innocent, insentient body is punished for it.

* * * *

3rd September, 1948

5. Three Anglo-Indian lady-doctors came from Bangalore. One of them had recently lost her husband in an air crash. She asked Sri Bhagavan:

Lady. - Is there rebirth?

Bh. - Do you know what birth is?

L. - O yes, I know that I exist now, but I want to know if I'll exist in the future.

Bh. - Past!.... Present!.... Future!....

L. - Yes, today is the result of yesterday, the Past, and tomorrow, the Future, will be the result of today, the Present. Am I right?

Bh. - There is neither past nor future. There is only the Present. Yesterday was the present to you when you experienced it, and tomorrow will be also the present when you will experience it. Therefore experience takes place only in the present, and beyond experience nothing exists.

L. - Are then Past and Future mere imagination?

Bh. - Yes, even the Present is mere imagination, for the sense of time is purely mental. Space is similarly mental; therefore birth and rebirth, which take place in time and Space cannot be other than imagination.

* * * *

22nd February, 1949

6. A well-educated North Indian came forward, prostrated to Sri Bhagavan and sat in the front line. He asked in excellent English:

Visitor - What is the cause and origin of the universe?

Bh. - Have you no worries of your own?

V. - Of course I have; that is why I want to know about Life, Death, Consciousness, etc.

Bh. - Begin with the beginning: who has Life, Consciousness, etc.? Have you, for instance, life?

V. - Of course I know I am alive, for I see my body.

Bh.- Do you always see the body? What happens to it and to the universe when you go to sleep?

V. - I don't know! It's a mystery.

Bh. - You may not know what happens to them, but do you for that reason cease to exist?

V. - I don't know.

Bh. - How do you then know that you exist even now?

V. - Now I have awareness and see my body moving and thinking.

Bh. - But you see your body also moving and thinking and being in all sorts of places while it is actually lying fast asleep in Tiruvannamalai.

V. - It is a mystery. Can I say that I, the permanent, am ever present and only my ego changes?

Bh. - So you think you are two persons: the permanent 'I' and the ego. Is that possible?

V. - Then please show me the way to the Real.

Bh. - The Real is ever-present, like the screen on which all the cinematographic pictures move. While the pictures appear on it, it remains invisible. Stop the pictures, and the screen, which has all along been present, in fact the only object that has existed throughout, will become clear. All these universes, humans, objects, thoughts and events are merely pictures moving on the screen of Pure Consciousness, which alone is real. Shapes and phenomena pass away, but Consciousness remains ever.

A few days later Sri Bhagavan gave a different answer to a similar question asked by Dr. Godel, a French Medical Officer of the Suez Canal. He told the doctor: "You must distinguish between the 'I', pure in it, and the 'I'- thought. The latter, being merely a thought, sees subject and object, sleeps, wakes up, eats and thinks, dies and is reborn. But the pure 'I' is the pure being, eternal existence, free from ignorance and thought-illusion. If you stay as the 'I', your being alone, without thought, the I-thought will disappear and the delusion will vanish forever. In a cinema-show you can see pictures only in a very dim light or in darkness. But when all lights are switched on, all pictures disappear. So also in the floodlight of the Supreme Atman all objects disappear."

Dr. G. - That is the Transcendental State.

Bh. - No, transcending what, and by whom? You alone exist.

Reflections on Life, Death, and Rebirth

7. News of someone's death was brought to the Master. Sage Ramana remarked: 'Good. The dead are indeed happy. They have got rid of the troublesome overgrowth — the body. The dead man does not grieve. The survivors grieve for him. Do men fear sleep? On the contrary they court it and on waking up the remark that they have had a happy sleep. Yet sleep is nothing but temporary death. Death is a long sleep.'

Reflection –Sage Ramana points out the glaring contrast in our behavior in the twin states of death and sleep, which are the same except in matter of duration. Of that too we cannot be very sure. We hate death, but run with might and main after sleep, so much so that if we remain sleepless for a few nights, we seek medical help and start swallowing sleeping tablets, if not also resort to drastic morphia injections. In the temporary death we call as sleep, we spread our beds and look forward to it.

In the long sleep we call as death, instead of feeling

happier still for the departed beloved who enjoys it, we put on long faces and mourn. The irrationality of our behavior would appear ludicrous to the man of wisdom but for the poignancy of the intense grief and terrifying fear which death inspires.

Sage Ramana perceives the body as a 'troublesome overgrowth' because it is superimposed on him — the pure being. Though he has a body he sees himself bodiless -videha. The body-'I' sense does not exist for him, yet the needs and diseases of the body continue to be 'troublesome'. The Videhais a Mukta (one who is liberated), sometimes called Videhamukta (one who is liberated after death). Devotees worship him as the manifestation of the pure Brahman, but the unintelligent call his state 'living death'. But then we are all working for this 'living death', and they who ridicule him too.

Sage Ramana continues:

8. 'If a man dies while yet alive he need not grieve over another's death. One's existence is evident with or without the body. Then why should one desire the bodily shackles? One should find out his immortal Self and be happy.'

Reflection -In the last note we have seen who the 'man who dies while yet alive' is. Naturally such a man does not mourn the death of anybody; for he knows their state and condition as he knows his own, and laughs with joy. Sage Ramana speaks from experience when he says that one remains the same under all circumstances and conditions 'with or without a body.'

9. A great devotee of Sage Ramana lost his only son - three years old. The next day he and his bereaved family came to the Ashram. The Sage seeing them said: 'Training of mind helps one to bear sorrow and bereavement with courage - the loss of offspring in particular. Grief exists only so long as one believes oneself to be of a definite form. If the form is transcended one would realize oneself to be eternal, having neither birth nor death. That which is born is only the body.'

Reflection –'Transcending the form' is a grand idea. What death destroys is only the form, and so long as we attach ourselves to the form we continue to feel the sting of death. But if by knowledge we come to realize that the form is not the person we love, we will be able to transcend grief and, in fact, death itself.

We are all in agreement that the beloved is not a mere shape, a colored picture, an inanimate substance, but a being, an entity which teems with life and intelligence, which thinks, feels, loves, wills, acts, and with which we establish relationships as father, son, husband, neighbor, friend, etc. The body, being devoid of intelligence, can, by itself, perform one of these functions, and, when life withdraws from it, it remains a lifeless decayed matter fit for cremation.

The 'mental training', which Sage Ramana suggests, will not only kill all sorrow at bereavements, but will also reveal to us the truth of our immortality, and thus save us from future birth and death. Hence the Scriptures (Srutis) lay down the law that any perceivable and conceivable object is the object of consciousness, and thus insentient, changeable and destructible. The subject or consciousness alone is sentient, changeless and indestructible.

10. **Sage Ramana says** - 'See how a tree, whose branches are cut grows again. So long as the life-source is not affected it will grow. Similarly the samskaras(subtle impressions or tendencies stored in the mind continuing from former lives as a result of one's own past karmas, or actions)sink into the heart in death: they do not perish. They are reborn. Just as a big banyan tree sprouts from a tiny seed, so the wide universe with names and forms sprouts forth from the Heart.'

Reflection - This is the rationale of rebirth. The samskaras, or impressions, left over at the close of one life become the seeds for the next. They are stored up in the Heart, from which a new body with new environments, new circumstances and new tendencies 'sprouts' forth at the right time to form the new life. As the tortoise withdraws its limbs into its shell, so do the lifelong (psychical) impressions gather together at the last moment and, along with the senses, withdraw into the centre of consciousness, to form the nucleus of the future birth. The Bhagavad Gita (One of the world's spiritual treasures; an essential scripture ofIndia in which Lord Krishna instructs his disciple Arjuna on the nature of God, the universe, and the path to liberation) puts this graphically:

'When the Lord acquires a body and when He abandons it, He seizes the senses and manas (mind) and goes with them, as the wind carries perfume from flowers.'

'Enshrined in the ear, eye, touch, taste, smell, and the mind, He enjoys the objects of sense.'

'The deluded do not perceive Him when He departs or stays or enjoys, swayed by the qualities (gunas - The three basic qualities of nature that determine the inherent characteristics of all created things. They are: sattva - purity, light, harmony; rajas - intelligence, activity and passion, and tamas - dullness, inertia and ignorance); the wisdom-eyed perceive Him.'

(Gita Chapter XV. Verses 8-10)

Thus the Lord equates the jiva (individual soul)with Himself, for it is He, the immortal and changeless, who takes bodies to enjoy the senses through them, discards them, takes new ones and so on. This is a scriptural confirmation of our immortality and divinity.With the rise of the body, the senses and all the psychical faculties also rise and spread a universe in infinite space and infinite time. Therefore the whole universe has its roots in the small cavity we call Heart.

Note: The Heart is the small cavity or the seat of Consciousness at the right side of the chest as experienced and expounded by Sage Ramanaas well; it is the real Self - all that is the manifest and the unmanifested.

Note - In the following, D stands for the devotee and M stands for the Maharshi Sage Ramana

11. **D:** 'If a person we love dies grief results. Shall we avoid grief by loving all alike, or by not loving at all?'

M: 'Both amount to the same thing. When all have become the one Self, who remains to be loved or hated? The ego that grieves must die. That is the only way.'

Reflection -We have already discussed the point that one who grieves is one who takes the body to be the beloved one. When the body dies the beloved one is believed to have died. Who is responsible for this error? The ego of course is the person who mistakes oneself for one's own body. But this ego is itself an erroneous conception, an imagined entity. The conclusion is therefore clear that the whole phenomenon is dud - the dead, the grief over the dead, and the one who is stricken with grief over the dead. It is an incubus created by the imagination, of which it is difficult to rid oneself. If a way can be found to kill the incubus, say, by a sadhana (spiritual practice) the hallucination will disintegrate of its own accord into the reality of the Self. In that case the love to which the questioner refers will have no occasion to manifest, because of the absence of duality of lover and loved, the Self being the sole existence.

12. **Sage Ramana says** - 'You ask if it is the ego that reincarnates. Yes, but what is reincarnation? The ego is the same but new bodies appear and hold it. Just observe what happens even (now) to your body. Suppose you want to go to London. You take a conveyance to the docks, board a steamer and reach London in a few

days. What has happened? The conveyance travelled from one part of the world to the other. The movements of the conveyance have been superimposed on your body. Similarly the reincarnations are superimpositions. Do you go to the dream world, or does it come to you? Surely the latter the same may be said of the reincarnations. The ego remains changeless all along.'

Reflection -The main point of this text is that what happens to the individual rises from inside oneself, though it appears to come from outside. Birth is the assuming by the individual –jiva (individual soul) or ego - of a body woven from inside oneself, like the dream body which rises from the dreamer and superimposes itself on the dreaming mind, or what is the same individual. This is the meaning of 'Do you go to the dream, or does it come to you?' Death is the temporary elimination of that superimposition, and birth is the reestablishing of it in a new form, and so on and on till jnana{true knowledge that one's self (atman) is identical with Ultimate Reality (Brahman)}brings the superimpositions to a radical end. This resembles the infinite number of webs which the spider spins out of himself for his temporary use.

The analogy of travelling demonstrates the fact that the individual himself remains always the same, and that the long journey (samsara-The world of change and becoming; the cycle of repeated birth and death in the material world) is not undertaken by the individual but by the number of vehicles one uses for the purpose.

The jiva(individual soul)constructs its own vehicles (bodies) and rides them for its own pleasure, as it were, according to the demand of prarabdha(destiny, part of one's karma to be worked out in this life)- the result of its behavior and its psychical impressions in its use of the previous bodies. It is therefore wrong to say that we die and are reborn, or that it is we who go round and round on the wheel of evolution. We remain always the same without beginning or end. Let us fix that firmly in our mind lest we lose ourselves in theories of Occultism, Behaviourism and the rest of their tribe.

13. D: 'Do intellect and emotions survive death?'

M: 'Before considering that, first consider what happens in your sleep. Sleep is only The interval between two waking, of these survive in this interval? They represent the body-consciousness and nothing more. If you are the body they always hold on to you. If you are not, then they do not affect you. The one who was in sleep is the one who is speaking now. You were not the body in sleep. Are you the body now? Find out this, and the whole problem will be solved.'

'That which is born must die. Whose is the birth? Were you born? How do birth and death affect the eternal Self? Think to whom these questions occur and you will know.'

Reflection -This is extremely interesting to those who are interested in their own death. You are awake now, and you will be awake tomorrow. But in between the two there is a gap of no-waking state. What happens to your intellect and emotions in that state? You may plead ignorance of what happens, but you do know that you exist then, otherwise you would not mention the gap, namely, sleep, at all: you would not say 'I slept for six hours last night,' admitting thereby that you undergo the experience of sleep as you undergo that of waking. If there were an interruption in your existence at night, you would end with every day and be a new person every morning. Then there could be no question of your being able to remember that you met so - and- so yesterday, or did such and such thing twenty years ago. There would be no memory of anything previous to this day, not even of your name, home, business or family relationship at all, for it would be as if you had taken a new birth. The fact that the memory of previous incidents, objects and of having again and again slept and wakened persists, proves your fixity, that you are a logical continuum, passing through a variety of experiences, sometimes pleasant and memorable, and sometimes the reverse. You are the thread on which all these experiences string themselves, like beads.

'Granting,' you may contend, 'that I exist in all these experiences and states and in all these years, how is it that I remember most of these experiences, but not those which happened only a few hours ago in my sleep?' The answer is, we are not concerned with the experiences at all; for memory, like the senses, returns to the Source in sleep and comes out again on waking. We are concerned only with your own existence and, as you admit its continuity in sleep, there remains nothing for us to do but to apply this to the state of after death. I think there should be no difficulty to do that. Taking our stand on the continuity of the jiva (individual soul) even in the absence of the body in sleep, we find that the possession of abody need not be the criterion for existence. That being the case, what valid evidence do we have to postulate extinction of existence with the extinction of the body? certainly none.

As for our intellect and emotions after death, they will go where they are even now going every night.

Sage Ramana's remarks now become obvious: 'The one who is in sleep is now in waking. You were not the body in sleep, so you are not it now. That which is born - the body - must die. You are not born so that you may die. Births and deaths do not affect you - the Self.'

14.D:'How were we all in our previous births? Why do we not know our own past?'

M:'God in His mercy has withheld this knowledge from people. If they knew that they were virtuous, they would grow proud; contrariwise they would be depressed. Both are bad. It is enough that one knows the Self.'

Reflection -The question comes from the Ashramites; it occurs in fact to almost everyone in the spiritual line. Sage Ramana rightly thanks merciful God for causing this oblivion before rebirth, or else the world would have been in complete chaos and life far more miserable than it is already under the present conditions. Apart from the pride or humiliation, of which Sage Ramana speaks, there are thousands of events and things which are better completely forgotten, and millions of people who had better remain unrecognized for one's own sake and for the sake of the people concerned. Problems would have arisen in such numbers and of such a nature as to possibly make the earth a plane unfit for a decent man to live in. We have therefore to say 'sufficient unto the day is the evil thereof', and offer thanks to God for drawing a heavy curtain between one life and another.

Yet we have all heard of some 'occultists', who claim the power to rend the curtain and see the past, and wonderwhat good has that done? Has it given jnana{true knowledge that one's self (atman) is identical with Ultimate Reality (Brahaman)}to the person whose past life is supposed to have been read, or even to the 'occultist' himself? If it does anything at all, it is to create serious doubts of its genuineness in some minds, and anabject, primitive faith in some others, both of which are definitely spiritually harmful. Why, therefore, dabble in such matters? Sage Ramana reminds us that the only knowledge worth acquiring is that of the Self, the rest is pure fantasy.

15. D: 'Where is the necessity for reincarnation? The theory of evolution is physically perfect. But for the soul further development may be required which happens after death.'

M: "Let us first see if there is incarnation before we speak of reincarnation. Who is the man: the body or the soul? You answer 'both together'. But you do notecase to exist in the absence of the body, say, in sleep. You call sleep temporary death. Therefore life is also temporary. If life and death are temporary, there must be something which is not temporary: that is the Reality. See for whom these questions arise. Unless the questioner is found, the questions can never be set at rest."

Reflection - Doubts about past births have been expressed by many people, more especially by those whose scriptures do not teach reincarnation. The questioner has found complete satisfaction in the theory of evolution without the necessity of rebirths and without deviating from his theological beliefs. But his questions carry in them their own solutions, if they are but carefully thought out.

In the first instance he admits the immortality of the soul and its continued development after death till perfection is achieved, yet he is unable to rid himself of the bias for the body, which he makes the partner of the soul in the synthesis of his self, or 'I'. On what ground does he give the body a place in the makeup of the 'I', he does not care to investigate. If the body is half his self, then this is no longer a homogeneous unit, but a hybrid compound of mortal and immortal substances, of which the immortal, which he calls the soul that survives death, is only a part, or half. Is this rational? Moreover, if the soul is not an integral whole, how is it possible for it to attain perfection in the evolution of which he speaks? Again, how does he know that the soul undergoes 'further development' after death? What does he, first of all, conceive the soul to be to require this development? Confusion becomes more confounded when he gives the body a share in his 'I', endowing it with sentience, with intelligence, when a little thinking would have convinced him to the contrary. By admitting mortality to the body, he has at once confessed to its insentience, for sentience never dies: it is eternal life. The body is thus insentient and therefore unintelligent; whereas the 'I' is pure intelligence as the knower of all things. Therefore the body is neither the 'I' nor a part of it.

As for rebirths, why does he find them illogical? If in this life he is born, as he admits he is, why cannot he be reborn? That which has caused this birth should be a valid cause for another birth. What makes him imagine that the cause of this birth of his has exhausted itself and can no longer be available for another birth, or a series of new births?

Let us illustrate this by a concrete example. A man marries because he has a desire for a woman. If the woman a little later dies, he may marry a second time, impelled by the same urge. But suppose he also loses his body in the meantime, what is he to do to satisfy this persistent craving? Naturally he has to take another body, as he had taken the present one for some desire or other.

Thus Sage Ramana tells us that there is no such thing as rebirth, what there is, is only assuming one body after another for the satisfaction of desires. If you do not want to take another body, by all means you are at liberty not to, provided you have ceased to crave for anything, thereby eliminating the cause of rebirth.

We have therefore to study our self before we enquire about evolution, reincarnation, life, death, etc., which is what makes the Sage advise the questioner to discover himself first.

Sage Ramana continues:

16. 'One sees an edifice in his dream. Then he begins to think how it has been built brick by brick by so many laborers and during so long a time, so also with the theory of evolution. Because he finds himself a man he thinks that he has evolved from the primal state of the amoeba.'

Reflection - This makes our sciences dream sciences. So they are. It is a well-known fact that scientists do not concern themselves with the absolute reality, which they leave to the philosophers to do, and remain satisfied with the physical reality, for example, the splitting and multiplication of the chromosomes, the proportional combination of the hydrogen and oxygen atoms to form the water molecule, etc. And when they step out of the physical into a non-physical area they get confused and confounded. When biologists, for example, speak of the evolution of life, they really mean the evolution of the form which the life inhabits, as we see before our eyes the evolution of the human body from the pinhead zygote to the size of the newborn babe, to that of childhood, adolescence, and full adulthood, and the gradual unfoldment of the mind in it. Scientists do not have direct contact with life to know what life is, whether it evolves or remains changeless. They cannot, for instance, directly perceive the life in the chromosome but can only infer it from the behavior of the chromosome, whose physical qualities they can directly observe like size, color, shape, movements, changes, constituents and so on.

Therefore those who believe in the laws of evolution must understand that their knowledge is very partial, and pertains only to the insentient universe, which alone can be perceived and can suffer changes.

As life is a closed book to the scientists, so also is life's other name - mind. Not their activities, but life and mind as they are in themselves, as substances, as 'First Principles'. If they knew the nature of the mind, they would have also known that all their endeavors were limited to a world which is essentially a dream, taking place inside their own consciousness. For at no moment can the scientist step out of his mind and say 'here is a real world which can stand by itself without me - without my mind'. When one is in a dream and is asked to step out of it to realise that it is a dream, one can shake oneself a bit and be out of the dream to the waking state to verify his old position. But in the waking dream jagrat (the waking state) it is not so easy, because the senses are then all out, fully entrenched in this their own dominion, of which they are the absolute monarchs. This is the reason why the scientist refuses to believe they are dreaming, and continues to imagine that one has crawled out of the amoeba into the monkey some millions of years ago, and out of the monkey some scores of thousands of centuries ago. How are we to convince them of this error that it is not the individual who has undergone all these metamorphoses, but the shapes of the bodies the individual has assumed? If the scientist can be convinced of this truth, then the scientist would presumably be also convinced that the amoeba, the monkey, and the millions of years are parts of the evolution of this, one's jagrat (the waking state)dream.

Who Am I? Who Am I? - Nan Yar?

The Teachings of Bhagavan Sri Ramana Maharshi

Translation by

Dr. T. M. P. MAHADEVAN

from the original Tamil

Published by

V. S. RAMANAN

PRESIDENT, BOARD OF TRUSTEES

SRI RAMANASRAMAM

TIRUVANNAMALAI, S. INDIA

INTRODUCTION

"Who am I?" is the title given to a set of questions and answers bearing on Self-enquiry. The questions were put to Bhagavan Sri Ramana Maharshi by one Sri M. Sivaprakasam Pillai about the year 1902. Sri Pillai, a graduate in Philosophy, was at the time employed in the Revenue Department of the South Arcot Collectorate. During his visit to Tiruvannamalai in 1902 on official work, he went to VirupakshaCave on Arunachala Hill and met the Master there. He sought from him spiritual guidance, and solicited answers to questions relating to Self-enquiry. As Bhagavan was not talking then, not because of any vow he had taken, but because he did not have the inclination to talk, he answered the questions put to him by gestures, and when these were not understood, by writing. As recollected and recorded by Sri Sivaprakasam Pillai, there were fourteen questions with answers to them given by Bhagavan. This record was first published by Sri Pillai in 1923, along with a couple of poems composed by himself relating how Bhagavan's grace operated in his case by dispelling his doubts and by saving him from a crisis in life. 'Who am I?' has been published several times subsequently. We find thirty questions and answers in some editions and twenty-eight in others. There is also another published version in which the questions are not given, and the teachings are rearranged in the form of an essay. The extant English translation is of this essay. The present rendering is of the text in the form of twenty-eight questions and answers. Along with Vicharasangraham (Self-Enquiry), Nan Yar (Who am I?) constitutes the first set of instructions in the Master's own words. These two are the only prosepieces among Bhagavan's Works. They clearly set forth the central teaching that the direct path to liberation is Self-enquiry. The particular mode in which the enquiry is to be made is lucidly set forth in Nan Yar. The mind consists of thoughts. The 'I' thought is the first to arise in the mind. When the enquiry ' Who am I?' is persistently pursued, all other thoughts get destroyed, and finally the 'I' thought itself vanishes leaving the supreme non-dual Self alone. The false identification of the Self with the phenomena of non-self such as the body and mind thus ends, and there is illumination, Sakshatkara. The process of enquiry of course, is not an easy one. As one enquires 'Who am I?', other thoughts will arise; but as these arise, one should not yield to them by following them , on the contrary, one should ask 'To whom do they arise ?' In order to do this, one has to be extremely vigilant. Through constant enquiry one should make the mind stay in its source, without allowing it to wander away and get lost in the mazes of thought created by itself. All other disciplines such as breath-control and meditation on the forms of God should be regarded as auxiliary practices. They are useful in so far as they help the mind to become quiescent and one-pointed. For the mind that has gained skill in concentration, Self-enquiry becomes comparatively easy. It is by ceaseless enquiry that the thoughts are destroyed and the Self realized - the plenary Reality in which there is not even the 'I' thought, the experience which is referred to as "Silence". This, in substance, is Bhagavan Sri Ramana Maharshi's teaching in Nan Yar (Who am I?).

T. M. P. MAHADEVAN

University of Madras

June 30, 1982

Om Namo Bhagavathe Sri Ramanaya

* * * *

Who Am I? - Nan Yar?

As all living beings desire to be happy always, without misery, as in the case of everyone there is observed supreme love for one's self, and as happiness alone is the cause for love, in order to gain that happiness which is one's nature and which is experienced in the state of deep sleep where there is no mind, one should know one's self. For that, the path of knowledge, the inquiry of the form "Who am I?", is the principal means.

1. Who am I?

The gross body which is composed of the seven humours (dhatus), I am not; the five cognitive sense organs, viz. the senses of hearing, touch, sight, taste, and smell, which apprehend their respective objects, viz. sound, touch, colour, taste, and odour, I am not; the five cognitive sense-organs, viz. the organs of speech, locomotion, grasping, excretion, and procreation, which have as their respective functions speaking, moving, grasping, excreting, and enjoying, I am not; the five vital airs, prana, etc., which perform respectively the five functions of in-breathing, etc., I am not; even the mind which thinks, I am not; the nescience too, which is endowed only with the residual impressions of objects, and in which there are no objects and no functioning's, I am not.

2. If I am none of these, then who am I?

After negating all of the above-mentioned as 'not this', 'not this', that Awareness which alone remains - that I am.

3. What is the nature of Awareness?

The nature of Awareness is existence-consciousness-bliss

4. When will the realization of the Self be gained?

When the world which is what-is-seen has been removed, there will be realization of the Self which is the seer.

5. Will there not be realization of the Self even while the world is there (taken as real)?

There will not be.

6. Why?

The seer and the object seen are like the rope and the snake. Just as the knowledge of the rope which is the substrate will not arise unless the false knowledge of the illusory serpent goes, so the realization of the Self which is the substrate will not be gained unless the belief that the world is real is removed.

7. When will the world which is the object seen be removed?

When the mind, which is the cause of all cognition's and of all actions, becomes quiescent, the world will disappear.

8. What is the nature of the mind?

What is called 'mind' is a wondrous power residing in the Self. It causes all thoughts to arise. Apart from thoughts, there is no such thing as mind. Therefore, thought is the nature of mind. Apart from thoughts, there is no independent entity called the world. In deep sleep there are no thoughts, and there is no world. In the states of waking and dream, there are thoughts, and there is a world also. Just as the spider emits the thread (of the web) out of itself and again withdraws it into itself, likewise the mind projects the world out of itself and again resolves it into itself. When the mind comes out of the Self, the world appears. Therefore, when the world appears (to be real), the Self does not appear; and when the Self appears (shines) the world does not appear. When one persistently inquires into the nature of the mind, the mind will end leaving the Self (as the residue). What is referred to as the Self is the Atman. The mind always exists only in dependence on something gross; it cannot stay alone. It is the mind that is called the subtle body or the soul (jiva).

9. What is the path of inquiry for understanding the nature of the mind?

That which rises as 'I' in this body is the mind. If one inquires as to where in the body the thought 'I' rises first, one would discover that it rises in the heart. That is the place of the mind's origin. Even if one thinks constantly 'I' 'I', one will be led to that place. Of all the thoughts that arise in the mind, the 'I' thought is the first. It is only after the rise of this that the other thoughts arise. It is after the - appearance - of the first personal pronoun that the secondand third personal pronouns appear; without the first personal pronoun there will not be the second and third.

10. How will the mind become quiescent?

By the inquiry 'Who am I? The thought 'who am I?' will destroy all other thoughts, and like the stick used for stirring the burning pyre, it will itself in the end get destroyed. Then, there will arise Self-realization.

11. What is the means for constantly holding on to the thought 'Who am I?'

When other thoughts arise, one should not pursue them, but should inquire: 'To whom do they arise?' It does not matter how many thoughts arise. As each thought arises, one should inquire with diligence, "To whom has this thought arisen?" The answer that would emerge would be "To me". Thereupon if one inquires "Who am I?" the mind will go back to its source; and the thought that arose will become quiescent. With repeated practice in this manner, the mind will develop the

skill to stay in its source. When the mind that is subtle goes out through the brain and the sense-organs, the gross names and forms appear; when it stays in the heart, the names and forms disappear. Not letting the mind goes out, but retaining it in the Heart is what is called "inwardness" (antar-mukha). Letting the mind go out of the Heart is known as "externalisation" (bahir-mukha). Thus, when the mind stays in the Heart, the 'I' which is the source of all thoughts will go, and the self which ever exists will shine. Whatever one does, one should do without the egoity "I". If one acts in that way, all will appear as of the nature of Siva (God).

12. Are there no other means for making the mind quiescent?

Other than inquiry, there are no adequate means. If through other means it is sought to control the mind, the mind will appear to be controlled, but will again go forth. Through the control of breath also, the mind will become quiescent; but it will be quiescent only so long as the breath remains controlled, and when the breath resumes the mind also will again start moving and will wander as impelled by residual impressions. The source is the same for both mind and breath. Thought, indeed, is the nature of the mind. The thought "I" is the first thought of the mind; and that is egoity. It is from that whence egoity originates that breath also originates. Therefore, when the mind becomes quiescent, the breath is controlled, and when the breath is controlled the mind

becomes quiescent. But in deep sleep, although the mind becomes quiescent, the breath does not stop. This is because of the will of God, so that the body may be preserved and other people may not be under the impression that it is dead. In the state of waking and in samadhi, when the mind becomes quiescent the breath is controlled.

Breath is the gross form of mind. Till the time of death, the mind keeps breath in the body; and when the body dies the mind takes the breath along with it. Therefore, the exercise of breath-control is only an aid for rendering the mind quiescent (manonigraha); it will not destroy the mind (manonasa). Like the practice of breath-control. meditation on the forms of God, repetition of mantras, restriction on food, etc., are but aids for rendering the mind quiescent.

Through meditation on the forms of God and through repetition of mantras, the mind becomes one-pointed. The mind will always be wandering. Just as when a chain is given to an elephant to hold in its trunk it will go along grasping the chain and nothing else, so also when the mind is occupied with a name or form it will grasp that alone. When the mind expands in the form of countless thoughts, each thought becomes weak; but as thoughts get resolved the mind becomes

One-pointed and strong; for such a mind Self-inquiry will become easy. Of all the restrictive rules, that relating to the taking of sattvic food in moderate quantities is the best; by observing this rule, the sattvic quality of mind will increase, and that will be helpful to Self-inquiry.

13. The residual impressions (thoughts) of objects appear wending like the waves of an ocean. When will all of them get destroyed?

As the meditation on the Self rises higher and higher, the thoughts will get destroyed.

14. Is it possible for the residual impressions of objects that come from beginning less time, as it were, to be resolved, and for one to remain as the pure Self?

Without yielding to the doubt "Is it possible, or not?" One should persistently hold on to the meditation on the Self. Even if one be a great sinner, one should not worry and weep "O! I am a sinner, how can I be saved?" One should completely renounce the thought "I am a sinner"; and concentrate keenly on meditation on the Self; then, one would surely succeed. There are not two minds - one good and the other evil; the mind is only one. It is the residual impressions that are of two kinds - auspicious and inauspicious. When the mind is under the influence of auspicious impressions it is called good; and when it is under the influence of inauspicious impressions it is regarded as evil. The mind should not be allowed to wander towards worldly objects and what concerns other people. However bad other people may be, one should bear no hatred for them. Both desire and hatred should be eschewed. That entire one gives to others one gives to one's self. If this truth is understood who will not give to others? When one's self arises all arises; when one's self becomes quiescent all becomes quiescent. To the extent we behave with humility, to that extent there will result good. If the mind is rendered quiescent, one may live anywhere.

15. How long should an inquiry be practised?

As long as there are impressions of objects in the mind, so long the inquiry "Who am I?" is required. As thoughts arise they should be destroyed then and there in the very place of their origin, through inquiry. If one resorts to contemplation of the Self unintermittently, until the Self is gained, that alone would do. As long as there are enemies within the fortress, they will continue to sally forth; if they are destroyed as they emerge, the fortress will fall into our hands.

16. What is the nature of the Self?

What exists in truth is the Self alone. The world, the individual soul, and God are appearances in it. Like silver in mother-of-pearl, these three appear at the same time, and disappear at the same time. The Self is that where there is absolutely no "I" thought. That is called "Silence". The Self itself is the world; the Self itself is "I"; the Self itself is God; all is Siva, the Self.

17. Is not everything the work of God?

Without desire, resolve, or effort, the sun rises; and in its mere presence, the sun-stone emits fire, the lotus blooms, water evaporates; people perform their various functions and then rest. Just as in the presence of the magnet the needle moves, it is by virtue of the mere presence of God that the souls governed by the three (cosmic) functions or the fivefold divine activity perform their actions and then rest, in accordance with their respective karmas. God has no resolve; no karma attaches itself to Him. That is like worldly actions not affecting the sun, or like the merits and demerits of the other four elements not affecting all pervading space.

18. Of the devotees, who is the greatest?

He who gives himself up to the Self that is God is the most excellent devotee. Giving one's self up to God means remaining constantly in the Self without giving room for the rise of any thoughts other than that of the Self. Whatever burdens are thrown on God, He bears them. Since the supreme power of God makes all things move, why should we, without submitting ourselves to it, constantly worry ourselves with thoughts as to what should be done and how, and what should not be done and how not? We know that the train carries all loads, so after getting on it why should we carry our small luggage on our head to our discomfort, instead of putting it down in the train and feeling at ease?

19. What is non-attachment?

As thoughts arise, destroying them utterly without any residue in the very place of their origin is non-attachment. Just as the pearl-diver ties a stone to his waist, sinks to the bottom of the sea and there takes the pearls, so each one of us should be endowed with non-attachment, dive within oneself and obtain the Self-Pearl.

20. Is it not possible for God and the Guru to effect the release of a soul?

God and the Guru will only show the way to release; they will not by themselves take the soul to the state of release. In truth, God and the Guru are not different. Just as the prey which has fallen into the jaws of a tiger has no escape, so those who have come within the ambit of the Guru's gracious look will be saved by the Guru and will not get lost; yet, each one should by his own effort pursue the path shown by God or Guru and gain release. One can know oneself only with one's own eye of knowledge, and not with somebody else's. Does he who is Rama require the help of a mirror to know that he is Rama?

21. Is it necessary for one who longs for release to inquire into the nature of categories (tattvas)?

Just as one who wants to throw away garbage has no need to analyse it and see what it is, so one who wants to know the Self has no need to count the number of categories or inquire into their characteristics; what he has to do is to reject altogether the categories that hide the Self. The world should be considered like a dream.

22. Is there no difference between waking and dream?

Waking is long and a dream short; other than this there is no difference. Just as waking happenings seem real while awake. so do those in a dream while dreaming. In dream the mind takes on another body. In both waking and dream states thoughts. names and forms occur simultaneously.

23. Is it any use reading books for those who long for release?

All the texts say that in order to gain release one should render the mind quiescent; therefore their conclusive teaching is that the mind should be rendered quiescent; once this has been understood there is no need for endless reading. In order to quieted the mind one has only to inquire within oneself what one's Self is; how could this search be done in books? One should know one's Self with one's own eye of wisdom. The Self is within the five sheaths; but books are outside them. Since the Self has to be inquired into by discarding the five sheaths, it is futile to search for it in books. There will come a time when one will have to forget all that one has learned.

24. What is happiness?

Happiness is the very nature of the Self; happiness and the Self are not different. There is no happiness in any object of the world. We imagine through our ignorance that we derive happiness from objects. When the mind goes out, it experiences misery. In truth, when its desires are fulfilled, it returns to its own place and enjoys the happiness that is the Self. Similarly, in the states of sleep, samadhi and fainting, and when the object desired is obtained or the object disliked is removed, the mind becomes inward-turned, and enjoys pure Self-Happiness. Thus the mind moves without rest alternately going out of the Self and returning to it. Under the tree the shade is pleasant; out in the open the heat is scorching. A person who has been going about in the sun feels cool when he reaches the shade. Someone who keeps on going from the shade into the sun and then back into the shade is a fool. A wise man stays permanently in the shade. Similarly, the mind of the one who knows the truth does not leave Brahman. The mind of the ignorant, on the contrary, revolves in the world, feeling miserable, and for a little time returns to Brahman to experience happiness. In fact, what is called the world is only thought. When the world disappears, i.e. when there is no thought, the mind experiences happiness; and when the world appears, it goes through misery.

25. What is wisdom-insight (jnana-drsti)?

Remaining quiet is what is called wisdom-insight. To remain quiet is to resolve the mind in the Self. Telepathy, knowing past, present and future happenings and clairvoyance do not constitute wisdom-insight.

26. What is the relation between desirelessness and wisdom?

Desirelessness is wisdom. The two are not different; they are the same. Desirelessness is refraining from turning the mind towards any object. Wisdom means the appearance of no object. In other words, not seeking what is other than the Self is detachment or desirelessness; not leaving the Self is wisdom.

27. What is the difference between inquiry and meditation?

Inquiry consists in retaining the mind in the Self. Meditation consists in thinking that one's self is Brahman, existence-consciousness-bliss.

28. What is release?

Inquiring into the nature of one's self that is in bondage, and realizing one's true nature is release.

THE LAST DAYS

The passage of great souls from the physical body frame at the time of earthly departure is death defying. The following is an account of the passing away of Sri Ramana Maharshi to the higher worlds, when his sojourn on Earth came to an end. These diary notes were kept by Sri S.S.Cohen an ardent devotee of Sri Ramana Mahrishi. It is worth noting the extraordinary events which took place during this time.

Friday, 14th April

Maharshi is in a very precarious condition. The whole morning has been spent by devotees in hushed gloom and with bated breath. After evening darshan (seeing a holy person), the unanimous verdict is that it is positively the last. The Master is now propped on large pillows, almost in a sitting posture, the head resting backward with open mouth, and two attendants briskly fanning him, to enable him to breathe freely – the battle for air, has thus started. At 7 p.m. oxygen is administered to him for about five minutes, but seeing it gave him no relief, he feebly asked that it should be stopped.

The situation was tense: about five-hundred devotees were outside in sad expectation of the solemn last moment. Blood relations, Ashram workers, a few old disciples, and some new aspirants went in by turn to have a last sight of him. When the end was known to be approaching, the whole congregation with one voice started chanting the Tamil hymns he had many years ago composed in praise of Lord Arunachala: "Arunachala Shiva, Arunachala Shiva, Arunachala!" till it came about 8-47. Many devotees grief stricken and beating their breasts, lost control of their feeling and rushed en masse to the small room where the sacred body lay, but Police officers immediately cordoned off the area till it was brought out and placed in the centre of the big darshan hall in yoga asana for all the people to pay their last respect to it. The news spread like wildfire to the town and the neighbouring villages and drew huge crowds. By 9-15, the crowd grew so thick, that it became necessary to give chance to all to pay their homage and pass the body in an orderly manner. A queue was thus formed – seven to ten broad – at a quick-march pace. It is still (11-55 p.m.) continuing unabatingly.

Around the sofa sat dozens of disciples, some chanting Maharshi's verses and other devotional hymns, but the others remained in silent contemplation. Sandal-wood paste and jasmine flowers now cover the body and incense burns by its side.

At about 9 p.m., Monsieur Cartier-Brassen, the French photographer, who has been here for about a fortnight with his wife, related an experience of his to me. "It is a most astonishing experience," he said. "I was in the open space in front of my house, when my friends drew my attention to the sky, where I saw a vividly-luminous shooting star with a luminous tail, unlike any shooting star I had before seen, coming from the South, moving slowly across the sky and, reaching the top of Arunachala, disappeared behind it. Because of its singularity we all guessed its import and immediately looked at our watches – it was 8-47 – and then raced to the Ashram only to find that our premonition had been only too sadly true: the Master had passed into Mahanirvana (all-pervading and deathless Selfhood)at that very minute." Several other devotees in the Ashram and in the town later told me that they too had seen the tell-tale meteor.

15th April, 1950

Many devotees kept vigil the whole of last night by the side of the sacred body; some snatched a few hours rest and returned early morning. The singing and chanting of Vedas continued throughout, as did the queue of worshippers till 11-30 a.m. today when the body was taken out to the South verandah for puja and abhishekam. Sri Niranjanananda Swami, the Sarvadhikari, assisted by his son Sri T. N. Venkataraman, poured over the sacred head dozens of pots of milk, curds, butter-milk, orange juice, mashed bananas and jackfruits, coconut water, etc., followed by many bottles of rose-water, attar, perfumes of all kinds and sweet smelling oils. Then enormous garlands of fresh roses and jasmines were placed round the neck and strewn all over the body.

The samadhi pit was dug 10½ x 10½ feet and seven feet deep. In its centre the masons isolated a small area of 4½ x 4½ feet and surrounded it by a wall built of granite stones, lime and cement. The remaining portion they filled with many cartloads of sand said to have been brought from the sacred Ganges and Narmada valleys.

At 6-30 p.m., the body, which by then had received the homage of not less than about 40,000 persons, was carried in a decorated palanquin reserved for the Deity of the temple to the samadhi. Here it was placed in the same yoga-asana into a bag made of the finest khaddar, which was then filled with pure camphor and lowered into the small area reserved for it. Then the pit was filled to the brim with camphor, salt, and sacred ashes to protect the body from worms and rapid disintegration, and closed with masonry work. The crowd was so intense that twenty policemen were hardly sufficient to control it.

Mr. Kaikobad, a Parsi devotee of the Maharshi, last night happened to be on the terrace of his house in Madras, when he saw the meteor, to which Monsieur Cartier-Brassen and others referred last night and intuitively associated it with the Mahanirvana of the Master and, without waiting for the morning, he immediately hired a taxi and came at top speed.

Miss H. P. Petit, who was sitting on the balcony of her house in Bombay, about a thousand miles away, also saw the shooting star at that fateful minute, at once guessed its meaning and wrote to a friend of hers in Benares that the Maharshi had passed away.

16th April, 1950

All the English and Tamil papers which arrived this morning from Madras gave wide publicity in banner headlines to the passing of the Maharshi. They also referred to the meteor which had been seen in the sky all over the State of Madras, hundreds of thousands of square miles, at 8-47 on the night of April 14, by a large number of people in different places and reported to the Press. These eye-witnesses had been struck by its peculiar look and behaviour, which led them to ascribe the strange phenomenon to the passing of a great spiritual soul. Such a mass of evidence speaks for itself, if evidence need be.

Glossary

Abhishekam: Sacred bathing.A religious bathing ceremony. During an elaborate bathing ceremony a deity is bathed not only in water, but also with milk, yogurt, butter milk, honey, clarified butter, sugar, and all kinds of fruit juices. After this bathing, the sacred image is dressed, ornamented, fed and praised with hymns accompanied with bells, drums and other instruments. This is especially the case with the worship of the Shiva Linga or the famous South Indian form of Vishnu known as Balaji.

Adi: First, beginning; used in compound words to signify original, prime,

Adi Plane: Adi means first. The Adi plane refers to the first cause, the divine light, the first plane, the undivided Lord, the Father or the Creator; it is from this plane that the forming of the other realms and further creative activity takes place.

Agni: The word Agni is Sanskrit for fire. Agni is The Hindu god of fire and guardian of humanity. It is the Vedic god of fire who presides over the Earth, one of the three chief divinities of the Vedas.

Aham sphurana: The throb of Self-bliss in the Heart.

Aham-vritti: The 'I'-thought. It the thought "I am" as opposed to thoughts about objects, feelings.

Akash: Ether; space.

Antahkarana: Means of perception; the thinking power

Anupadaka: Self-existing, without vesture or without clothing or without any additional veil. A term applied to certain self-created gods.

Arunachala: The holy mountain in South India where Sage Sri Ramana Maharshi spent all his adult life. Also the mountain represents the symbol Linga of the god Shiva.

Arupa: A compound word meaning "formless," but this word formless is not to be taken so strictly as to mean that there is no form of any kind whatsoever; it merely means that the forms in the spiritual worlds are of a spiritual type or character.

Arupadevas: Formless celestial beings.

Ashramam: Hermitage, the abode of a sage.

Astral Body: One of the subtle bodies and is seat of our physical consciousness, feelings, emotions, sympathies and antipathies. We have this in common with the animal kingdom.

Atma: The essential Divinity, or light of consciousness, in each individual; often translated into English as "Self".

Atmic: Of or pertaining to the Atma.

Bhagwan: Commonly used name for God; a title used for one like Sri Ramana Maharshi who is recognized as having realized his identity with the Self

Brihadaranyak: One of the major Upanishads; Sanskrit philosophical treatise that sets forth teachings maintained by sage Yajnavalkya who elaborately describes the sole greatness of the Absolute Self, the nature of Its existence, the way of attaining infinite knowledge and immortality.

Buddhi: Intellect; faculty which enables the mind to perceive objects in the phenomenal world.

Buddhic: The level of consciousness where the oneness of all life becomes apparent.

Darshan: Seeing; vision.

Devas: A god or celestial being, of which there are various classes; celestial deities; beings living in the higher astral plane, in a subtle, non-physical body that are endowed with great piety, tremendous lifespan, and superior mental and physical prowess. They are entrusted with specific powers for the purpose of universal administration

Devachan: A Sanskrit word, meaning the dwelling place of the gods; the shining land; heaven; the higher realm above the astral; is the fulfilling of all the unfulfilled spiritual hopes of the past incarnation, and an efflorescence of all the spiritual and intellectual yearnings of the past incarnation.

Devaraja: King of gods.

Dhruvam: Secure or eternal

Ego: The expression of the Jivatma on the atmic, buddhic and causal planes.

Etheric Body: This is one of the subtle bodies and is also called the life body. This provides the force of life, growth and reproduction within organisms. We have this in common with the plant kingdom.

Houri: A nymph of paradise; a voluptuously beautiful young woman; one of the dark-eyed virgins of perfect beauty believed to live with the blessed in Paradise

Indra: King of the Devas (demi-Gods) and god of rain and thunder.

Individuality: The expression of the ego in the causal body.

Jivatma: The individual soul or self; a spark of the divine fire.

Jnani: A Self-realized person, a sage; one who has attained realization by the path of knowledge, sage.

Kama: Desire; wish; love.

Kama-loka: Desire world; the semi material plane, to us subjective and invisible, where the disembodied "personalities," the astral forms, called Kama-rupa remain until they fade out from it by the complete exhaustion of the effects of the mental impulses that created these eidolons of human and animal passions and desires.

Kama- rupa: The desire form; the desire body created by a person through the mental and physical desires and thoughts in connection with things of matter. After death it becomes the vehicle in the kama-loka of the usually unconscious higher principles of the person that was. These astral forms remain until they fade out from the astral plane due to complete exhaustion of the effects of the mental impulses that created them. This body is part of the transformed astral body and is a result of human experiences over a number of lives.

karma: Action; work; deeds; the Law of Karma is the universal law of cause and effect, and the continuing process of action and reaction, accounting for the interpenetration of all phenomena. Thus our present thoughts, actions, and situations are the result of what we have done in the past, and our future thoughts, actions, and situations will be the product of what we are doing now. Individual karma results from this process.

Maharshi: Great rishi or sage.

Mental body (lower): One of the subtle bodies which is the vehicle of human intellectual thinking. This has developed over many lives as part of the transformed etheric body by the ego.

Monad: Jivatma; a spark of the divine fire.

Personality: Is transitory and is the expression of the ego in the physical, astral and lower mental bodies.

Pramada: Swerving from abidance in the Absolute.

Rupadevas: Celestial beings having form.

Samsara: The realm of relativity; the process of worldly life; the bondage of life, death and rebirth.

Sastras: Sacred scriptures; a religious or scientific treatise

Siddhis: Supernatural powers; extraordinary powers that

may be acquired through spiritual development.

Ulladu Narpadu: Forty verses on that which is; title of the main work composed by sage Sri Ramana Maharshi.

Upadesa Saram: Essenceof Instruction; title of another main work of sage Sri. Ramana Maharshi.

Yogabrastha: One who has slipped from yoga.

BIBLIOGRAPHY

Aiyer, C.S. (1982). Quotations from the Maharshi. The Mountain Path. (Vol. 19, p.23)

Cohen, S.S, (2003). Guru Ramana. Tiruvannamalai: Sri Ramanasramam.

Muruganar (2005). Guru Vachaka Kovai. Tiruvannamalai: Sri ArunachalaRamana Nilayam.

V.S. Ramanan (Pub.) (2002). Maharshi's Gospel. Tiruvannamalai: Sri Ramanasramam.

V.S. Ramanan (Pub.) (2003). Talks With Sri Ramana Maharshi. Tiruvannamalai: Sri Ramanasrama